PRAISE FOR THE WORK OF

H. R. Coursen

"An emerging area within the broader field of performance-centered Shakespearean criticism concentrates on televised performances, and to it no one has contributed more in recent years than H.R. Coursen."
Philip McGuire, Studies in English Literature

"H. R. Coursen provides an elegant reading of the play's textual history, sources, structure and themes, criticism, and performance history."
William Worthen, on A Guide to *The Tempest in* Studies in English Literature

"It is indeed remarkable that such an encyclopedic amount of information and so many well-informed judgments could be compressed into this relatively small book. A rewarding and valuable study."
James Lake, Shakespeare Bulletin, *on* Shakespeare in Space

Shakespeare Translated

Studies in Shakespeare

Robert F. Willson, Jr.
General Editor

Vol. 15

PETER LANG
New York • Washington, D.C./Baltimore • Bern
Frankfurt am Main • Berlin • Brussels • Vienna • Oxford

H. R. Coursen

Shakespeare Translated

DERIVATIVES ON FILM AND TV

PETER LANG
New York • Washington, D.C./Baltimore • Bern
Frankfurt am Main • Berlin • Brussels • Vienna • Oxford

Library of Congress Cataloging-in-Publication Data
Coursen, Herbert R.
Shakespeare translated: derivatives on film and TV / H.R. Coursen.
p. cm. — (Studies in Shakespeare; v. 15)
Includes bibliographical references and index.
1. Shakespeare, William, 1564–1616—Film and video adaptations.
2. English drama—Film and video adaptations. 3. Film adaptations. I. Title. II. Series.
PR3093.C675   822.3'3—dc22   2004027476
ISBN 0-8204-7839-3
ISSN 1067-0823

Bibliographic information published by **Die Deutsche Bibliothek**.
Die Deutsche Bibliothek lists this publication in the "Deutsche
Nationalbibliografie"; detailed bibliographic data is available
on the Internet at http://dnb.ddb.de/.

Cover concept by Nancy E. Randolph
Cover design by Sophie Boorsch Appel

© 2005 Peter Lang Publishing, Inc., New York
275 Seventh Avenue, 28th Floor, New York, NY 10001
www.peterlangusa.com

All rights reserved.
Reprint or reproduction, even partially, in all forms such as microfilm,
xerography, microfiche, microcard, and offset strictly prohibited.

This book is for Ken.

Contents

Introduction 1
1 *Romeo and Juliet* 25
2 *Hamlet* 57
3 *Othello* 95
4 *King Lear* 115
Conclusion 133
Citations 145
Bibliography 155
Index 161

Reprinted with permission from Disney Publishing Worldwide.

Introduction

I will look at the issues of "translating" the Shakespearean *praxis*—that is, the action imitated[1] into formats that alter setting and/or language. We have some grasp of the Shakespearean setting, of course, a less sure sense of costuming, and a firm grip on the script or scripts that we inherit. I will look at those scripts, assessing them for their ability to "recontextualize." That assessment itself will be controversial, since no consensus exists on "Shakespearean meanings." A *thematic* approach, however, will suggest what can be brought forward in time and what cannot. The media define what can occur within them. They are changing and thus represent a dynamic that must be accounted for when they are confronted by a Shakespearean script. My definition of the media, too, will arouse controversy, since few agree on what film or television *is*. The discussion cannot be abstracted from political and economic considerations. Indeed, I will make a few comments on the *political* logic of late capitalism that will make readers of the "centrist" position leap with outrage. It has never been my intention to serve the status quo; however, my approach will be labeled "reactionary"[2] as it has been in the past, and rightly so this time. Much of what follows is a reaction. I cannot, for example, claim that the inherited text, no matter what its complications and variations, is irrelevant to the process of production.*

No doubt television represents a "dumbing-down," a numbing, a willingness on the part of its audience to accept less and less. The Shakespeare "off-shoots," as Ruby Cohn calls them,[3] that appear on TV prove as much. Another culprit, I think, is the jargonization of Shakespeare. We have moved away from the plays and into a critical thicket that says little about them, and often says wrong things about them. For example, when Daniel J. Vitkus says that "Othello enacts his own punishment and damns himself by killing the Turk he has become,"[4] he tells us something that the play will not support. It is true that Othello, typically, has expanded upon his own damnation in Luciferian terms, but the play does not pursue the downward curve that he describes. Furthermore, Vitkus misses the crucial duality that Othello emphasizes. Othello does commit suicide—but that is just personal. What he does is to execute an enemy of the state who happens to be himself. He assumes command for the last time and at last validates the heroism that has been attributed to him by himself and others. Perhaps the action does involve his Christian soul. He may suggest as much if his word is "Judean," as in the First Quarto, a reference to Judas, who would be the first person to be damned within a Christian dispensation. What happens is that body politic properly extinguishes body natural.

Shakespeare wrote plays. He can only be understood within that framework. Any other version of "understanding" is a misunderstanding. Even when production is adduced, however, it is sometimes cited incorrectly. Peter Donaldson calls Loncraine's *Richard III* "a widescreen color film [that] uses, reframes, and alludes to many other media, including black-and-white and silent cinema, 35-mm still photography, photograph-based silk-screen graphic art, wireless telegraphy and tickertape, recorded and amplified 'live' sound, and, in the final moments, digital collage."[5] That is true of Loncraine's techniques, but it does not follow that Loncraine's many variations show Richard to be a "modern media-reliant dictator,"[6] as Donaldson says. I complained in my response that the film might have been interesting had Loncraine treated Richard as Donaldson claims he does.[7] In fact, it is Prince Edward and King Henry who use the telegraph at the beginning of the film. In their rush toward modern techniques of information gathering, however, they have forgotten to post any guards! We see Clarence use a camera. We see Richard looking at a film of his coronation and at a photograph of the executed Hastings. Where do we see Richard *use* any medium other than a microphone at Edward's coronation ball? Where is Goebbels? Where is Leni Reifenstahl? Donaldson's effort to link Richard with Hitler fails (as does Loncraine's). Stanley, meanwhile, is in charge of Richard's "horse"—meaning cavalry. The line, amazingly, is left in the filmscript. But Stanley wears the wings of the RAF and he apparently has the *only* airplane. The media-savvy Richard has not gotten around to adding airplanes, or since he is supposed to be alert to the latest technical advances, warning systems like radar that were coming into being before World War II on both sides of the English Channel. His

Tiger Tanks and Panzer divisions exist, it seems, without the other parallel developments in offensive and defensive military techniques. That is one issue that modernizers have to face. It is particularly apparent in a film that pays attention to its historical moment. It was not an issue in the stage production from which the film emerges. There we could fill in details as the production encouraged us to explore the zone of our suspension of disbelief.

The basic problem with modernizing *Richard III*, though, is inherent in the received script. Richard suffers a nightmare before his final battle that frames itself in medieval terms. Ghosts appear out of his guilt and condemn him. "Despair!" they say, as if he were Faustus being pulled down by a specific Mephistopheles. He frames his guilt in the tradition of a *debat* between body and soul. He is both fool and king, but can say nothing good of himself. The truth is the finding of "guilty!" The evil person cannot detach himself from his evil. It stares at him across the terrible gulf he has created between will and the self that he cannot eradicate. This, of course, is an insight deriving from Augustine and Bernard of Clairvaux. It cannot find a place in a modern setting. Al Pacino, as he searched for *Richard*, made sure that Richard's soliloquy after awakening took place in the "medieval" setting of The Cloisters, one site of the several in Pacino's journey of exploration. To have it occur on the streets of a late 1990's New York City would have been interesting, as throngs poured from subway entrances, but it would have been as wildly anachronistic as were Ian McKellen's words in a modernistic 1937.

And that is what I will argue about in the scripts that have been brought forward in time in recent productions. Will the script permit a recontextualization in something resembling our times? I would assert that when a script will *not* translate effectively into a specific updated setting, no reason exists for it not to be presented in a period that will permit its issues to emerge with power. Why does the period have to be our own? Science fiction and fantasy demonstrate that we as an audience can accept and enjoy worlds that are not our own. In fact, that is a major premise of the two genre—and of a lot of productions of Shakespeare as well. Shakespeare should not demand a dumbing-down, which is sometimes the same as a "bringing-up-to-date," but, all too often, that is what Shakespeare gets in film and on TV.

Shakespeare, no doubt, is an adjunct of the profound narcissism of America. Since he is "good," association with him is also "good." Narcissism nowadays, according to Christopher Lasch, involves the imitation of successful behavior.[8] That means that association with Shakespeare in advertising or teenage "culture" is inevitable. And since adults, it seems, imitate teenagers, the association filters upward. Coppélia Kahn, for example, accuses high school teachers of teaching Shakespeare because it is the trendy thing to be doing: "teaching Shakespeare provides for many undervalued, overworked, and underpaid teachers a sense of cultural entitlement. No other author conveys such clout ... In the bleak working conditions teachers endure in schools ... no wonder they seek ... a sense of professional worth conferred by the glamour of teaching the bard; no wonder they fall victim to bardolotry. They pass this snob appeal on to their students."[9]

Having worked with 75 high school teachers in five National Endowment for the Humanities Summer Seminars and in 2004 with a dozen wonderful teachers in Professor Samuel Crowl's workshop at Ohio University, I do not believe that teaching Shakespeare in high school manifests a teacher's self-indulgence. I am confident that the vast majority of those teachers do *not* turn out the students that Professor Kahn encounters—those who "hate Shakespeare." It is true, however, that attaching Shakespeare to something or attaching oneself to Shakespeare can be a version of narcissism. If anything characterizes our "culture" in 2004, it is narcissism. A President of the United States can say publicly that he can't think of any mistakes he has made while in office. Is that just the pressure of a news conference as he maintains? I am puzzled, particularly since this President has allied himself with a religion that has its basis in guilt.

Perhaps the most glaring recent act of narcissism has been Mel Gibson's projection of himself, physically and emotionally, into his film *The Passion of the Christ*. It is an act of stunning egotism that will lay up more treasure for Gibson on this earth—not that he claims to want it. For the purposes of a study of Shakespeare, Gibson's example is salutary. It stresses the text. Since the speakers utter Aramaic and Latin, Gibson relies on subtitles, pulling the eyes of even those who can understand the language to the bottom of the screen. Stuart Klawans suggests that Gibson is pretending to "make [a] literal transcription... of a text."[10] That means that narrative materials added without "biblical authority"—however tenuous that would be in itself—are validated simply by their inclusion in the film. And there are many in Gibson's film. Klawans says that "textual literalism in film has been primarily a matter of false claims, misdirection, illusionism, and irony."[11] Gibson, says Klawans, is "dead serious, as if textual literalism could in fact be achieved." The effort is based "on a text believed to be inerrant."[12] The Pope is reported to have said of the film, "It is as it is"—though the Vatican has disavowed that ex cathedra imprimatur. But Gibson is saying what the United States administration has said about its vague monster—"The War on Terror." If you dissent, as Klawans says, "you disagree with revealed truth."[13] The film is a gift to the absolutists.

That is perhaps an antidote to the "feel good" Jesus who knows no pain but alleviates all pain without side effects like headache, nausea, or sudden death. Frank Rich complains that "authentic spirituality [is] missing in this jamboree of bloody beefcake."[14] David Denby suggests that "Gibson can brush aside the work of scholars and historians because he has a powerful weapon at hand—the cinema—with which he can create something greater than argument: he can create faith."[15] In other words, seeing is believing. Gibson had the money to make the film and then, in an act of surpassing hubris, to behave like the crucified Christ when people did not like the film. That is "the anti-Christian sentiment," he says.[16] Or, as Gibson says in response to the criticism of Frank Rich, "You try to perform of love even for those who persecute you."[17] He has it several ways at once. As Denby says, "Gibson's timing couldn't be more unfortunate: another dose of death-haunted religious fanaticism is the last thing we need."[18]

The film has been seen, however, as evidence of *our* narcissism, not Gibson's. The emphasis on physical pain tells us of the agony that Christ went through for those who believe. "In sermons, however," says Kenneth L. Woodward, "the emphasis all too often is on the smoothly therapeutic: what Jesus can do for me."[19] As H. Richard Neibuhr says, "A god without wrath brought men without sin into a kingdom without judgment through the ministrations of a Christ without a cross."[20] In other words, Gibson's narcissistic imitation of Christ is necessary to remind us of our own narcissistic need to embrace only the convenient Christ who saves without bleeding.

Does it follow that our own association with Shakespeare, as teachers, is an attempt to confer upon ourselves an unearned superiority? It certainly is true that those who sell things to us do associate Shakespeare with their product. We live in a society premised, it seems, on "consumer confidence." Were we to stop buying, not only would we be filled with a sudden emptiness but the economy would collapse around us. The result is that as terror alerts move up the spectrum we are urged to redouble our travel and shopping. "This doesn't concern you," we are told, "Go ahead and play." Condoleeza Rice, meanwhile, looks at ominous memos and, instead of asking for "more detail" (as a good teacher would), complains that the memo is too vague for anything but a shoulder shrug. In other words, what we receive must reflect back to us precisely what we want, or it is irrelevant. Some genius started a rumor before Thanksgiving 2001 about a terror attack on shopping malls. That caution resonated, of course, since we were supposed to be mobbing the malls as we "went on with our daily lives" and let the experts subdue the terrorists. And in that instance, they did keep Osama at bay—another of those "successes" about which we will never hear. And when a politician speaks, he is there, as David Brooks says, "to say things people in the audience already agree with so they can applaud their own ideas."[21]

Shakespeare, then, becomes part of this often self-defeating pattern of postmodern life—"post" because we have discovered nothing with which to replace "modernism." In looking at mostly recent examples of Shakespearean references and reshapings in film and on TV, I take for granted their reinforcement of narcissism—whether it is just to tell an old story a new way to better sell the film or the products invading the spaces around the TV production, or whether the example represents a more obvious association with Shakespeare to better sell a specific product. The mirror is always in place, suggests Barbara Hodgdon, because the "audience's ritual values coincide with Hollywood's ideological ones."[22] That is to say, shopping and selling are twin halves of a single event. Almost invariably, the Shakespearean source illuminates the moment of its appearance—sometimes by creating a useful analogy with the drama surrounding it, sometimes by becoming its own highlight within a murky context, and sometimes by creating an instant and easily available reference. *Romeo and Juliet*, for example, invariably means "young love" and the use of that play is the most ubiquitous in today's teenage culture.

Shakespeare was "conservative," as the politics of his time and the needs of his pocketbook dictated, so that his incorporation into a status quo shopping society should not be surprising. It is not accidental that a radical script like *King Lear* has not been recently made into a film. A radical version of it appeared from Peter Brook at the end of the indefensible war in Vietnam, over three decades ago. Would another extreme version of it show us where we are today—assuming that no production could be passive toward its material? Perhaps.

One problem today, however, is that the kingdom of America is divided in another way—between word and action, between an espousal of "freedom" and its suppression, between a President who associates himself with a "culture of life," but whose adopted state brims to overflowing along its death row and who exports "shock and awe" to people who, he says, "hate us for our freedoms."[23] The American President can preside over the destruction of a middle-class "safety net" (the poor among us having been totally abandoned) while asserting that "I believe we have a duty to free people."[24] The ability to discern the hypocrisy that some zeitgeists have found in Shakespeare's politicians is not available to us today. I find that hard to fathom, but I assume that people have bought into the Prince Hal myth—the young man whose wild youth did not promise the sobriety and steadiness of leadership as he maneuvered his country into a dubious war.† We follow and, once there, "stay the course," as long as young people from the lower middle to lower classes are there as our proxies. We will not "cut and run," particularly since there is no "we the people" involved. In other words, Shakespeare is no longer an interrogative agent, as in the many films that appeared just before the turn of the millennium that defined the qualities of modernism and postmodernism, as Courtney Lehmann shows.[25] Shakespeare has lost his "negative capability"—once demonstrated in Michael Kahn's powerful antiwar *Henry V* (1969), where Kahn took a script often produced as a jingoistic justification for the use of force and had the dead of Agincourt rise to greet the conquering Henry as he returned to England. Shakespeare today is a functionary of a status quo that is devolving toward a police state. One of the reasons, I believe, is that Shakespeare is now expressed in a virtually impenetrable language that only its practitioners can grasp. That does not include the many of us who are responsible for teaching the plays to high school students and college undergraduates. Another reason may be that, as Richard Burt argues, neither liberal nor conservative academic values pertain any more to Shakespearean production:

> The problem for liberals is that there is no longer a Shakespeare icon, a token of Victorian imperial power for them to subvert from the margins; the center is already decentered, the original is already hybrid, the authentic is already a simulacrum. The problem for the conservatives is that there is no Shakespeare at the center for them to uphold.[26]

My students and I enjoyed *Shakespeare in Love*, in spite of some of its humor, meant to make self-styled sophisticates smile. My issue with the film is that it tends to place Shakespeare in the long-discredited autobiographical context invented by Edward Dowden. (I discovered, though, during talks I gave in this country and in several foreign countries in the 1990s that Luhrmann's *Romeo and Juliet* had, inevitably, a greater impact on adolescent students.) When discussing *Shakespeare in Love*, I do not find it helpful to know that the film treats "the relationship between poetic labor and sexual expenditure, the pressures of the marketplace, the instability of the commodity form, and masculine desublimation as a key to creativity."[27] I can follow much of that and perhaps even translate it into a discourse that will work in an undergraduate classroom. I am not sure of "sexual expenditure," however. It smacks more of the exhausted, postcoital lover whom Keats projects onto his urn than of Will and Viola in the film. I get lost, however, as I hit "masculine desublimation." Does that mean that sublimation—the only "defense-mechanism" that works—has to be activated *and* dismissed before the poetry can flow? Perhaps. If so, then the writer is correcting Freud, who argues that art is merely a response to psychic pain. While I do not hold such a limited view myself, for Freud art would be the sublimation, not the response to it. Does the writer mean "repression"? That is a process distinct from sublimation. Or does "desublimation" mean an erasure of that psychic activity? At any rate, rather than try to accommodate myself to what is a foreign language to an aging New Critic, I simply confess to my bafflement before it. I would also assert that performance critics have always accepted the postmodernist tenet of "instability." Whatever the "commodity form" may be (does the writer mean "drama as commodity," "script as commodity within a marketplace," both?), every new production of a Shakespeare play is an interpretation of that script and thus a tacit demonstration of a given script's instability.

Shakespeare scholars have adopted the jargon and clichés of academic fashion, perhaps inevitably, but unfortunately for those of us who still teach the plays to students reading many of them for the first time.‡ Those students may, however, have "experienced" a play before they encounter it in a classroom. It is difficult for many students to avoid references to *Hamlet* or *Romeo and Juliet* in their televisual environment. It may be that we as teachers can build on that "knowledge." It may be that we must combat it. Hamlet as someone who delays, or who looks at a skull and says "To be or not to be," or Romeo and Juliet as representatives of different cultures or as *merely* victims of a disapproving older generation—these clichés may well inhibit an intelligent reading of the script.

The hollowing out of intrinsic content for the sake of trendiness is not confined to scholarship, of course. It can invade even "serious" drama, as described by Charles R. Forker. Forker calls Mark Rylance's *Richard II*, at the London Globe in 2003, "a man constantly trying to control his emotions through nervous giggling and self-parody. Strikingly original as this approach is, its results are perverse, virtually stripping the character of royal dignity and reducing the iconicity of kingship with its divine-right gravitas to silliness. Given the secularity of our times and the soap opera image of the Windsors in modern-day Britain, [Director Tim] Carroll may have reasoned that audiences can no longer swallow the concept of Shakespeare's kings as links between the human and the celestial. But Richard's tragedy, as Shakespeare conceives it, is so bound up with the protagonist's painful attempt to reconcile his anointed status with his human inadequacies that the complexities of royal identity—theological, national, and personal—become central to anyone who pays attention to the text. Rylance's quirky trivializing of the crown, together with the solemnity it enshrines, makes Richard's surrender emotionally barren and politically of no deeper import than of competence replacing impotence. With the cosmic implications of deposition largely ignored, Carlisle's eloquent defense of royal indefeasibility might just as well have been omitted."[28] Rylance's excesses as actor are sometimes controlled by the strength of the cast around him, as in his Royal Shakespeare *Hamlet* at Stratford, but not the version he brought to the United States, where his virtuosity was not balanced by a strong cast and thus merely called attention to itself and away from his character. In the latter production he demonstrated the shallowing out of nuance and complexity apparently demanded by our televisual expectations.

A "postmodernized" production of *Richard II* may well obscure the ways in which the play depicts a paradigm shift, in the sense that Thomas Kuhn uses the concept, from the ceremonial, hierarchical status quo that Gaunt celebrates and that Richard inherited and squanders in multiple ways—having his uncle murdered, leasing out royal lands, denying sequence and continuity to himself and England by seizing Gaunt's estates—to the dynamic, competitive "new world" into which

Bolingbroke is inevitably drawn. By the end of the play, kingship is up for grabs and the Wars of the Roses loom on history's horizon. Can the play suggest that we may also be in the midst of a paradigm shift from a constitutional government to a state of martial law? Perhaps, but only if it explores the issues that are there in the script.

I have argued in the past that Shakespeare shows us where we are as a culture. That so many Shakespeare scripts were adapted as one- or two-reel silent films was not just an effort by the filmmakers to enhance the "prestige" of their product. It was also a means whereby they learned how to tell a story via visual sequence and title cards. That so many Shakespeare films appeared as the millennium was about to swing meant that the films were showing us where we were and were not. This thesis has been argued by, among others, Courtney Lehmann, but for me the implications of the films are just as clear in political as they are in cultural terms. As Thomas Hughes reminds us, technology has never been value free.[29]

If Shakespeare scholarship is any criterion, we cannot express ourselves clearly anymore. As scholars and critics, we should. Instead, we reflect society's imprecision. Zbigniew Brzezinski has argued that to declare war on terror is like declaring war on blitzkrieg.[30] Blitzkrieg was the product of a state. That is the issue that Bush has been unable to grasp. "Terror" is not necessarily state-sponsored, so we make war on *concept*. That makes sense, of course, when a nation is driven by ideology. When the Nazi tanks rolled into the Ukraine, they *were* greeted with flowers. The Ukranians hated Stalin. But the Slavs were inferior to the Aryans. Nazi oppression quickly turned the population against the illusory liberators. Ideology is ultimately empty of content but full of superficial symbols—outstretched arms and gigantic flags. Julie Taymor's brilliant *Titus Andronicus* (2000) reveals a world of empty rituals. Rome has hollowed out. Shoes are filled with dirt. It is an old ceremony, the meanings and origins of which have long been forgotten. And, suddenly, American flags and "God Bless America" stickers become ubiquitous emblems of depths of hatred and insecurity that remain unfathomed by those who display them.

James Mann's *Rise of the Vulcans: The History of Bush's War Cabinet* (2004) chronicles the careers of those who have come together under Bush, who assert an America "whose military power was so awesome that it no longer needed to make compromises or accommodations ... with any other nations or groups of countries."[31] As in Vietnam, however, military dominance is not enough. There, we were defeated by an enemy without an air force. And only a bunch of West Pointers, poor boys, and Lyndon Johnson paid for that. Barbara Garson's *MacBird* (1967) could appear during Lyndon Johnson's tenure, suggesting that he had a hand in John Kennedy's demise. As yet, as far as I know, no comparable dramatic parody has appeared for Bush.[§] One would think that the plays that demonstrate hubris at its height, *Lear* and *Coriolanus*, for example, would be popular these days. But perhaps the artistic community is as cowed as the polity and the media seem to be. *Richard II* shows a bad leader invoking divinity even as his actions cause his throne to crumble out from under him. But it has not been politically relevant, as far as I know, since the gimmicky RSC production of 1972 got a lot of unearned resonance out of Watergate.

We live in a Manichean universe where we struggle against evildoers. The only tragic element in this battle of good vs. bad may be the hubris of the righteous warriors. If so, the results seem already catastrophic, as the self-proclaimed side of the good seems intent on pulling the rest of the world down with it—acre by acre, tree by tree, child by child. It may be, though, that the nightmare, like Macbeth's dramatized reign—historically over a decade—will be brief. Gibson's film may be the apogee of the bizarre misperception that history is somehow subject to imposed definition. Elaine Pagels has demonstrated that the history of the gospels—their inclusion or exclusion from the Bible—and the four canonical gospels themselves suggest remarkable variation in the ways that they deal with Christ. "Many," she says, "tend to assume that only one side can speak the truth, while others speak only lies—or evil."[32] The same words could be applied to Michael Moore's tendentious and unconvincing *Fahrenheit 9/11*.

As Louis Menand says, "The intellectual investment in the Iraq war is much scarier than the financial involvement. Moore's movie never treats it."[33] Moore, then, participates in the dumbing-down represented by simplifiers like Reagan and, worse, gross misrepresenters like Bush ("All crime is hate crime," "They hate us for our freedoms").

While Shakespeare consistently deconstructs simple-minded attitudes, the plays are seldom allowed to do so on film or TV. If they do, they probably fail commercially, as *Titus* did. Shakespeare is permitted to show us very little these days, except how to sell products. Shakespeare as subversive, as "oppositional," has disappeared. One reason—and this is always implicit in my analysis—is that the media themselves have lost their ability to distinguish *within* themselves. On

20 May 2004, the General Accounting Office (GAO) announced that the Department of Health and Human Services was in violation for having passed off a piece of propaganda on Medicaid as an authentic news report. Just what an authentic news report is these days, the GAO did not specify. Frank Rich writes compellingly of the administration's effort to inflect the invasion of Iraq through the heroic Jessica Lynch.[34] Even without the dark mirror of her apparent opposite, Lynndie England, Lynch's story quickly evaporated. She did not fight off her attackers with a knife once her carbine was empty. She was not maltreated by the evildoers who captured her. They tried to return her to the Americans but were fired upon by her countrymen. The narrative was shaped to avoid other issues during the invasion—the confusion that caused the attacking force to destroy civilians as it "shocked and awed" Iraq, for example. Jessica was welcomed back to Elizabeth, West Virginia, on 23 July 2003 with a parade that was televised nationally. A few days after CBS showed the pictures from Abu Ghraib (28 April 2004), Lynndie England's photo was removed from the pantheon of heroes at the Fort Ashby, West Virginia P.O.

Shakespeare in the new millennium is designed to tell the story that specific interests want told. This does represent a change from the Shakespeare who invariably, but not overtly, reflected the cultural moment of a given production. If that cultural moment is primarily commercial, however, then that is the moment that is reflected. If, for example, *Romeo and Juliet* or *Hamlet* are scripts in which the adults behave badly (as they do) and the youngsters behave well (as they can be shown to do with sympathetic casting and editing), and if the goal of production is to sell things to the younger market, then the emphasis of the productions is predictable and inevitable.

"Recontextualizations" abound, and I will mention a few that have been amply examined or that do not warrant a fuller treatment.

Random allusions to Shakespeare in film are many, of course, and lie outside my purview. Early in Howard Hawks's *Only Angels Have Wings* (1939), for example, Pancho (Pedro Regas) spouts some Spanish from which the English word "Shakespeare" emerges. Geoff Carter (Cary Grant) asks what he said. Sparks (Victor Kilian) translates. "'A man can die but once. We owe God a death.' I think it's from *Henry the Fourth*." Yes. Somehow, Pancho knows Feeble's lines from Part Two. The only person in the film who dies, however, is the ubiquitous Thomas Mitchell, who breaks his neck after pranging in a Ford Tri-

Motor. Pedro's reference, then, is more to threatening atmosphere—storms, mountains, and inadequate aircraft—than any fatalities the film ultimately deals out to the characters.

Macbeth seems invariably to be recreated within a criminal society. This approach will never work, simply because the world of the play is explicitly Christian, and even depends on specific Christian usage for one of its greatest scenes. It is one thing for a ghost to appear in *Joe Macbeth* (1956) and for Lily MacBeth (Ruth Roman) to sneer at her husband (Paul Douglas), "You saw yourself in a yellow mirror." It is quite another for Banquo's image to deny Macbeth his place at a table that represents a Eucharist. That is the resonance beneath the scene in 1606 and it can be recaptured in modern productions, as in the Trevor Nunn (Thames TV, 1979), for example, with its solemn music and communal loving cup. In the play, Macbeth can express the destination of his victims only in the terms available—"to heaven or to hell," "if it find out heaven." That is the world Macbeth inhabits, in spite of his desperate wish for a Manichean universe that would give him a place to stand and fight. That is what he means when he talks of "cancel[ing] the great bond that makes [him] pale" and that is something that gives him "terrible dreams that shake [him] nightly." He can no more escape external nemesis than he can the *magister interior* coded within him. That is also true of Lady Macbeth, of course, who perceives the murk of her own damnation.

The wonderful comic actor, Paul Douglas, is too amiable to portray an ambitious criminal underlord. But the fault is not in the stars, as it were, because no "supernatural dimension" exists in this world, as the film's primary critic, Robert F. Willson, Jr. says.[35] A fortune teller—Minerva Pious ("Mrs. Nussbaum" of "Allen's Alley")—is hardly an instrument of darkness sent to "betray" Joe to the "deepest consequence" of damnation. On seeing Banky's Ghost at the dinner party, Joe asks, "Which one a you guys done this?" Nor can the fireworks display during which the hoodlum, Michael Battaglia (John Parker Torturro) is killed in *Men of Respect* (1991) be anything but a pale imitation of the stars falling from the skies predicted by the film's occultists. That suggests that Michael will live beyond his lease of nature and survive even until the ending of the world. He apologizes to his wife, Ruthie (Katherine Borowitz) after the shattered banquet with a powerful "Sorry I ruined your party." The film ends with another heir to the corrupt kingdom being greeted as a "man of respect." As in the Polanski film, where Donalbain goes off to seek the predictions of the Weird Sisters, evil is an endlessly recyclable commodity in this world on the far side of King James I. Nor can a rundown housing estate in *Macbeth and the Estate* (BBC2, 1997) and its small-time drug dealers be a metonymy for a kingdom and its nobility. Nor can a potential fastfood empire, as in *Scotland, PA.* (Lot47/Abandon, 2002), be analogous to the dimensions of the original play, where crimes smash against the face of the cosmos. Here, the Duncan figure is murdered by being dunked in a vat of french fries oil and the Lady Macbeth figure gets a spot of grease on her hand that she cannot wash away.[36]

Macbeth is a "chain of being" play, as the bleeding Captain suggests with his similes: "Yes, as sparrows eagles, or the hare the lion." After the murder, the natural order is turned upside down: a mousing owl rises up to down a falcon, "tow'ring in her pride of place." This worldview represents a reversion for a Shakespeare who had already written the syncretic and ambiguous *King Lear*, but it shows what happens when you kill a king. It is an "occasional play" that must be returned to its occasion—as production can still do—in order for it to release its power. I can conceive of contexts in which much of it might work—Hollywood in the 1920s, for example, possibly an ecclesiastical setting—but only production of the original script can make its anachronisms vivid again.

That crooks are trying to behave like legitimate businessmen reverses the *Macbeth* narrative in which loyal citizens become the serpent under the innocent flower. Criminals seem regularly to knock off the chief or the head of the rival gang—witness Chicago, from whence much of our criminal mythology emerges. The splendid funerals with their flower-filled phaetons suggest that crooks function in a world where fate works against them. "Crime does not pay," we were told as children by *Gangbusters*. But Macbeth is not a criminal to begin with, so the analogy would have to be a successful and law-abiding person deciding to kill his boss. The *tragedy* of Shakespeare's play lies in Macbeth's decision to act against his own better nature and pull fate onto the field against him. And, in his case, the nemesis is God.

The Taming of the Shrew can be easily placed in a contemporary setting, as Gil Junger proved with his *Ten Things I Hate About You* (1999), where the *praxis* is recreated in a West Coast high school.

In *The Flirting Widow* (1930, directed by William A. Seiter), Mr. Faraday (Claude Gillingwater) refuses to permit his daughter, Phyllis (Flora Bramley) to marry until her older sister, Celia (Dorothy Mackaill) finds a husband. The local candidate, Raleigh (William Austin) simply will not do. "In that outfit you look almost like a man," he says to Celia. "With that moustache, so do you," she replies. Celia writes a letter to a nonexistent Colonel John Smith, who turns out to be real (Basil Rathbone) and who shows up at the country estate. After that, the film collapses into a sequence of ludicrous plot complications designed to fill out the hour.

Cole Porter's *Kiss Me, Kate!* appeared as a film in 1953, with Howard Keel and Katherine Grayson and as a TV program in 1958, with the original stage stars, Alfred Drake and Patricia Morison, directed by a pioneer of Shakespeare on TV, George Schaefer. Although it includes "Brush Up Your Shakespeare," the show has been excoriated in recent years as if it were some combination of the Inquisition, Slavery, and the war in Vietnam.[37] The *Moonlighting* version (25 November 1986) places Cybill Shepherd and Bruce Willis in their usual roles, but this time in a "Shakespearean" setting. Jack Oruch has dealt with the production conclusively.[38] Like its parent play it uses an effective frame. Jonathan Miller excised the frame in his Puritan version for BBC (1980), but *Moonlighting* director, Will MacKenzie, shows a young man eager to watch the show dispatched to do his Shakespeare homework by his mother. He reads *Shrew*, recontextualizing it into an episode of the show his mother is watching downstairs. He finishes and rushes down, only to find the show's final credits gliding past. "That's okay," his mother says. "It wasn't very good tonight anyway." An amusing documentary about the Joseph Papp New York Shakespeare Festival *Shrew* (1981), with Meryl Streep and Raul Julia, features responses from audience members. One woman says, "It's such a silly subject nowadays." Her boyfriend interrupts, "But it's not silly!" She goes on, "I can't believe how many people were applauding when he did that my horse, my ass bit." He reaches below camera for her hand. "That scene is a good representation of what our relationship strives to be!" She flings his hand away and gives him a glance meant to wither the foliage in Central Park. Another woman says, "It's a fantasy that is very dangerous for men. Who could be as appealing, wonderful, and strong as Petruchio? " Her husband silently goes cross-eyed beside her.

A Midsummer Night's Dream finds its way into *Dead Poet's Society* (1989) and *Get Over It* (2001), as students struggle to produce versions for their schools. In the former, Robin Williams plays a teacher who dismisses a quantitative method of teaching poetry that never existed (the easier to dismiss) and substitutes a system in which the students must idolize him as "Captain, my Captain." In the latter, Martin Short is as much of a megalomaniac, a drama teacher who demeans the students who step into his hubristic atmosphere. One of his memories of triumph on the stage is his speaking "To be or not to be" to the skull of Yorick.

Robert F. Willson, Jr. suggests of the first version of *The Goodbye Girl* (1977) that the inner play (*Richard III*) parallels the outer narrative: "the wooing of Lady Anne ... is analogous to Dreyfuss's effort to win over an embittered and skeptical Mason. Both ladies are at first convinced that their wooers are simply egotistical 'actors,' but in the end succumb to their advances with utter acceptance of vows of love and faith. It may be that Simon intended a kind of in-joke here for the benefit of Shakespeareans ... it could be argued that Simon has used the *Richard III* as something of a play within the play, reflecting on and providing insight to the rich comic texture of an otherwise conventional situation comedy."[39]

In contrast to Patricia Heaton's character in the 16 January 2004 version on TNT, Marsha Mason's Paula is softer, more ironic, at moments almost amused at the absurdity of her situation. She transmits the vulnerability that is often the element that elicits audience sympathy. Richard Dreyfuss's Elliot is also ironic, of course, and not particularly likable. Heaton's Paula alternates between whiney and shrill. She comes off as stereotype—a composite of qualities that males reject from their own personas and therefore project onto the woman. She becomes a function of the gaze of the male unconscious. Jeff Daniels's Elliot is unbelievably accommodating without convincing us for a moment that he could fall in love with this woman. The hurtful line "Now I know why the others left," delivered after one of Heaton's tantrums, signals a remarkably slow learning curve. Heaton does, however, convince us that she is very insecure, particularly when she cues Daniels about their initial sexual encounter the night before and then rejects his willingness to agree. And she transmits the attitude of a certain New York type superbly. This is the person who has come from somewhere else and who has somehow survived in the Big City and is damned if she will share its hard-won secrets with anyone. Yet, when she is mugged and has her purse stolen—an event more typical of the late 1970s than it is today—she berates Elliot for not getting the purse back for her.

It is difficult to draw any parallel between Richard III-Lady Anne and Elliot-Paula. In the original, Elliot claims that Richard "wants to hump Lady Anne." In the present production, he says that Richard "wants to get Lady Anne in the sack." In each, he asks to play Lady Anne. Elliot in each production does make a flattering (or sexist) early reference to Paula's rear end. Otherwise, Elliot claims—and we believe him—that he has no wish to have a sexual relationship with Paula. No analogy to Lady Anne's reliance on male sponsorship is developed. Unless we know *Richard III*, we will not learn from *The Goodbye Girl* that Richard killed Anne's young husband and the Henry VI whose funeral procession Anne is leading. The "gay Richard" concept—based apparently on the young princes in the Tower—would seem to torpedo the effort to relate inner play with the other narrative. The *Richard III* elements include Elliot's inability to utter the opening soliloquy (Dreyfuss can get the first ten words out. Daniel keeps working on the first word), a rehearsal that Elliot and his Lady Anne conduct in his bedroom, part of I.2 in rehearsal, and a sequence of moments from the first and only performance. But what aspects of these moments reinforce the love story? Dreyfuss's Richard III is amusing. He signals his disagreement with his interpretation as he goes, possibly an analogue to his attitude about sharing the apartment with Mason. Daniels's Richard is so radically overplayed as to destroy any possibility for any analogy with the surrounding plot. The possibility was there—if Paula and Richard had been depicted as overbearing tyrants, using unfavorable circumstances from which to launch their attacks against the amiable Elliot and Anne. The line "I'll have her, but I will not keep her long," which comes in Richard's soliloquy at the end of I.2 (not I.4 as the Simon script calls the scene between Richard and Anne) is not in Simon's playtext. It would refer to Tony, the actor who has left Paula as the play opens, and might foreshadow the threat of Elliot's departure. I was confused in each of *The Goodbye Girl* productions by the overtly gay performance of Richard. In each the Director says, "We'll use it as subtext." It was far more than subtextual in each production but so over the top in the current offering that *no* subtext (even the actor's disapproval of what he was doing) could have worked beneath the performance. Daniels's Richard was indeed an insult to his friends in the gay community, as Daniels's Elliot (but not Dreyfuss's) said it would be. It is barely possible that Dreyfuss would have played Puck in his previous performance, but not credible that Daniels would have. Lysander, perhaps. That instant of script should have been changed even if Lucy (Kate Eisenberg) might not have recognized that it was Richard Powell's role in the 1935 film.

Heaton's characterization may emanate from the change in zeitgeist since 1977, as signaled by *Thelma and Louise* (1991) and *First Wives Club* (1995), but it makes her meltdown into a loving, wall-papering dependent at the end all the more incredible. Even Mason's softer depiction does not play convincingly against Diane Keaton's emergence from dependency in another 1977 film, *Annie Hall*, or Jessica Lange's skeptical Julie at the end of *Tootsie* (1982). One result of Heaton's shrill Paula is that her daughter, Lucy, here becomes a victim, as opposed to the "adult" depicted by Quinn Cummings in the original film.

Simon's updatings include Elliot's receiving the key to the apartment via FedEx, not airmail special delivery, a change from Alexander's to Bloomingdale's (on sale) for Paula's initial shopping spree, an alteration in reference from "gay liberation" to "the gay community," a change from "Tatum O'Neal" to "a young Shirley Temple" (is she more accessible in 2004 than Tatum O'Neal?), from "grass" to "drugs" in Paula's list of prohibitions as Elliot moves in, a raise in Elliot's equity rate from $240 to $600 a week, a change from Spencer Tracy to Jack Nicholson as someone who bombed in his first Broadway play, from Subaru to a Toyota hybrid as the car that Paula hawks, the addition of cable television stations among the many media outlets condemning Elliot's Richard, and so on. The newer version does occur in a zone free of cigarette smoke.

The Director (Richard Benjamin) in the second version does not call Richard a "queen who wants to be king." He calls *Richard III* a "Greek tragedy," and does not mention Olivier's interpretation.

The suggestion of role reversal is picked up in each production. In the 2004 version, Paula goes on and on during her tantrum about telling Elliot what he should be saying about "last night," eliciting his "Now I understand why the others left." That line is not in the original—though why Elliot is still around in the remake is a mystery. In the remake, Elliot calls Paula "crackers" and the script shifts into *The Taming of the Shrew* mode, as Elliot says. He becomes "more shrew than she" (as Curtis remarks in that play) and Elliot pulls off his stunt with the fire escape. No changes or updatings, though, can help when Paula insists on remaining in New York to do the wallpapering instead of going off to California with Elliot. Her domesticity is convincing—as Liz Taylor's was not in the 1966 version of *Shrew*—but it puts her (and us) back in the 50s.

One critic noted that "While goodbye doesn't mean forever, maybe it should."[40] The script does not age well. And, of course, it suffers the inevitable diminution suffered by any film made for TV. Its clichés emerge. Its conviction wanes. The commercials reign.

Fred Wilcox's *Forbidden Planet* (1956) ushers in a fascination with space, in being lost there, and in future times when stars will throw their spears. I find it surprising that *The Tempest* has not found itself reconfigured in futuristic contexts more often since the film appeared. It is still enjoyable, featuring an engaging robot and the superb special effects of *Oz*'s A. Arnold Gillespie.[41] Paul Mazursky's 1982 *Tempest* is a tepid offering in which a New York executive (Paul Cassevetes) suffers a mild midlife crisis. Raul Julia's endearing Kalibanos makes the film worthwhile.

The NBC version of *The Tempest*, which aired in December 1998, is set in the Confederacy of 1865. The thematic links with the American Civil War would seem to emerge from the "freedom-bondage" concept that runs through the play and illustrates in different ways the conflicts of Ariel, Caliban, and Ferdinand. Here we have an irrelevant Gator Man, played by J. Pyper-Furgeson, who wants his bog back, and an Ariel, played by Harold Perineau, who combines Caliban *and* Ariel. The "spirit" can become a crow at any moment he chooses, but he also does a lot of the domestic chores. As an unfreed slave, who learns about the Emancipation Proclamation two years after it has been issued, he wants to join Grant's army on the way to Vicksburg.

The production resembles a story of voodoo thrust upon a Civil War reenactment, or perhaps a nightmare of Mr. Hightower, Faulkner's preacher in *Light in August,* whose sermons keep rumbling off into the dust of one of Jeb Stuart's cavalry columns. The voodoo is promising (a la Gloria Naylor's *Mama Day*), but the production places the narrative in a specific 1865, and makes Ulysses Grant a subhero, thereby introducing a host of issues the script does not raise and blurring beyond distinction what the script does invite a production to explore. A specific time period is seldom a good environment for the translation of a Shakespeare script to any medium, and that is particularly true for television, where a limited field of depth cannot accommodate a lot of details. Here, it doesn't matter.

The special effects "from the same masters who dazzled in last spring's miniseries, *Merlin*,"[42] are tame and tiny, as they must be on a medium that lacks the scale for the spectacular and that usually translates the supernatural in to the psychological.[ll] We learn all we need to know when we are told that "the teleplay is by veteran TV writer James Henerson, whose work [includes] 'I Dream of Jeannie' and 'Bewitched'"[43] —two shows that emerged from the very different personae of their resident witches. Had Prospero been played by Vanessa Redgrave, as in a recent London production ....

The major problem with the production is its remarkable lack of believability. Television is a medium of soap operas that treat in tedious detail the reasons for meaningless actions, or that show persons whose stories reveal the poverty of the human experiment. Peter Fonda's Gideon Prosper is a victim of both strains of these twin displays of futility. The sudden effort to lynch him—he is, after all, chief landowner of the area—is as improbable as his deliverance from the rope.

His motivation to stay in the swamp grows more and more implausible as pressure is brought to bear on him to develop a conscience. The effort here is to parallel the development of Shakespeare's Prospero, but NBC's Prosper is more a puppet of the plot—a Pinocchio—than a recognizable character struggling with a moral or ethical dilemma. Why does he object to his daughter's elopement with her handsome Union officer? Prospero has reasons for slowing the romantic pace of Ferdinand and Miranda, but to change the motive into an apparent hatred of Yankees is to introduce yet another irrelevancy to the story. Since the swamp is right around the bend from the old plantation, Gideon can go after his brother at any time. His excitement at hearing that his brother is near is incomprehensible. After Prosper's storm, Katherine Heigl's Miranda, little homemaker that she is, gets herself offcamera by saying that she is going to check on the house. We remain breathless until she returns to report that nothing of the vine-woven, bark-covered Tarzan treehouse has perished. At another moment, after Gideon is plugged through the breastbone by his brother, Anthony (John Parker Glover is a terrible shot until asked to shoot offhand from a rocking boat), I thought that we were going to be asked to clap our hands and say that we believe in "Dat Ole Black Magic."

At the end, rewards are handed out. The production answers the still-vexed question of Caliban by showing that Gator Man gets his swamp back because he had courage. It is a wonder that Gideon does not hand the cowardly blusterer a purple heart. As Prosper, Miranda, and Fred leave the island, Gator Man stands on his deck. No one waves goodbye. What does work is Anthony's sneering refusal to accept his brother Gideon's hand at the end, even though a firing squad awaits him. But we wonder, given this blank Prosper and this perfidious Anthony (who has committed far worse than *The Tempest*'s Antonio), why the hand has been offered in the first place. Since the action is heavily influenced by a voodoo priestess appearing as a face out of flames, the sudden advent of a "Christian" set of values has not been prepared for. *The Tempest* may be more pagan or cabalistic, more Giordano Bruno or Cornelius Agrippa, than a reflection of Richard Hooker and the reformed church, but it does have a strong Christian rhythm. How could it not? "After all," as Barnaby Dobree, writing of the final plays, says, Shakespeare "belonged to a Christian country; he had been brought up on the Bible; so its ideas, its familiar phrases, would naturally occur to him."[44] Here, we cannot believe in either pole of the play's syncretic value system.

I sought some equation between Gideon Prosper and the Bible's Gideon. In the Book of Judges, Gideon is one of the citizens oppressed by the Midianites. After a lot of negotiation with God, which involves tearing down the altar of Baal, tests in which a fleece left out over night is alternately wet with dew when the ground is dry or dry when the ground is wet, and the reduction of his army from 22,000 to 300, Gideon drives the enemy out, killing most of them, including the princes, Oreb, Zeeb, Sebah, and Zalmunna. It is a great story, but I could not find any parallel between it and this version of *The Tempest*.

The production reminds us of our own dispensation by constantly interjecting commercial breaks, at what the directors must have deemed moments of unbearable suspense. Many of them were for what must be the worst television shows imaginable. If the spots selected to promote these shows are so crashingly unfunny, for all of the artificial laughter that floats around them like dead leaves, why would anyone be tempted to watch them? At other moments, since the production appeared only a dozen shopping days before Christmas, the mosquito-buzzing swampland of the Mississippi Delta was juxtaposed against the snowflakes, balsam trees, colored lightbulbs, and other clichés of a white, middle-class Christmas.

Freeing the slaves was necessary and overdue, but it was only a secondary reason for the American Civil War. I assume that the production meant us to infer the knowledge that the "brave new world of Reconstruction" became a version of the old world very quickly. What on earth is executive producer Raskin talking about when she says, "We loved the banishment and the isolation, in this case, in terms of North versus South"?[45] That statement signals incoherence at the heart of the project.

I asked myself a) whether the production would have been successful without any knowledge of *The Tempest* to get in the way, and b) whether the production enhanced our sense of the source. In each case, I answered no. The production itself is tedious, elongated beyond its intrinsic content and centered on a mere Scrooge. Its connections with the original script are so tenuous or simplified that it distorts rather than illuminates. Unlike other works of art—painting and sculpture, for example—the plays of Shakespeare permit us to inhabit them in our time and, inevitably, *with* our time. This production simply abandons its originating source and gives us a far lesser thing in its place.

It will be objected, rightly, that my critique would not even occur were it not for the production's linkage with Shakespeare's play. True. Without that connection this *Tempest* would have passed unnoticed, its radical inconsistencies merely those of television melodrama. Our expectation of the medium is a fragment of Aristotle's "final cause," the effect of the work of art on the observer. This *Tempest* can be said to have met our expectations for television, which are low. Television is in its infancy—and likely to stay there. We learn about it, however, as it encounters the Shakespearean script and struggles to find the right balance between a heavy concept and a bare stage.

Gus Van Zant's *My Own Private Idaho* is a gloomy and incoherent film and thus popular among post-modernist critics. It would deserve no mention here except in that it employs the *Henry IV* wayward son, drunken surrogate father motif. "If Shakespeare is only window dressing," says Kenneth S. Rothwell, "the movie belongs to" what he calls "the parasitic" category, which includes "only fragments of Shakespeare... not deeply embedded in the film's main plot."[46] I would suggest that *Idaho*, in places, is what Rothwell calls "a recontextualization [that] will keep the plot [of the Shakespeare play] but move Shakespeare's play into a wholly new era and jettison the Shakespearean language."[47] Rothwell's second category includes the film or TV production that uses Shakespeare— an actual production— to "mirror"[48] the offscreen lives of the actors. *A Double Life* (1947) and *Kiss Me, Kate!* (1953) are examples, of course, but *Idaho* does not really fit a category that uses Shakespeare as "mirror." Kathy M. Howlett views Van Zant's film positively, as dissolving "the binary opposition between high and low culture to reveal the vitality of the

Shakespearean text given an American context."[49] I would argue that the "Shakespearean text" is absent from the film.

As I write, in the Spring of 2004, I predict that Shakespeare will become more and more the servant of mere commerce, if not condemned outright as heretical and banned from production, that is, unless accommodated to reinforcement of the powers-that-be. We exist in America not just "under God," but under a President who believes that "our rights were derived from God" and that "God wants me to be president."[50] At this point, it seems that the Democrats share God's wish. But then, as Frank Rich remarks, "In the fear game, the Democrats are the visiting team, playing at a serious disadvantage ... they can't suit up officials at will to go on camera to scare us."[51]

Notes

[*] Cf. Lynda Boose and Richard Burt: the text is "a referent no longer there... [films] reconstruct a Shakespeare narrative in some new realm of the imagination" (*Shakespeare: The Movie*. London: Routledge, 1997, p. 1). How can something be *reconstructed* if it is not there already? On the erasure of the text as a perceived source of contemporary adaptations or offshoots of Shakespeare, see Richard Burt, "Introduction." *Shakespeare, The Movie, II* (London: Routledge, 2002), pp. 14–36.

[†] Having written that, I discover the parallel in Harold Meyerson's op-ed piece, "Prince Hal vs. King Henry" (*Washington Post* on-line, 28 April, 2004). "You don't build a record if you don't show up," he says of Bush's National Guard service. "'Young and irresponsible'... Bush was Prince Hal."

[‡] For a sampling of the theory that drives much of the current criticism of Shakespeare and the media, see Walter Benjamin, "The Work of Art in the Age of Mechanical Reproduction." *Illuminations*, Hanna Arendt, ed., Harry Zohn, trans. New York: Harcourt, Brace, and World, 1968, pp. 219–253; Theodor Adorno and Max Horkheimer, "The Culture Industry: Enlightenment as Mass Deception." *Dialectic of Enlightenment*, John Cumming, trans. New York: Continuum, 1972, pp. 120–167; and Frederic Jameson, "Postmodernism and Consumer Society." *The Cultural Turn: Selected Writings on the Postmodern: 1983–1998*. London: Verso, 1998, pp. 1–20. Perhaps Shakespeareans were the last to know, but Mark Greif announces the demise of theory in "Life After Theory," *The American Prospect*. 13/8 (August 2004): pp. 62–65. With the election of Reagan, Greif says "it began to seem that in fact everything *apart* from culture had been lost overnight to an unsuspected revolutionary conservatism" (64). Theory, Greif argues, has created its own wilderness, from which no escape is possible and from which no light emerges. Many of us were attracted to performance criticism because we realized that "theory" had little if anything to say about the plays. Productions of them invariably do project new insights into the texts

as *scripts*. But theory and that undramatic sector known as new historicism still hold sway in Shakespeare studies, as witness some of the seminars offered by the 2004 meeting of the Shakespeare Association of America: Histories of the Book: Marginal Practices in Early Print Culture, Theorizing Global Shakespeare Pedagogy, The Future of Presentism and the End of History, Global Trade: Discourses and Practices, Cloistering the English Woman: Shakespeare and Beyond, The Principle of Pleasure (a seminar that deals with the pleasure derived "from reading and writing about Shakespeare," as opposed to experiencing the plays in production), and so on. These seminars will produce some brilliant work, I have no doubt, but will also undoubtedly add to what Russell Jacoby calls the "tidal wave of unreadable faux-theoretical monographs." "The Three P's: Publishing Perishable Prose," *New York Times Education Life* (1 August 2004): 4.

§ Harold Bloom's "Macbush" (*Vanity Fair* [April 2004]: 286–287) employs Tamburlanian overreaching as much as it does its Shakespearean source and is at least as much a parody of textual scholarship as it is a satire about the Bush regime.

‖ On television's reduction of the supernatural to the merely psychological, see Alan Dressen, "The Supernatural on Television." *Shakespeare on Film Newsletter* 11/1 (1986): 1 and 8.

On *The Tempest* offshoots, *Yellow Sky* (1948) and *Age of Consent* (1970), see Daniel Rosenthal, *Shakespeare on Screen*. London: Hamlyn, 2000, p. 149.

Chapter One
Romeo and Juliet

It may be, as Douglas Lanier suggests, that "postmodern democratization" has erased the "outmoded divide between high and low culture." Lanier goes on to argue that "one overarching aim of recent Shakespeare films has been to definitively establish the screen image ... as the principal vehicle for sustaining Shakespeare's cultural authority in a post-theatrical, post-literary age."[1]

I would suggest that *Romeo and Juliet* is one of the chief agents of that authority, and that the process began long before Theodor Adorno, Walter Benjamin, Frederic Jameson, et al[2] identified it for us. Most teachers of the play are aware that many of their students will have already had an experience with Shakespeare's *Romeo and Juliet* in some form or other. If I were teaching the play, I'd ask, "What do you know about *Romeo and Juliet*?" Shakespeare's version may end up surprising students who "already know the story." And the students' versions are likely to amaze the teacher.

Romeo and Juliet is easy to "recontextualize," as the current jargon has it. It is a simple story—two teenagers fall in love, in spite of the objections of the young woman's parents, and die as a result of parental priorities and Romeo's impetuously wrong conclusions. Furthermore, while the play is set in a Catholic country, no inhibiting "cosmic imperative" interferes with modernizations. Richard III's guilty soliloquy as he awakens before his final battle sounds wildly anachronistic in a 1937 setting, and *Macbeth* does not translate well to the criminal sphere in spite of all the efforts to make that concept work. *Macbeth*'s medieval premises are calculated to show what it is to kill a king within the complete and comprehensive dimensions of the "chain of being." It may be fascinating to find Hamlet trapped in "a system that turns all art to commerce and subjects all idealities to control,"[3] but *Hamlet* becomes a trifle less portentous when the Ghost disappears into a Coca-Cola machine, a postmodern purgatory. All corporations may inform against Hamlet, but heaven and hell are not usually part of the corporate equation. The major error that adaptations of *Romeo and Juliet* make is to differentiate the two lovers via class, race, or origin. Shakespeare's immediate source, Arthur Brooke's *Romeus and Juliet* (1562), emphasizes the "equal state" of the Montagues and Capulets. Brooke, in fact, makes that equality the source of the "envy" out of which "black hate and rancor grew." The play claims that the "two households" are "alike in dignity." The feud—easily understood if the lovers are differentiated in any way other than by gender—is a "given." It is not to be "understood," but to be felt as a terrible power that undermines any prospect of a comic ending. A pagan fatality broods over the lovers—they are "star-cross'd," as the chorus informs us, and thwarted by "a greater power than we can contradict," as the Friar says to Juliet. Romeo can "defy" the "stars," but the inherited feud that seeps along the sewers of Verona is reflected by a zodiac that looms irrefutably above the fist he shakes at it.

Today, of course, the source of the lovers' problems can be defined in other ways. A 2003 commercial for Nextel Walkie-Talkies begins with a view of a proscenium arch in a theater, framing a familiar play. Juliet looks down from her balcony as Romeo, below, commits suicide because of miscommunication. The Friar exclaims "Kids!" in amused exasperation. This trivialization interestingly underlines the private world in which cell-phone users live. They pay no attention to their immediate environment when all is focused on the voice at the other end of the line. Romeo and Juliet live in such a world—inhabited only by a third party, the Friar—and their inability to communicate within it dooms them. That is a more complicated message than the commercial delivers, of course, but the commercial demonstrates one more time the pervasiveness of this play and these characters in our culture and how they exemplify our failures and our expectations. We wiser beings can look back with a certain amusement at flaming youth. We wiser beings can avoid such misconceptions. We also avoid extremes, of course, and find that the heyday in our blood is tame. That is the lesson of cell-phone use. It is the detachment we desire, as much as the contact. The proscenium arch at the outset of the commercial permits us to suspend our disbelief. The product permits us to maintain that suspension. We are constantly rehearsing for a play that never begins, or we maintain a stance of distant observers of someone else's drama. The cell phone becomes a metonym for a post-literate, completely vicarious existence.

Here are some examples of my thesis: a version of the story has already been told to many of its audience members before they encounter Shakespeare's play. Some of the examples are clearly and merely designed to sell a product. Others pull the play into a cultural context deemed desirable—that is, a zone within which products are likely to sell simply because money is so readily available.

In *Daddy Long Legs* (1919), Mary Pickford's Juliet forgets her lines during her school's graduation production and has to be cued by the woman playing Romeo (Jeanne Carpenter). It doesn't matter. Pickford is at her loveliest as she mimes "Oh yes!" and continues the play. "Who is that?" ask Daddy Longlegs (Mahlon Hamilton) and a younger suitor (Marshall Nieland) in the audience. The film was remade twice. Jean Negulsco's 1955 version (with Fred Astaire and Leslie Caron) has Fred discovering Leslie in France and thus does not incorporate the play-within-a-film.

In *A Day at the Races* (1935), just before she is about to bilk Groucho Marx's Mr. Quackenbush, Esther Muir's Miss Marlowe tells her accomplice, "Don't worry, by the time you knock on that door, I'll have that moth-eaten Romeo doing the balcony scene."

The lovers of *Romeo and Juliet* were seldom teenagers in the 1930s. In *Hold that Kiss* (1938), Morgan Wallace says to a long-faced Dennis O'Keefe, "Good morning, Romeo. Has something gone sour between thee and thy Juliet?" Yes, but only temporarily. After mutual practical jokes, these two adults O'Keefe (30 in 1938) and Maureen O'Sullivan (27) kiss and make up. Since Dennis is a clerk at a travel agency and Maureen works at a dress shop, this Romeo and Juliet couple functions within the same economic plane. And it can hardly be called a cross-cultural relationship.

In *The Wizard of Oz* (1939), Jack Haley's Tinman pauses along the yellow brick road and suddenly hears "Romeo, Romeo, wherefore art thou Romeo?"

In *Stagedoor Canteen* (1943), a soldier (Lon McCallister) discovers Katherine Cornell serving oranges at the Canteen where stars—from Broadway, in this instance—have volunteered to wait on the military. He asks her whether she remembers the balcony scene. She does. They recite it back and forth across the cafeteria's rails, as Judith Anderson looks on. "Hey! What's slowing up the line?" demands a Marine. "A little unrationed ham being served," Katherine says, referring to the wartime rationing that had gone into effect. She looks sadly after the lad going off to war with only the vicarious memory of having played Romeo to Cornell's Juliet to sustain him.

And the script could be played for laughs in 1943. As he raises the poison to a seemingly dead Juliet, Cantinflas, in the Mexican film *Romeo y Jolieta*, directed by Miguel M. Delgado, condenses Romeo's "Here's to my love." "Salud!" he says.

In a 1956 MGM film, *These Wilder Years*, directed by Roy Rowland, a pregnant teenager, Suzie (Betty Lou Keim), explains to Steve Bradford (James Cagney) why she did not marry the boy who impregnated her. "Our parents hated each other," she says, "so we had to meet in secret. He was a jet pilot. He did not come back" (presumably from Korea). "The Montagues and the Capulets!" Bradford exclaims. "Who?" Suzie asks. Innocent of Shakespeare, the girl has made up a story that happens to parallel Shakespeare's play, suggesting that the narrative—the *praxis*—is prior to and independent of the play. That Suzie's explanation is untrue—she is a child of poverty, not the daughter of an oil baron, and her lover said that her pregnancy could have been caused by "sixteen other guys"—only emphasizes the story's ubiquity. Her lover's excuse is the same one Cagney had used twenty years earlier to escape responsibility for his lover and their son.

On 5 May, 1962, "The Case of the Ancient Romeo" became episode 151 of *The Perry Mason Show*. A prop sword is replaced with a "live" one, and Romeo (Steve Brock, played by Rex Reason) kills Tybalt (Franz Lachman, played by Jeff Morrow). Perry (Raymond Burr) and Della (Barbara Hale) just happen to be in the theater that evening. They witness a variation on the scheme that Claudius and Laertes construct and on the substitution of an actual dagger for the killing of Banquo in *Macbeth*. Since Lachman is also the director who has brought in a new Juliet (Patricia Huston) to replace the woman who should get the role (K.T. Stevens), the motive is clear. Brock has killed Lachman in revenge for this casting decision. The show does take us into the typical Mason courtroom, in which the camera closes-up on various guilty-looking faces. Then, however, Director Arthur Marks works a variation on the usual format. Instead of having someone confess in the courtroom, as Perry's intimidating elimination of all other options swings the finger inexorably toward the guilty party, Perry returns everyone to the theater. He places everyone in the position he or she was in when the sword was switched. During the reenactment, the guilty person is in the down-right, or vulnerable, stage position. That blocking proves prophetic. Another innocent person is free to have a few post-revelation drinks with Perry and company and another evildoer is left to the humane hospitality accorded by the LAPD.

It is more than coincidence that the stage version of *West Side Story* appeared in 1957, and that one of Peggy Lee's songs was written in

1958: "Romeo loved Juliet / Juliet, she felt the same. / When he put his arms around her, / He said, Julie baby you're my flame. / Thou givest fever, when we kisseth, / Fever, I'm afire. / Fever, yes, I burn forsooth." *West Side Story* and Peggy's "Fever" herald the advent of a teenage culture that has burgeoned since. Many of the great Broadway shows had been produced by the late 1950s. While Harry James and Benny Goodman soldiered on, most of the big bands were gone. Glenn Miller had disappeared, the Dorsey Brothers were dead, and Fred Astaire was old. Elvis, the Beetles, and rock and roll were arriving as the musical center of the new adolescent culture. By 2003, the teenage clothing market alone had become a $70 billion a year industry. I am told by someone who knows this sort of thing that, while we once hoped to dress as adults dress—I can remember my first pair of long pants in 1938—we now dress as teenagers dress. So, it is not surprising that a play that treats the difficulties of first love and the issue of parental interference should now be the play we encounter most often as we pick our way through the thickets of postmodern life. The play, of course, is full of linkages between love and death—it was a ubiquitous metaphor in the plays of the 1950s—and it recapitulates the process of adolescence. As Peter Blos argues in his classic study, *On Adolescence*, the adolescent alternates between mourning and being in love. He or she senses the loss of childhood and simultaneously yearns for the perceived pleasures of adulthood.[4]

And, of course, the adolescent process invites parody. After I gave a talk on *Romeo and Juliet* at José Ramon Diaz-Fernandez's splendid conference on film in 1999, sponsored by La Universidad de Malaga, I was told that a Bugs Bunny version of the balcony scene exists. I have been unable to track that one down, but perhaps some Loony Tunes aficionado or ada can help me. That sequence itself would impress the scene on a youthful imagination long before it had encountered Shakespeare's version.

In and Out, a trivial film of 1997, shows Joan Cusack as an English teacher—almost obligatory for recontextualizations of *Romeo and Juliet*—wandering drunk after having been jilted on her wedding night. She encounters her former student Cameron (Matt Dillon). They recite lines from the balcony scene—though the English teacher in her corrects him at one point—then dance, as Patsy Kline's voice emerges from the tavern behind them, changing the street into a make-believe ballroom.

A 1998 ABC cartoon shows a balcony collapsing under the weight of its Juliet. "What blocks the light from yonder window?" Romeo has just asked. He is kayoed and carted off like just another injured football player. A substitute Romeo appears offering a juicebox, but Juliet perseveres, even if her new Romeo, now dead in the play, has to scratch his nose in real life. Will a future audience of *Romeo and Juliet* say, "No! The balcony is supposed to collapse!" Never underestimate the power of a first experience. Will future audiences of *A Midsummer Night's Dream* realize that they have already seen "Pyramus and Thisbe" on ABC?

In a 1998 commercial for Visa, Steve Young, then quarterback for the 49ers asks how his date is doing. "A bit chilly," she says. "What am I thinking of?" Steve asks. He takes his jacket off. His date prepares to receive it over her shoulders. The camera pans to the left, where sits Jerry Rice, then Steve's favorite pass catcher. Steve places the jacket over Jerry's shoulders. First things first. Jerry Rice had been where Steve Young wanted him to be many times. Jerry is where the unnamed young woman does *not* want him to be. The threesome goes to the theater. Three tickets slide out from the box office. To *Romeo and Juliet*, of course. The very title of the play by 1998 is a synecdoche for romance, but three tickets suggest an unwelcome triangle.

Another 1998 commercial shows a hapless Romeo unable to find the side of his body in which his heart doth hop as a balcony-inhabiting Juliet emotes above him in German. It is all very "vooden." "Ve Germans don't do vromance. Ve do beer!" says a Germanic voice as a bottle of Beck's bangs down in front of us.

I will look at some of the films and television shows that use *Romeo and Juliet* directly, or resemble it in some basic way.† The usual resemblance occurs in parental objection to an often cross-cultural or cross-racial relationship, a warping of Shakespeare's "households ... alike in dignity" format. Films like Josef von Sternberg's *An American Tragedy* (1931, with Frances Dee, Phillips Holmes, and Sylvia Sidney) and *A Place in the Sun* (1951, with Elizabeth Taylor, Montgomery Clift, and Shelley Winters), both versions of the Dreiser novel, don't fit, since the "Romeo" figure has a pregnant girlfriend on his hands—until she drowns. *Love Story* (1970), although it incorporates the objections of the aristocratic Brewsters to their son's marriage to an Italian girl, won't work since neither Romeo nor Juliet dies of a wasting disease. Nor am I dealing here with films of the play—though great ones have been made. The 1936 version with its superannuated stars, Shearer and Howard, is underrated. Although a function of the '30's "star system," its black and white photography is often superb. Zeffirelli's high-renaissance *Romeo and Juliet* of 1970 captures the generational conflict inherent in the script and rife in American society at the time. Luhrmann's smashing 1996 production may have been undermined by woeful acting in the main roles, but its pace, its setting in the caldron of Mexico City, and its ironic use of religious iconography make it a wonderful film. *Shakespeare in Love* uses *Romeo and Juliet* to demonstrate that people in love can exchange each other's roles and say each other's lines within the singleness of their passion. The lovers (Joseph Fiennes and Gwyneth Paltrow) blend their voices and beings into a figurative and literal duet as the camera cuts back and forth across a river that, for a few magic moments, does not divide but joins. The blending is reinforced by the merging of gender—the "Juliet" figure plays Romeo and a boy actor (Daniel Brocklebank) plays Juliet (and even complains that his dress makes him look like a pig). Unfortunately for the existential couple but happily for the fictional Shakespeare's career, Paris-Wessex (Colin Firth) makes off with Juliet.

The narrative seems inescapable. It existed, of course, in various guises before Shakespeare dramatized it—in Masuccio of Salerno, Luigi da Porto, Bandello, Boaistuau's translation of Bandello into French, and Brooke. It can be traced back at least as far as Ovid's tale of Pyramus and Thisby, which Shakespeare treats in *A Midsummer Night's Dream*, another play about young love and parental interference. It can emerge independent of Shakespeare's adaptation of the narrative. This persistence suggests that the story is archetypal, even if Shakespeare's play has engraved the archetype into Western culture. Jameson argues that narrative is designed to sustain the status quo,[5] and certainly in the 21st century *Romeo and Juliet* would be a major engine of the teenage consumer culture. But like other scripts, *Romeo and Juliet* can occasionally be subversive, even as it is presented in and encoded by modern media.

Balzac's version of *Romeo and Juliet* is *Eugenie Grandet*, in which a nasty (and latently incestuous) father drives his daughter's lover away. That she is not his natural daughter (as we later learn) is significant, of course, since she and Charles are supposedly first cousins. The novel makes a great silent film, *The Conquering Power* (1921), directed by Rex Ingram, with Alice Terry, Rudolph Valentino, and Ralph Lewis. The film begins with an interesting disclaimer: "You, Great Public, do not like the costume play. Life is life. So we make our story of today." The public would soon change its collective mind, of course, and the film is set and costumed in a 19th century French mode, as opposed to something resembling Harding's "normalcy," or Gatsby's mansion. Charles (Valentino) is given to wild and extravagant parties, however, even as his father Victor (Eric Mayne) goes bankrupt. Charles is dispatched to the provinces, where live wealthy but miserly Grandet (Lewis), his wife (Edna Demaurey), who looks like Marie Antoinette awaiting execution, and his lovely daughter Eugenie. She is besieged by suitors—a pompous squirt (Ward Wing) and the final failed result of the local aristocracy (George Atkinson). Grandet, recognizing the immediate attraction between Charles and Eugenie, plays the suitors off against each other. "I would rather see my daughter dead than married to Charles Grandet," he says. Eugenie, of course, overhears this echo of Shylock and Capulet. Pere Grandet bilks Charles of what is left of Victor's estate and sends him off to Martinique, but not before Eugenie gives Charles the golden coins her father has given her—one on each birthday. Pere Grandet intercepts Charles's letters to Eugenie. Pere Grandet tells Charles that Eugenie is to be married. "I do not deem it advisable that you correspond with her any longer." Believing that Charles is to be married, Eugenie finally accepts the dry-prune Bonfors (Atkinson). Charles returns and visits the garden where he and Eugenie had fallen in love. She arrives and shows him her empty ring finger. They show each other the tokens they have exchanged—a key and a cross. Bonfors looks out the window at their embrace and realizes that he's had it.

In one of the film's great scenes, Grandet is visited, a la Richard III, by ghosts—in this instance, of his brother, Victor, and Grandet's wife, who died after he had attacked her for defending Eugenie. Grandet is crushed by the gold he has hoarded, suddenly come alive as a malevolent material god. "Someday your gold will crush you," a peasant (Eugene Pouyet) predicts as Grandet forecloses on him. Gold becomes a "baby" that Grandet rocks in a cradle. But the infant becomes a monster. "I am gold. Now you are mine!" The scene inspired Stroheim's *Greed*, though much of the hallucinatory material in that film was cut. Another wonderful moment comes when Eugenie hears that Charles has returned to Paris. The subtle changes in Terry's expressive face epitomize the silent screen technique that makes these films so satisfying. The film's title cards occasionally lapse into the Victorian, D. W. Griffith style of sentimentality that those cards could display in the early days of feature-length films: "Woman's is the passive part—the web of life interwoven with love, sorrow, and hope."

Eugenie looks at the statue of the Virgin in her garden and the nest that a bird has built in a nearby tree. "While the man busies himself with the present and looks to the future with consolation." Plenty of other women just beyond the horizon? The film is much better than its written premises might suggest.

When Valentino asked for a raise from the $250 a week that Metro was paying him, he was offered another $50 per. He left for Paramount. *The Sheik* appeared later in 1921. The woman who adapted Balzac's novel for the screen, June Mathis, also left Metro for Paramount. She wrote *The Saphead* for Buster Keyton, along with *Blood and Sand* for Valentino, *Greed*, and *Ben-Hur*.

Romeo and Juliet has been a part of popular culture for a long time, but its negative ending has not. The preview for the 1936 film does not suggest that the story will end gloomily and tombily. In the 1939 film, *Andy Hardy Gets Spring Fever*, Judge Hardy (Lewis Stone) surprises Andy (Mickey Rooney) by reciting part of the opening chorus. Even the older generation experienced romance at some distant moment in the past! Andy redesigns Shakespeare's play so that he is an Admiral in the Navy and Ann Rutherford is a Tahitian maiden who falls into a volcano. In his *Romeo and Juliet*, Andy, landing on a foreign shore, borrows from *The Tempest* and exclaims "She speaks English!" as he encounters Talulla (Rutherford). She explains: "Many moons ago, a steam canoe like the one that brings you, came here across the great sea. But the storm came and so she sink. One white god like you is saved. He marry native girl. She my mother. He my father." "This beautiful olive-skinned creature is a daughter of the U.S.A.!" Andy exclaims. Again the Romeo and Juliet story is reconfigured as a meeting of different cultures. Andy angrily chastises Talulla for her supposed infidelity—really excoriating Miss Rose ("a rose by any other name," of course) Meredith (Helen Gilbert), with whom Andy believes himself to be in love and whom he has seen kissing her fiancé upon the latter's arrival backstage. So the play-within-the-play suddenly creates a Pagliacci moment. The racist assumptions—white god and olive-skinned maid—are very much the same that inhabit the much later Pocahontas films of Disney, but in the latter they are used more consciously and political correct. In the 1939 film, although Talulla leaps into a volcano, Andy and Polly end up happily smooching.

The negative mythology is distanced from the comfortable middle-class life of the Hardys and girlfriend Polly. *Romeo and Juliet* is a metaphor for young love, of course, but in the Andy Hardy series and in films about young people in the late 1930s the goal is adulthood and the illusory completion that it confers on teenagers. The deaths of Romeo and Juliet are not a metaphor for teenage life but a contrast to it. The aspirations of any culture at any given moment in history will find their resonance in Shakespeare—but it will be a different resonance.

The film does make one major error. Rose quotes Lorenzo from Act Five of *Merchant of Venice*:

> How sweet the moonlight sleeps upon this bank!
> Look how the floor of heaven is thick inlaid
> With patens of bright gold.

"That's from *Romeo and Juliet*!" Andy exclaims. Director "One Shot Wally" Van Dyke does not correct the error. How many generations have searched for those lines in *Romeo and Juliet*?

We hear Tchaikovsky's *Romeo and Juliet* Overture (1870) for the first time on film behind Norma Shearer and John Gilbert in a Technicolor balcony scene in *Hollywood Revue of 1929* (directed by Charles Reisner, though the *Romeo and Juliet* scenes are ostensibly directed by Lionel Barrymore). Irving Thalberg, MGM chief, was fascinated by Tchaikovsky. The Overture would be the personal theme of the two "young" lovers in the 1936 film with Norma Shearer and Leslie Howard, directed by George Cukor. The Overture also makes a brief and obtrusive appearance at the end of a film without a musical accompaniment—MGM's *Tarzan the Apeman* (1932, directed by W. S. Van Dyke). As Tarzan (Johnny Weissmuller) and Jane Parker (Maureen O'Sullivan) and Cheetah (Cheetah) stand on a promontory to survey their jungle domain, we suddenly hear the music. Ah, yes! This is a version of *Romeo and Juliet*. O'Sullivan, though Irish, plays a British woman in the film. Tarzan, though a displaced aristocrat in the Edgar Rice Burroughs' fiction, is just inexplicably "there" in the film, a creature of the jungle. This is probably the first time, then, that film emphasizes the radical differences between the two lovers, as opposed to the "both alike in dignity" context of Shakespeare's play.

The 1936 *Romeo and Juliet* starred a 36-year-old Shearer and a 42-year-old Howard. At the time, the stars' creaky knees were not much remarked. Shearer as a young girl was ludicrous at times—though she was nominated for an Academy Award—and Howard played Romeo (as the text signals) as a man in love for the first time. It was still Depression America, and the conquest of the marketplace by teenagers was still 25 years away. The film did not bomb, as mythology has it. It made a healthy $1,200,000. The problem was that MGM's Irving Thalberg splurged, spending $2 million on the film—the last vehicle he would create for his wife, Norma. Thalberg died as the film was being released in the autumn of 1936. In 1936, however, films were media for mature stars, and the issue of their age was not often broached. Joan Crawford—who lost a lot of roles to Shearer at MGM—did offer this critique of the film: "I couldn't wait for those two old turkeys to die—could you?"

A wonderful "alternative" version of *Romeo and Juliet* did occur in 1936. In an episode directed by Gordon Douglas, "The Little Rascals" perform the play in a barn. Their sign announces "Sattiday Mattinnay. Spanky Presents Romyo and Julett ... by Spanky and Shakspeer." Alfalfa (Carl Switzer) makes his first entrance as Romeo only to be interrupted by a chicken (a graceful allusion to Chaucer's Nun's Priest, probably not grasped by all). Romeo must chase the chicken out before he can truly say, "Ah—alone at last!" The performance itself is almost destroyed when Darla (Hood) refuses to play opposite Alfalfa, who has been eating onions. Buckwheat (William Thomas) substitutes for Darla, therefore introducing a boy actor in the woman's role and the cross-racial format that seems to characterize modern interpretations of the story. Buckwheat, too, objects to the onions and pushes Alfalfa's ladder from the balcony. He and the ladder slash through the curtain that Spanky (McFarland) has hastily thrown down. But all ends well as the company shares the pile of pennies that the spectators have paid as they exited.

A 1936 film that does include the unhappy ending of *Romeo and Juliet* is MGM's *Rose-Marie*. It opens with Jeanette MacDonald and Allan Jones performing Gounod's *Romeo Et Juliette*. The opera-within-a-film includes a lavish Capulet party, a program illustration of the balcony scene, a snippet of sword play, a shot of Juliet and Friar Lawrence, and the virtually simultaneous deaths of Romeo and Juliet. Costar Nelson Eddy was so jealous of Jones's tenor voice that Eddy insisted that Jones's solo, "E lucevan le stelle" from Puccini's *Tosca* be cut from the film.

The Tchaikovsky Overture occurs briefly on Richard Carlson's car radio in *The Dancing Coed* (1939, directed by S. Sylvan Simon). By this time, the Overture is clearly associated with Shakespeare. It sounds under an actorly voice (Eugene Radovitch) saying, "All the world's a stage, and all the men and women merely players." Jacques's clichés cue Lana Turner's brainstorm to hire two actors to play the fathers that the president of Midwestern University (Walter Kingsford) has summoned to respond to their children's publishing of pictures embarrassing to the institution. The film does have a whiff of the disparity between the two principals in that Turner is a hoofer posing as a coed to win a contest, while Carlson is an authentic college student, if such a thing exists. Earlier, a conference in the college paper's newsroom had been conducted in front of a poster for the Midwestern University production of *Hamlet*. The poster alludes to the disguise and investigation elements of the film's plot. The film features a sparkling performance by Ann Rutherford, fleeting glimpses of Veronica Lake and Robert Walker, and a too-brief solo by Artie Shaw's great drummer, Buddy Rich. See his longer solo in MGM's *Thrill of a Romance* (1945), when he was with Tommy Dorsey.

Romeo, Juliet and Darkness (1959), aka *Sweet Light in a Dark Room*, a Czech film directed by Jiri Weiss, takes place in Prague in 1942, just before the assassination of Reinhard Heydrich, Reichsprotector of Bohemia and Moravia. Hana (Dana Smutna) plays a Jewish girl hidden in an attic room by Pavel (Ivan Mistrik). The film opens with a Jewish family, the Wurms, packing a handcart and on their way to the railway station for transport to Dachau. A neighbor says goodbye. "See you again." It is a parody of the goodbyes of a normal society, in which the man leaves town for another job. Mr. Wurm shrugs. The Wurms and their wagon disappear down an empty avenue in a haunting deep field shot. The neighbor himself is later taken away by the Gestapo. One of Pavel's classmates is pulled from class. His name appears on a long list of executions, and two flowers show up on his empty desk. The girlfriend of a Nazi officer moves into the Wurm's apartment: "Has the place been cleaned out now that the Jews have left?" The girlfriend (Karla Chadimova), however, is not above making a pass at Pavel, or bringing Pavel's mother (Jirina Sejbalova) a jacket of Mrs. Wurm's to be altered. Pavel abandons his very blonde girlfriend (Blanka Bohdanova) and falls in love with Hana. Although Hana has become a nihilist, she is won over by Pavel's existentialism. They talk about the possibility of a future together as they gaze at the stars above Prague. They dance and imagine sunlight and flowers, a place for them beyond the dark room in which she hides. The German officer's girlfriend's yapping dog threatens to reveal Hana's hiding place. Paul kills the dog. The dog's owner, however, suspects that someone is hiding in the attic.

By this time, the assassination attempt on Reinhard Heydrich has been made. He lived from 27 May to 4 June 1942. During this week,

Prague rumbles with tanks and armored cars, and echoes with ubiquitous public address announcements. The film captures a constant of good recontextualizations of *Romeo and Juliet*—a rise in violence in the society surrounding the evolving love affair.

The Nazis searched 30,000 buildings in Prague looking for Heydrich's killers. He was buried in Berlin on 9 June, after a service featuring Hitler's eulogy and Seigfried's Funeral March from *Gotterdammerung*. His assassins, Czech volunteers Josef Gabcik and Jan Kubis, who had parachuted into the area near Prague from Great Britain, were discovered in the Karol Boromejsky Church and finally committed suicide, along with their lookout Josef Valcik on 18 June. On 10 June— legend has it as a result of Hitler's putting his finger down randomly on a map of Czechoslovakia—the village of Lidice was obliterated. The allies knew that the assassination of Heydrich would elicit a brutal response, but apparently felt that his rise to higher positions would be more of a risk. A more cynical motive may have been that Nazi repression would reawaken Czech resistance. Heydrich had virtually succeeded in "pacifying" Czechoslovakia prior to his assassination. Heydrich was the only Nazi leader specifically targeted by the Allies for assassination during World War II.‡ (Admiral Isoroku Yamamoto was assassinated when his plane was shot down by U. S. Army P-38s in the Pacific Theater on 18 April 1943.)

Realizing that she is trapped and that her presence will condemn many of those who live in the apartment building, Hana rushes into the street. We hear the shots and the coup de grâce outside the locked gate of the building. The film's intentionally bleak camerawork and the sotto voce love scenes that contrast with the blaring public address announcements make this result feel inevitable from the first. At the outset, the Wurms move down the avenue without a voice raised in their defense. Nothing could have saved them. At the end, nothing can save Hana.

Romeo, Juliet and Darkness has the tonality of several films made immediately after World War II in the "neorealist" mode. The mutter and clank of tanks thorough the boulevards of Prague could be footage from a documentary. The film's dark frames and abrupt cuts are reminiscent of Rossellini's *Open City* (1945), De Sica's *The Bicycle Thief* (1948), and Andraez Wajcla's film from Poland, *Kanal* (1957). *Hangmen Also Die* (1943) is a fictionalized account of Heydrich's assassination, directed by Fritz Lang, with a screenplay by Lang, Bertolt Brecht, and John Wexley.

The linkage between *Romeo and Juliet* on film and teenage America (and from there to the rest of the Western world) really begins in 1961, with *West Side Story*, of course, and also with Peter Ustinov's *Romanov and Juliet*. Sandra Dee (Juliet) had become a teenage favorite with *The Restless Years* (1959)—an early teen high school flick—and her portrayal of Gidget. The Ustinov film emerged into a market suddenly aware of the teenage dollar.

This is a lightweight affair in which Ustinov engineers a romance between Dee, daughter of the American ambassador to the five-mile square duchy of Concordia, and Igor Romanov (John Gavin), son of the Russian ambassador. The film is indebted to Peter Seller's *The Mouse that Roared* (1959), in which Grand Fenwick attacks the United States in order to obtain needed foreign aid. Ustinov's Concordia wishes to remain free of international interference. Ustinov makes the mistake of introducing himself and his tiny country to the United Nations in refusing to break a tie vote on an amendment to an amendment that no one understands but that is deadlocked along Cold War alliances. Ustinov plays all the voices in the roll call with which the film opens on Manhattan's east side. Back in Concordia, via an ancient Forker Tri-motor, he finds himself besieged by offers. From America: oil, munitions, schools, and last year's missiles. From the Soviet Union: tractors, grain, a power plant, and a visit from the Bolshoi Ballet. Concordia's primary industry is the production of postage stamps with obvious errors on them. To accept advanced aircraft would be impossible, Ustinov explains, because their landing speed would roll them into foreign territory.

As romance blossoms between Juliet and Igor, war looms over Concordia.

Ustinov is aware of the Shakespeare connection. A brooding Igor is compared to Hamlet. Concordia's drill sergeant resembles Falstaff instructing Wart in the use of the caliver. The wife (Tamara Shayne) of the Russian ambassador (Akim Tamiroff) touches the feather on the hat her husband has given her like Bottom inspecting an ear. Both Igor and Juliet are summoned to their wedding from the balconies of their embassies.

A subplot that involves Juliet's former boyfriend, Freddie (Rik Van Nutter), and the female Russian officer (Suzanne Cloutier) that the Russian Ambassador has selected for Igor ends happily. They fall in love, reinforcing the happy ending of the main plot and, presumably, the pacific closure of the Cold War.

Watching the film during the never-ending war on terrorism, it is easy to forget that 1961 was one of the high points—or low points—of the Cold War. The Bay of Pigs invasion occurred on 17 March 1961. The Cuban Missile Crisis, which came close to eliciting an atomic exchange, played out in October of 1962. The Limited Test Ban Treaty, which emerged from these very dangerous years, was signed in 1963. This lightweight film may have seemed overly escapist back then.

Sandra Dee's first starring role was in Helmut Kautner's *The Restless Years* (1958), an early teen flick in which two outcasts fall in love. Melinda (Dee) has a dotty mother (Teresa Wright) who makes beautiful clothes for her, while Will Henderson (John Saxon), son of a failed air-conditioner salesman (James Whitmore), has just moved back with his family to his father's hometown. It is the last stop, it seems, on Mr. Henderson's downward ride to bankruptcy. He and his wife (Margaret Lindsay) do not want Will to see Melinda because of her illegitimacy and the ongoing stigma of Mrs. Grant's strangeness. She is waiting for a letter from the man, inevitably a trumpet player, who seduced her 16 years before under the town bandstand and left her with a daughter. She even runs to the mailbox at night, just in case there might be a special delivery letter from him. Henderson wants Will to meet the children of important people so that Henderson can sell his air conditioners. The "play" within the play, introduced by the obligatory English teacher (Virginia Grey) of this genre, is not *Romeo and Juliet* but *Our Town*, the quintessential voice of small town values that will no doubt prove a favorite among the movers and shakers of the film's Libertyville, who put a smiling façade in front of its malicious teenage cliques; failed businessmen; mad women; and drunken, bedridden wives. Melinda wins the role of Emily, but is seen taking off the wedding dress that Will has unconvincingly demanded that she wear while he helps her rehearse. In Libertyville, this doffing of a symbol of purity is translated into evidence of unchasteness and, since Melinda is only 16, of indictable transgression. Her rival Polly (Luana Patten) spreads the word. Having chased Melinda and Will to the notorious bandstand—an improbable action dictated by the play on which the film is based (*Teach Me How to Cry*, by Patricia Joudry)—Mrs. Grant becomes convinced that her own terrible moment is repeating itself. But as she is confronted by Melinda and Will, Mrs. Grant is forced to recognize that her former lover will never return. *Our Town* is never performed within the film, events having overtaken drama. The film, though, suggests that time has moved on from the Grover's Corners, where the stubborn conservatism of the milkman's horse is an issue, to a point where the present-day Emily and George do savor what they have and will not be forced to look back through the salt of nostalgia on what they have lost. Although Will is going away, so that his father can at last reach his proper level and manage a grocery store in Toledo, he promises to return. The film ends with a calm and smiling Mrs. Grant telling the postman that she is not expecting a letter. But Melinda gets one from Will. They have escaped the cycle of inevitability. Things will work out in the next generation. The film, then, with its 16-year-old daughter and its emphasis on the triumph of time emerges from the archetypes that inform *The Winter's Tale*. And it is another precursor of the many *Romeo and Juliet* variations to come. The film shows how teenagers behaved back then—even to the detail of their sliding across the bench seats of the automobiles to get to the driver's seat as opposed to getting in on that side. As for the adults, Whitmore hands an open bottle of beer to his wife so that he can keep both hands on the wheel as he drives off, can get the car into high gear, and say, "Hand me that beer, please."

Los Tarantos (1963), directed by Francisco Rovira Beleta, deals with rival gypsy families. It begins with a fight on a street in Barcelona. Members of one family destroy the flower cart of another. Juana (Sara Lazana), daughter of the wealthy gypsy Camison (Antonio Prieto), wanders up to the hillside where Soledad (Carmen Amaya) conducts her Flamenco school. There, a wedding celebration is in progress, a marriage approved enthusiastically by both families. Juana dances well enough to win Soledad's approval. Juana and Raphael, Soledad's son (Daniel Martin), fall in love. At the beach, they engage in an underwater kiss, seemingly an inevitable way for the modern Romeo and Juliet to conceal their love. The cause of the feud emerges, though. At some point years before, Camison had wished to marry Soledad. She married another man. Camison had him killed. Now, Soledad goes to Camison. "My son and your daughter are in love. I give you my son," she says. Camison turns his back on her. After Curro, the Paris-Tybalt figure (Jose Manuel Martin) beats Juana, Soledad confronts Camison in "Los Tarantos," a gypsy bar (still there at Placa Reial 17 de Barcelona), and tells him that the conflict must stop. We should have been together long ago, she admits. Juana runs to Raphael—he is not there. She faints and falls to the cold ground in front of his roost. He finds her. Is she dead? He holds her—a pieta—and her left arm moves. He takes her up the ladder. Curro tracks them down and kills them. He is, in turn, cornered in the Camison stables and killed. The cycle of killing and revenge is powerfully depicted. But at the end, the boy and girl, who have been the go-betweens for the young lovers, stand in front of Raphael's tree house. The boy catches a pigeon and hands it to the girl. The action suggests reconciliation in the next generation more effectively than the ridiculous golden statues promised at the end of the original play or the silent ending of *West Side Story*, where the chastened Jets pass in front of a grieving Maria. The two youngsters of *Los Tarantos* have already engaged in a prelude to love.

Since Soledad and her family make their meager living by dancing, it is not surprising to find Flamenco occurring at all hours and during all seasons. Especially noteworthy in this vivid film are the dance by Mojigondo (Antonio Gades)—the film's Mercutio—in the predawn Las Ramblas section as the nozzles whisk the streets clean, the vibrant score composed and played by Spain's great guitarist, Peret, and the masterful Flamenco dancing of Carmen Amaya, in her last film—she died in November 1963). The film is doubly elegiac in that much of it was shot in the Somorrostro district of Barcelona, since lost to development. The film was nominated for best foreign picture of 1963, but lost to Fellini's *8½*. Alfredo Mana's *La Historia de los Tarantos*, the play on which the film was based, was made into a successful ballet in 1997 for the Ballet Nacional de Espana. *Los Tarantos* deserves to be reissued with English subtitles. As a musical/dance version of *Romeo and Juliet*, it ranks with Prokofiev.

James Ivory's superb *Shakespeare Wallah* (1965) is filled with elegiac snippets from Shakespeare that reinforce the decline of British cultural influence in post-independence India: Cleopatra's farewell to Antony, and Ophelia's "And will he not come again?" for Polonius. An actual Anglican funeral service echoes against the alien culture surrounding the tiny plot that "is forever England." As it develops, the film also provides transgressive moments—an audience's interfering with the final scene of *Othello* and with the marriage scene of *Romeo and Juliet*—in the latter instance, an example of corrupted ritual.

After their night together—their "real-life" Romeo and Juliet moment—Lizzie (Felicity Kendal) offers to give up her career for Sanju (Shashi Kapoor), a parallel to Juliet's willingness to disavow her identity. Lizzie is met with silence. Why? Perhaps Sanju's narrow code is now asserting itself in spite of his seeming emancipation from cultural bounds, as evidenced by his confession that he can barely recall the Sanskrit he learned at school. And she has already transgressed, not just, as he has complained, by "showing herself" on stage but by sleeping with him. "So would I 'a done, / By yonder sun, / And you had not come to my bed." Perhaps he does not understand his own silent rejection. For Lizzie, like Juliet, it is "all or nothing" first love. That is not true of the more experienced Sanju. In her penetrating analysis of the film and its cultural ramifications, Valerie Wayne argues that "Sanju's attraction to Lizzie seems inseparable from his attraction to the culture of Shakespeare and the world of the theatre."[6] If so, he has somehow fallen in love with the roles she has played and not with the woman, even as he has objected to her playing those roles. If so, he is baffled when the woman offers herself free of the culture with which he is infatuated. His visit to her dressing room before a performance—itself a transgression of tradition—then, has signaled his fascination with the make-believe and its construction. The interrupted marriage scene works out from the theatrical frame into permanence in the film. The marriage will never occur. Lizzie leaves on a boat for England, a "home" she has never visited.

The film dramatizes a conflict between Shakespeare and an emerging Indian "culture." No matter how debased the indigenous films made by Sanju's girlfriend, Didi (Praveen Paul), may be, Shakespeare represents the voice of the occupier. Rather than being absorbed into the culture—as in America, for example—Shakespeare is banished from it, bundled up with English rule.

Everytime We Say Goodbye (1986), directed by Moshi Mizrahi, is a shallow film, notable for an early starring role for Tom Hanks as David and a moving performance by Cristina Marsillach as Sarah, the Sephardic woman with whom Hanks falls in love. He is a Yank with the RAF in Jerusalem in 1942 on leave while he recovers from injuries. In falling in love with Sarah, he is, of course, attempting to cross into a rigidly traditional society. He is the son of a Presbyterian minister and in a British uniform. He cannot win many points with Sarah by refusing to visit the supposed tomb of King David, who is, after all, part of John Knox's heritage as well as of hers. While Sarah's family loves all things British—marmalade, whiskey, the King and Queen, fish and chips, and soccer—Sarah's nasty mother (Gila Almagor) declares her "dead." Her much more sympathetic father (Avner Hizkiyahu) says "You'll no longer be my daughter." The family steals her clothes to keep her from meeting David. Her plight is mirrored by that of her friend Victoria (Anab Atzmon), who marries an RAF pilot

(Benedict Taylor), repents, and realizes that she'll be a pariah no matter what happens. Helped by an understanding brother (Avi Keidor), though, Sarah descends from the balcony outside her room and walks barefoot to David's apartment.

Even though Sarah inexplicably agrees to marry her cousin Nessem (Moni Moshonov), love prevails, and the film's theme song "A Nightingale Sang on Berkeley Square" (1940) plays on. The other song that informs the film is "Bluebirds Over the White Cliffs of Dover" (1941), a hopeful tune from the dark early days of World War II. The title of the film is also the title of a song by Cole Porter that did not appear until 1944, so I assume that that is a coincidence, although the song asks, "Why the gods above me, / Who must be in the know, / Think so little of me, / They allow you to go." The title derives from the film's consistent pattern of hellos and goodbyes. "Everytime we meet, it's just to say goodbye," David complains and, at the end, as David is returning to duty, Sarah parodies him—"I know. You have to go."

Late in the film, once David has returned to his unit, we are told that it is "November 1942." The film occurs, then, during the time that Rommel forced the British to withdraw from Bir Hacheim and the Gazala Line. On 13 June, British forces were hurled back into Egypt. The South African garrison at Tobruk surrendered, and the British made a stand at El Alamein, only 75 miles from Alexandria. If that battle is lost, the way is open to Palestine and beyond. By St. Crispin's Day (23 October 1942), Field Marshall Montgomery, having taken over the British Eighth Army from General Ritchie, was ready for the second battle of El Alamein, which led to Rommel's eventual defeat. The Afrika Korps, of course, had been depleted by the need for tanks and manpower by the all-devouring Russian front.

That history makes this film a strange experience. Except for a reference to Hitler by one of Sarah's civilian brothers, the war and its imminent threat does not intrude on the daily life of Palestine and its inhabitants. None of its males are even in uniform. That no shadow of Nazism looms over Palestine may explain the film's unbelievable quality. All of the resistance to David comes from Sarah's family, none from the dangerous task of flying a Spitfire in combat in an environment hostile to Rolls Royce engines even if no one is shooting at you. A fighter pilot, even if offduty, studies his manuals. He "flies the plane" even when in some half-asleep, half-awake zone at some unnameable hour in the early morning. Even love does not intercept that process.

China Girl (1987) is a moody *noir* in color, shot in the borderlands between Little Italy and Chinatown in New York. The border is Canal Street, with the Italians living north of it, the Chinese to the south. A Chinese restaurant opens in the forbidden territory. That transgression seems odd, since there's a Chinese restaurant right across the street. The trespass foments trouble between the "greaseballs" and the people "who squint even when the sun ain't shining." In addition to racial epithets, the film is full of foul language. Perhaps needless to say, Tony (Richard Panebianco) falls in love with Tye (Sari Chang). The relationship is without chemistry, indeed without motivation, as the two sneak around so that they can gyrate, each in a world of his/her own, to disco music. Film, a light-sensitive medium, can capture passion, as television never can, but there is none here. The cross-racial, cross-cultural relationship is doomed, of course, as the violence of the younger generation boils over in spite of the efforts of the elders to cool it. One web-page commentator suggests that the ending is even worse than that of *West Side Story* (because in *China Girl* both young lovers die). That is the comparison, however. *China Girl* is a *West Side Story* without the song and dance. In the minds of some viewers, the Bernstein musical has intervened as "source." Something similar happened to *O*, based not so much on *Othello*, as on O. J. Simpson. *O* was then intercepted by Columbine and its Shakespeare-quoting murderers ("Good wombs have borne bad sons"). That history suggests that suburban high school massacres are not to be exploited lest that offense arouse sensibilities that will not be disturbed by the murder of a white man and woman by a black man. *China Girl* does have a fascinating opening credit line, as the words "China" and "Girl," printed to look like oriental characters, pass each other—"China" going up, "Girl" moving down. The film also has an occasional brilliant shot—a clothesline with ghostly long johns being pulled past a tenement wall by an invisible hand as a thunderstorm begins, and a chicken being plucked in the kitchen of a Chinese restaurant. In *China Girl*, the male lead is called "Romeo," even though his name is Tony—something that seems to happen in other films as well, regardless of the name of the character (*Los Tarantos* and *Romeo Must Die*, for example). As far as I can tell no female lead not named Juliet is ever called "Juliet," as a catchall name for a female lover. I assume that the lack of crossover results from society's convention that the woman is never the aggressor in a relationship, merely a function of the "Romeo gaze." That stereotype, of course, ignores Juliet's assertive and courageous character in the play.

Tony Howard says that Disney has "politically corrected *The Tempest* in *Pocahontas*"⁷ and, while *Pocahontas* (1995) does have overtones of *The Tempest*, it is much more a version of *Romeo and Juliet*. The film begins with men boarding a ship and singing "We'll all be rich and free, / Or so we've been told / By the Virginia Company." The ship runs into a storm worthy of the opening scene of *The Tempest*, and John Smith leaps into the ocean to save his inept friend, Thomas. Ratcliff, the scheming commander of the expedition sneers at his crew as "witless peasants." John Smith muses of yet another new world, "What could be different about this one?"

The Native Americans, meanwhile, are singing after their victory over a rival tribe, and are ready to return to their ahistorical stasis. When Chief Powhatan asks for his daughter, Pocahontas, he is told that "she goes wherever the wind takes her." Powhatan has plans for her. She will marry the stone-faced Kocoum. "Even the wild mountain stream must someday join the river." But she resists the cyclic status quo of her tribe. "You never step in the same river twice," she says, quoting Heraclitus. There's always something new just around the river bend, she knows, even though she wonders whether all her dreaming is over. All of this sounds vaguely like Johnny Mercer's "Moon River." Much of recent Disney music seems to have been slightly rescored and rephrased from other tunes—perhaps as reinforcement, perhaps merely as plagiarism. Pocahontas imparts her dream of an arrow spinning then stopping to Grandmother Willow. What should she do? She should listen to her spirit, of course. Spirit is emblemized by a wind on which bright-colored leaves float. Pocahontas, like *West Side Story*'s Maria, knows that "Something's Coming!"

That something arrives as "clouds" harassed by myriad gulls. They are the sails of Ratcliffe's ship, an ominous arrival, not a morally neutral natural phenomenon. John Smith and Pocahontas meet almost immediately, of course, and fall in love, even if she "doesn't understand a word" Smith says. In *The Tempest*, we are privy to the background of the characters and thus are not surprised, as they are, that they all speak the same language. In this film, Pocahontas and Smith quickly overcome the barrier without the use of a handheld dictionary. The Indian maiden is, of course, in tune with all the creatures and rhythms of nature. Smith's eyes open like those of Fitzgerald's Dutch sailors "face to face for the first time in history with something commensurate to their capacity for wonder." As Smith and Pocahontas sneak out at night to rendezvous, Ratcliffe insists that his men dig for gold. "The gold of Cortez, the jewels of Pizarro, / Will seem like mere trinkets by this time tomorrow." "They are ravenous wolves," says Powhatan's medicine man. Pocahontas explains to Smith that the only gold in this new world is the kernel of an ear of maize.

The romance deepens, but when Kocoum—a kind of Paris-Tybalt figure—is shot by Thomas, who is defending Smith, war looms. Both sides cry "Savage!" and the battle is about to be joined when Pocahontas, realizing that the arrow of her dream is the arrow of John Smith's compass, places her head on the block next to Smith's and persuades Powhatan not to fight. The only belligerent on the other side is Ratcliffe, who is captured by his own men and carried aboard his ship in chains. Pocahontas sets up the sequel by refusing to join Smith on his return trip to England. "I'm needed here."

This, then, is one version of the modern Romeo and Juliet story. The lovers are very different—geographically, racially, and linguistically. But their love unites the groups they represent, or at least keeps the two alien entities from going to war. The lesson of acceptance in a multicultural environment is clear. "Savages?" Pocahontas asks. "You mean—not like you." Historical accuracy is tailored to fit the allegory. Perhaps the history of the white settler on this continent and the Native American is not suitable for an animated version. The film operates with familiar stereotypes—noble native, noble white man, rapacious aristocrat—but it strikes me as a far less insidious piece of indoctrination than *The Lion King* films.

At the end of *The Lion King* (1994), all the animals of the jungle had made a pilgrimage to Pride Rock to bend to the new heir being held up by the wise baboon, Rafiki. Ah—but "it's a girl!" In *Lion King II: Simba's Pride* (1998), King Simba tells his daughter Kiara not to wander into the Outlands, but she must perforce wonder what's there. There she meets Kovu, a male cub, who saves her from drowning after a frightening episode with alligators. Kovu is an Outlander, of course. Kiara is reminded of her dynastic destiny and asks, "What if I don't want to be Queen?" She continues to assert a sense of her "body natural": "Can't I just be me?" in the face of her father's insistence that she must subsume her own sense of self into that larger imperative. He has also said that "We are all one family under the sun," but it is a different story under the moon. Kovu grows up, having been programmed by the scheming Zima to infiltrate Simba's pride. He returns from the Outlands, and he and Kiara fall in love, of course. Kovu is banished to the east after Simba accuses him of setting an ambush from which Simba has narrowly escaped. Zima had intimated that Kovu was part of such a plot. All nature—but no sword-wielding angel—drives Kovu out. He embraces the carefree doctrine of "Hakuna Matata" espoused by Pumbaa and Timon. Kovu is no longer a crown prince, heir to Pride Rock. "What's in a name?" Timon says, wafting any sense of family or heritage away. Meanwhile, a heartbroken Kiara says to Simba "He loves me for *me*!" Kiara pleads for Kovu. "You'll never be Mufasa!" she says to Simba, adducing the magnificent former king whom Scar had betrayed. This insult is the equivalent of Juliet's renunciation of her Capulet heritage. Kiara follows Kovu into exile, and they reunite on a snowy hillside that turns green as they exchange affectionate nuzzles. Their song— "There's a perfect world, shining in your eyes"—is a blatant rip-off from *West Side Story*. (A worse example of bad taste is the film's parody of a then ubiquitous commercial in which two bimbos rip off their clothes to fight to the skin about whether a lite beer is less filling or tastes better as drooling adolescent boys look on.) Kiara rejects Kovu's suggestion that they run away and begin a new pride. "If we do," she says, "they'll always be divided." They begin a return journey to Prideland. Zima and her followers launch their attack. It is modeled on Olivier's Agincourt, with crosscutting between each army as they gradually reach a gallop. The mano-a-mano between Simba and Zima resembles the squaring off of Henry and the Constable in the Olivier film. Kiara and Kovu attempt to arbitrate, but Zima attacks anyway. Finally, as all revengers must, she tumbles to death, into a river suddenly released from its dam of logs, an analogue to the explosive passions in which their possessors must drown. "My flag will fly / Against a blood red sky. / That's my lullaby!" she had sung. Now, as opposed to Zima's "wake up call," another modernized *Romeo and Juliet* is realized: the lovers have brought together the feuding factions. The pride is reunited, as the exiles from the Outlands are accepted, and all of nature pays homage to the four figures atop Pride Rock. Mufasa's voice rumbles from the sky in an analogue to God's voice at Christ's baptism (Matthew 2: 16–18). "Well done, my son." We are one. But one what? Kiara has integrated her political and emotional selves, true, but the "message" is still vividly hierarchical. This is not Coleridge's "We are all one life." We are one as long as all nature accepts the authority of those standing atop Pride's Rock. The film validates their authority, of course, but in 2004 that validation is a bit scary in the "you are either with us or against us" climate of post-9/11

America. Doug Stenberg argues that the reactionary nature of Disney's "message, the traditional readings of the plays, and the inculcation of those readings in films like *The Lion King* will most likely be challenged by an increasingly 'multicultural' America. [Meanwhile] Disney will rely on what has worked for centuries."[8]

Wishbone featured an articulate and imaginative Jack Russell Terrier, and ran from 1995 to 1998. Aimed at children 6 to 11 years of age and designed to introduce them to literature, and the fact that a past exists, its episodes included "Cyranose," "Bone of Arc," "The Hunchdog of Notre Dame," "Frankenbone," and "Shakespaw" (which I have not seen). The show was filmed, as opposed to taped, to enhance the quality of its images by way of the light-sensitive medium. It got to *Romeo and Juliet* quickly, in episode four, "Rosie, Oh Rosie, Oh!," in April 1995. Wishbone, sans leash, is captured and sent to the pound, where he finds himself in a cage next to a beautiful beagle named Rosie. Wishbone is redeemed, but Rosie remains, in spite of the wishes of teenager Samantha, who cannot convince her father to let her adopt Rosie. Samantha is permitted to take Rosie home for a brief visit. Wishbone, a neighbor dog, finds Rosie. They frolic. Rosie is captured by Animal Control and returned to the pound. Interspersed with this narrative are Wishbone's fantasies of *Romeo and Juliet*—the Capulets (with just a note or two of Prokofiev behind them), the ball (in which Wishbone wears a mask), the balcony scene, and Romeo's departure from Verona. Wishbone gets back to the pound to find only a dog bone, with rose attached, in the cage where Rosie had been. Wishbone imagines the tomb scene. He accepts the ovation given him by the invisible theater audience. Back in his terrier guise, he learns that Rosie has been adopted. Wishbone, rose-bone in mouth, prances happily out of the pound to seek her out.

The show, indeed, introduces the major sequences of *Romeo and Juliet* in an opulent proscenium format. The ending shows that, although Juliet and her inamorata, Wishbone, lie in the Capulet monument, there's rewarding applause once the curtain closes, and a world beyond the unhappy ending the stage has depicted. Most children, I think, will accept the fact that Wishbone is a dog playing roles in his vivid Terrier imagination, and will not demand that Romeo be a dog when they come to Shakespeare's play. Part of that hope, of course, rests with the actor playing Romeo.

Titanic (1997) tells the story of a poor young artist among the happy and kindly folks in steerage who falls in love with a penniless upper-class young woman whose mother (Frances Fisher) insists that her daughter marry a nasty rich boy (Billy Zane). The Romeo-Juliet-Lady Capulet-Paris (Tybalt) outline is clear. So are the stereotypes. As the ship is sinking and people are plunging into the killing North Atlantic, Rose (by any other name—Kate Winslet) and Jack (Leonardo DiCaprio, Luhrmann's Romeo) lean over the railing. "Jack—this is where we first met!" she exclaims.[9] First things first. Jack describes himself as "a tumble weed blowin' in the wind," stealing from The Sons of the Pioneers and Bob Dylan, while Rose, now 101 and looking back, can say "A woman's heart is a deep ocean of secrets." They are not worth diving for. The film might have done something with the ship, as opposed to merely recreating it physically. Shortly after the tragedy of the Titanic in 1912 (and it was one—*hubris* was at its heart), Thomas Hardy constructed a terrifying myth of "alien" yet inevitable lovers in his great "The Convergence of the Twain," waiting until "the spinner of the years says, 'Now!'" The poem conveys the same fatality of the opening chorus of *Romeo and Juliet*. The film's little love clichés diminish the grandeur of the event and drain the narrative of its inherent mythology.[§]

On 1 March 1999, Bill Cosby has a dream—or nightmare. Before going to bed, he has coached his niece (Jurnee Smollett) on Juliet's "Wherefore art thou Romeo" speech. She is bewildered. So is he. "I just don't get Shakespeare," he says. "It's no fun saying something if you don't know what it means," she says. Wiseguy Griffin (Doug E. Doug) says, "Yes it is, isn't it, Mr. Cosby." He falls asleep and in his dream tricycles into his kitchen, only to be met by Shakespeare (Tom Conti). Cosby tricycles out, only to be confronted by his late sixth grade teacher, Mrs. Wilson (Eugenia Collingwood). He must "get it," or else. Griffin wanders by, saying "To be or not to be" and holding the skull that Hamlet, it seems, must carry these days as he says those words.[11] Cosby's wife Ruth (Phylicia Rashad) greets him at the local coffeehouse with Lady Macbeth's mad scene, but he refuses to come to bed. Outside, on the sidewalk in Queens, Goneril and Regan complain about Lear. Cosby intervenes. "This guy has worked all his life and you are turning him out?" Now he gets it. "There's nothing, either good or bad, but thinking makes it so," says Shakespeare. "Now, you're quoting me!" Cosby says. Shakespeare has explained Cosby to himself, as Mrs. Wilson said he would. Now Cosby can go to his friend's retirement party and explain his frustrated, depressed friend to himself. Shakespeare's pedagogy is contagious. At the end, Cosby explains "wherefore" to his niece. "'Wherefore' doesn't mean 'where?' It means 'why?'" "Oh, I get it!" she exclaims.

This show is a demonstration of empowerment, since earlier, on 22 October 1987, guest star Christopher Plummer had embarrassed Cosby's Cliff Huxtable by placing him "in an uncomfortable position as the meaning of a line [is] unclear and he seems to be the targeted audience."[10]

Romeo Must Die (2000) is billed as a martial arts film designed to show off the considerable talents of Jet Li. He escapes from prison in Hong Kong while in chains, suspended from a ceiling, and surrounded by guards. When he is pummeled in a "touch" football game, he learns that it is fair to hit the person carrying the ball. So he hands off multiple times to people he then beats up. His final confrontation with another expert, like most fights on film, looks as if it could go either way until he wins. Li's family and the African American O'Day family are fighting for control of the Oakland waterfront. Like Li, the daughter Trish (Aaliyah) is an outsider in her own family. Li has been serving a prison sentence for his father (Henry O). Trish runs a shop.

Each family kills the troublemakers within it and blames the other family. After a final gunshot, which we are meant to assume may have hit Li (but is actually the sound of his father's suicide), he and his girlfriend walk unchallenged past a phalanx of blinking blue lights somehow summoned to the site. All of this is scarcely believable, of course, but that is the point. It is a fantasy in which, finally, evil has been eradicated a la *Richard III* and virtue survives.

The film was almost universally panned, but critics missed its parody. It combines kung fu and hip hop in an impossible stew, makes sure that the "love" between Han Sing and Trish includes nary a kiss, and names its black family O'Day. That has to be intentional. It is true that an American League African American outfielder is named O'Leary, and that his great-great grandmother was not implicated in the Chicago fire, but the film's straining of credulity is intentional. The kung fu sequences are illustrated by x-rays of skulls cracking and spines severing—surely meant to raise the same kind of laugh as Jackie Chan's intentional clumsiness does, and Li pauses to change direction in midair in ways that Auguste Vestris never contemplated. The artificial quality of the film is signaled as Trish's fat bodyguard (Anthony Anderson) pretends to be Chicago Bear middle linebacker, Brian Urlacher, by way of a video game. That the "Oakland" waterfront is Vancouver is another giveaway, but what proves parody is that O'Day wants to bring professional football to Oakland on the 40th anniversary of the Raiders' debut. After a 4–12 season in 2003, that hope achieves a kind of wry humor, but Cannon, Marcus Allen, Biletnikoff, Tatum, Stabler, Otto, Blanda, Madden, Al Davis, Shell, Tim Brown, Upshaw, Branch, Bo Jackson, and others, would have been startled to be told that Oakland was without a professional football team, as would the millions of boys who have rebelled identically by wearing black Raiders caps backwards as an emblem of the rebellious outlaw status the team has enjoyed all these years (as opposed to "America's Team," the drug-riddled Cowboys). A final tip-off is that the police, absent throughout a sequence of gangland massacres, show up unalerted but en masse at the end of the film after the elder Sing's suicide. The lovers have not reunited warring families—the family members are all dead—but they are alone at last.

It is a spoof, of course, but nowadays satire can be difficult to distinguish from "serious art."

The 27 November 2001 *The Gilmore Girls* episode, "Run Away, Little Boy!" features a teacher (Lorna Raver) who breaks her class into groups and assigns each group one act of *Romeo and Juliet* to perform. She had done this previously with *Richard III* and got versions using the Mafioso, the Roman Empire, and—her favorite—the final days of the "Sonny and Cher Show." Since the Comedy Hour ran from 1971 to 1974, no one in Professor Anderson's class could have remembered it. The class members must be addicted to reruns. The productions will count, Professor Anderson says, for half the student's grade. And so they set to work. Rory (Alexis Bledel) is cast as Juliet by her director Paris (Lisa Weil), a young woman driven to get into Harvard. Rory, it seems, is well known to be chaste, Paris argues, and thus will be a fetching, if tomb-bound, Juliet. Meanwhile, back in Stars Hollow, Rory's mother Lorelai (Lauren Graham) has broken up with Max and is desperately trying to return an Italian ice-cream maker sent to her as a wedding gift. Lorelai wants to achieve "closure." The Romeo assigned to Rory's group, Tristan (Chad Michael Murray) is booted out of school, so Paris must now play Romeo. In the class's performances, the balcony scene is played as Neanderthal, with Romeo wearing a bearskin and holding a club, Juliet standing on a rock in leopard skin and holding a dinosaur's thigh bone. In the fight scene, boys in business suits kill each other with cell phones.

Lorelai's breakup with Max is meant to contrast with Rory's reconciliation with her boyfriend Dean (Jared Padelcki). Rory had given Tristan a kiss at a party. "Oh—that was *you*?" Tristan mocks when she tells him to keep quiet about that momentary infidelity. Dean works at a store that has a special on "Assorted Gourds," so we are meant to sympathize with him against the privileged troublemaker, Tristan, the Tybalt figure. But Rory likes Tristan because he's handsome and dashing and does not hawk gourds. She hates to see him go, but uses that emotion as subtext for her very successful Juliet.

I assume that the show is meant to place the maturity of the teenagers and their ability to function splendidly under the pressure of a sudden cast change against Lorelai's simpering immaturity. If so, it makes its point. The show is a version of the pagan worldview wherein mere human beings struggle maturely in view of a petty and petulant pantheon.#

A more challenging adaptation, "Romeo and Cher," an episode of *Clueless*, aired on 13 December 1996. It may have had its genesis in the 1995 film from which the series was spun. In the film, Mr. Hall (Wallace Shawn) the English teacher asks where Christian Storvitz is. Cher (Alicia Silverstone) tells Hall that poor Christian is in Chicago with his father having been the subject of a custody battle. "I think it is a travesty on the part of the legal profession," Cher complains. Mr. Hall thanks Cher for that perspective. But she, at least, is aware of the ways in which adolescents are torn apart by the adult world. The name "Christian Storvitz" itself is an oxymoron.

In the television episode, Mr. Hall (still Wallace Shawn) has assigned *Romeo and Juliet* and is monitoring the scenes and speeches the students have selected. Amber (Elisa Donovan) sings "Who's the pretty girl?" from *West Side Story* and explains to Hall that it is the musical version of the Shakespeare play. Instead of asking her to expand on that—thus opening up the huge area of art, music, and dance that has been inspired by Shakespeare—Hall labels the performance "unacceptable." He goes on to say that "she seems to think that every assignment is open to interpretation." Hall typifies the often terrible teachers who inhabit these films and television shows, of whom Robin Williams's "Captain, my Captain" in *Dead Poet's Society* is probably the worst. In the *Clueless* episode, Mr. Hall is an agent of the rigid world in which these affluent teens are bound. The high school is no longer Beverly Hills, as it was in the film, but Bronson Alcott. The idealistic founder of the Temple School would be appalled were he to visit the institution that dishonors his name.

The young people live in a zone where their own disposable

allowances dictate a strict response to relationships. Sean (Sean Holland) cannot buy his new girlfriend a camisole, Cher (Rachel Blanchard) advises him. "That's a six-month gift." And that applies only if the two are exclusive partners. Note paper? "Summer fling! 'I'll write you. I can't wait to see you next July!'" A gold bracelet means "you've already met her parents and have been going out for a year." A dream candle means "caring, but not *too* caring." Finally, after Sean and his girl break up, Cher gets the dream candle.

Cher—"An Ordinary Girl," as her theme song proclaims—falls in love with Skyler (Michael Patrick Crane) the son of her father's rival in the potato chip industry. Though forbidden to see each other, they meet at a mall, she pondering "What's in a name" on an upper walkway, he standing in front of the scene's obligatory pool and fountain. The theme is Nino Rota's "There's a place for us." It shifts to a snippet of Tchaikovsky as Skyler rushes up the escalator, then settles into the appropriate insipidness of the Carpenters' "Close to You." Skyler and Cher reinvent the potato chip, thus bringing their fathers together in partnership. The teen relationship ends, though, when she wants to see a Brad Pitt flick. He yearns for Jim Carrey in *Monkey Boy*. She realizes that "I say 'potato...'", "And I say 'spud'?" Skyler asks. Somewhere, Cher has acquired a grasp of sophisticated Fred-and-Ginger song lyrics. Skyler hasn't a clue. "Separated by artistic differences," she says philosophically.

This episode demonstrates that its characters are pulled by the strings of expectations they only dimly perceive. They can afford anything but the awareness that they can afford anything. Whether they are adults driven by profit or teens controlled by a built-in pattern of expectation and trendiness, these people come at us from the world of television and reflect the world in which we live (as does the TV set when turned off *or* on). Barbara Hodgdon argues that the "high school milieu—a hierarchical culture divided along lines of class, gender, and race—mirrors early modern culture in ways that perhaps no other aspect of American life does."[11] One notices that no older women are present in this episode, though there's a portrait in Cher's entrance way—probably her absent mother.

Save the Last Dance (2001)—with its distant echo of Zelda Fitzgerald—tells of a teenage girl whose mother is killed rushing to her daughter's ballet audition for Julliard. The girl fails, of course, and is sent off to live with her father in a gritty Chicago neighborhood. At a virtually all-black high school, Sara (Julia Stiles) quickly makes friends with Chenille (Kerry Washington) and is soon learning hip hop from Chenille's brother, Derek (Sean Patrick Thomas). Their cross-racial love affair is far more *Romeo and Juliet* than *Othello*, though perhaps the only time we believe in it is when Sara pretends to be affectionate with Derek in order to shock an older white woman (Brenda Pickleman) on a commuter train. Derek takes Sara to a ballet—Tchaikovsky, not Prokofiev. The latter's Capulets would have lent some reinforcing threat to the main plot. Suffice it that Derek convinces Sara to audition again in spite of her guilt over her mother's death. Derek is tempted to ride off with Malakai (Fredo Starr, the Tybalt figure here) on a revenge mission, but backs out at the last minute. Chenille accuses Sara of taking one of the few good black men left, after "the drugs and the drivebys," the analogue to the dangerous lanes of Verona. Sara breaks up very unconvincingly with Derek. Nevertheless, he shows up in time to salvage her audition. She is off to Julliard. Derek is off to Georgetown. Malakai is off to jail. Chenille stays with her baby son.

A thread that the shallow script does not pursue is that of Sara's father, Roy (Terry Kinney), a down-at-the-heels trumpet player. "He's pretty good—if you like jazz," Sara says dismissively. While he accompanies Sara to her audition, he is never seen again. The only other evidence of an older generation is the school's principal (Ora Jones), who greets Sara, but is not seen again, and Chenille's grandmother (Dorothy Martin), who appears once and disappears. Since the father is a jazz musician, he might have approved of Sara's relationship with Derek against stereotype, but, as far as we know, he knows nothing about it, and remains the cliché of the failed father.

Clearly, while cultural differences cannot kill love, authority can, as in *China Girl*. And sometime authority fails, as in *Romeo Must Die*, and in Shakespeare, where Egeus is overruled in the matter of Hermia by a greater power than he can contradict. The Nazis represent that fatality in *Romeo, Juliet and Darkness*. The recent versions of *Romeo and Juliet* either reinforce hierarchy or challenge it. The Disney films clearly support the status quo. Any "oppositional" energy in recent productions, however, is usually defined by the authority of the teenage marketplace. In *The Gilmore Girls* episode, Rory is an exemplary young woman following her heart and her intelligence. She is still, however, inextricably bound by the strict and, in her case, puritanical rules of the world as she perceives it. Paris, with her drive to attend Harvard, is more controlled by society's expectations for her than is Rory. Although an adolescent, Paris is already a nasty "adult." She will have no trouble with the GMAT when she takes it, graded as it is against a model essay already in the computer. Rory, bless her heart, might offer original insights on her GMAT and suffer as her work conflicts with the preferred response. The "ordinary girl" Cher is a conspicuous consumer who has studied the footnotes to the rules, and can be mildly ironic within the rigid demarkations by which she lives. The script—like so many others of Shakespeare—can say opposite things, depending on who is telling the story. While the play is usually a function of the marketplace within it and surrounding its production, it can be more than that. The subversive elements of any script often keep it alive in meaningful ways, as in an older film like *Shakespeare Wallah*, even as commerce employs the plays more and more as an adjunct to selling products, or promoting the way of life within which those products are consumed. Suffice it that most students "know" the story before they encounter Shakespeare's version of it.

Thanks to José Ramon Diaz-Fernandez and Alfredo Michel Modenessi for sending me the Spanish and Mexican examples of Romeo and Juliet, *and to Harry Keyishian for* Stagedoor Canteen.

Notes

* On *West Side Story* as "the greatest film musical ever made," see Daniel Rosenthal, *Shakespeare on Screen*. London: Hamlyn, 2000, pp. 126–27.
† Richard Burt cites two productions that I have not seen: "spin-offs of *Romeo and Juliet* such as *Solomon and Gaenor* (dir. Paul Morrison, 1999), about a Welsh woman and a Jewish man set in 1920's Wales, and *Broken English* (dir. Gregor Nicolas, 1996), about a Bosnian woman and a Maori set in contemporary New Zealand, [that] consistently synchronize racial differences with linguistic and religious differences." "Slammin' Shakespeare," *Shakespeare Quarterly* 53 #2 (Summer 2002): 207. For other offshoots and derivatives that I do not discuss, see Tony Howard, "Shakespeare's Cinematic Offshoots," *The Cambridge Companion to Shakespeare on Film*, edited by Russell Jackson (Cambridge: Cambridge University Press): 297–298. Burt also lists several other obscure offshoots in his notes to his Introduction to *Shakespeare, The Movie, II* (London: Routledge), pp. 30–36. See also the Alas, Poor Yorick catalogue, Film Adaptations (Spring/Summer 2004): 9.
‡ For an alternative version of Heydrich's assassination that casts suspicion on the Nazi leaders themselves, see Sven Hassel, *Gestapo* (New York: Bantam, 1996), pp. 162–164.
§ See Steven Biel's brilliant *Down with the Old Canoe* (New York: Norton, 1996) for an analysis of the Titanic mythology as zeitgeist has altered it from April 1912 to Ballard.

11. At least two other productions show a Hamlet figure saying "To be or not to be" to a skull. In *Pocahontas*, it is Shakespeare on the streets of London. In *Get Over It*, it is Dr. Desmond Forrest Oates (Martin Short)—another example of awful high school teacher—daydreaming of his grand theatrical past. Students may be puzzled when they get to *Hamlet* to find no skull accompanying that stultifying soliloquy or no "To be" directed at the skull that pops up later on.

\# Allessandra Stanley calls "The Gilmore Girls" a "mother's pipe-dream," apparently because Lorelai gets to depict the adolescent. If chronological adults behave like children, children must try to behave as adults. "That ['O.C.'] also has a large adult following suggests that youth-obsessed baby boomers relate best to teenagers." Or try to. Or think they do. Stanley argues that, on teenage TV, "Teenagers see themselves and one another as grown up. Everyone else is either a child or very, very old." Beyond that relative neutrality, "what is striking these days is how often the parents are depicted as purely evil—in other words, exactly how their children view them." "The Ancient Days of Teenage Drama." *New York Times* (2 April 2004): Arts 1.

Chapter 2
Hamlet

One of the great detective stories is that of Oedipus, as rendered by Sophocles. We the audience know that Oedipus himself is the guilty person he seeks, the one who has killed his father, married his mother, and brought a plague to the city of Thebes, of which he has become king. We watch in helpless fascination as Oedipus discovers the truth. Shakespeare goes Sophocles one better in *Hamlet*. Here, we have *two* detective stories on a collision course. Hamlet wants to find out whether the king, Claudius, really did kill Hamlet's father, the former king. Claudius is intent on discovering what is wrong with the crown prince, his nephew Hamlet, who has been acting very strangely.

Furthermore, *Hamlet* is a story of revenge. This basic story goes back to the Old Testament and Homer. In the Elizabethan configuration, the revenger is usually less powerful than his adversary, often feigns madness, and invariably achieves his revenge through a situation that the evil person sets up or agrees to—a banquet or a play. Claudius, in *Hamlet*, encourages the play-within-the-play, "The Murder of Gonzago," and arranges the final duel in great detail with Laertes. The evil person inevitably falls into his own trap; in this case a reverse-eucharist in which the poisoned wine he has prepared kills his wife and adds to his own final agonies. This is "poetic justice," as when Macbeth believes that the prophecies of the Weird Sisters predict good things for him. We as audience members tend to associate with the revenger and thus enjoy the "wild justice" of his vengeance. It takes five acts, of course, before the revenge does take place. *Hamlet* is an unusual revenge play in two ways: a) Hamlet scarcely raises the moral issue of revenge for his own consideration, and b) the Ghost does *not* ask Hamlet specifically to kill Claudius. That is Hamlet's inference.

The revenge play is a special subcategory of tragedy.[1] If *Hamlet* is a tragedy, the hero Hamlet makes it so. But when? He must revenge, as the Ghost asks him to do, and set "the time...right," as he says of his mission. That means more than adjusting a clock. It means that he must restore Denmark to health. We notice that no rituals go right in Denmark. Until the murder of the former king is solved and the political situation is set right, Denmark suffers from a kind of spiritual plague in which normal rhythms and the sacraments themselves go awry or cannot function. The opening changing of the guard is confused— the wrong person issues the challenge. The marriage of the new king and the former queen is haunted by a recent royal funeral. The former king has been killed without receiving last rites, as he complains. Claudius cannot pray. Polonius is denied a funeral, as Laertes complains. Ophelia dies as a result of a reverse baptism, sinking to "muddy death" rather than rising cleansed into newness of life. She receives a "maimed" funeral, further disrupted by a brawl between her brother and her former lover, whom his mother had hoped would marry Ophelia. A ceremonial duel is a death trap for both participants. Hamlet forces poisoned wine down the throat of a dying man. Finally, a new king comes in and orders a new funeral. That last sequence is appropriate in a sense, in that it is the "King (and Prince) are dead, long live the King" formula, but we notice that, in this Christian climate of Denmark, none of the efforts to contact God succeed. By the end, the royal line of Denmark is extirpated.

How can Hamlet set the time right? How can Hamlet return Denmark to the healthy oneness with God's universe that it enjoyed before the murder of the former king? How can Hamlet restore Denmark's sacramental premises? His only opportunity is in the play he presents before Claudius. It is his idea. It has the potentiality, as he suggests, of striking a guilty party "so to the soul" that that person "presently"—meaning at once—"proclaim[s]" his guilt. The allusion ("guilty creatures sitting at a play") is to a woman in Lynn, England, who confessed to her husband's murder during a play that depicted a similar episode.[2] Drama—the imitation of an action, in this case a version of "This is Your Life"—can have a powerful effect upon the guilty conscience. The play fails, of course, but is that because Claudius flees? The text suggests that it is Hamlet, not Claudius, who breaks up the play: "He poisons him i' th' garden for his estate." If so, this is that act that dooms Hamlet, just at the point when the inaction of which he has so often been accused might have saved him. One cannot argue what does *not* happen in a play, except when the character himself has suggested what might happen. We go into the play scene believing that Claudius may confess. He has already demonstrated a tortured soul ("How smart a lash that speech doth give my conscience!"). If Claudius confesses, Hamlet becomes king as a result of a bloodless coup and Denmark returns to its positive relationship with the surrounding supernature. Claudius would face appropriate punishment, of course, but he might manage to save his soul. The potential confession does not occur, of course. If the play is a tragedy in the formal sense of the word, the positive ending is canceled because Hamlet interferes with his potentially redemptive play-within-the-play and, in so doing, dictates the final scene, in which almost everyone dies. As Auden says, "With a Greek play, we say 'what a pity it had to be that way.' With a Shakespearean tragedy, we say 'what a pity it should have been that way when it could have been otherwise.'"[3]

Such a reading makes *Hamlet* a coherent and well-constructed drama that builds toward the explosive moment of "Gonzago," where the two detective stories collide in midcareer. Hamlet determines that Claudius is guilty of the former king's murder. Claudius realizes that that murder is what has been on Hamlet's mind. But as an immediate result of the play-within, Claudius cannot pray, and Hamlet, thinking the voice behind Gertrude's curtain (arras) may be that of the king, kills Polonius. Nothing good comes of "Gonzago." The Players leave Elsinore wondering what *that* was all about. Suffice it that a good production of the play can follow the curve upward to the moment of confrontation as the play-within breaks up and then pursue the denouement, which is made up of the events after the climax. After "Gonzago," the physical and perhaps eternal fate of almost everyone we see is sealed.

A director editing the script for performance would be wise to ask: how is this play put together?

Is the climax Hamlet's unwillingness to kill the apparently praying Claudius? Is the climax Hamlet's sudden killing of Polonius, as if the sword Hamlet has just put up very reluctantly has leaped through the curtain almost of its own accord? These are the candidates that critics tend to nominate as the action that determines Hamlet's fate. Each, however, is a result of the "Gonzago" scene, and (regardless of what Hamlet says about it) its failure. The later scenes are moments discerned amid the wreckage. That "Gonzago" is the climactic moment of the play has been pretty well accepted by stage directors,[4] and it is on stage and in other performance media that *Hamlet* lives. Nowhere else.

The "thematic" approach to the play, though thoroughly discredited by postmodernist critics, helps in suggesting what the script permits in recontextualizations and what it prohibits. This approach suggests one method whereby Shakespeare organizes his play. This assumes that the play *is* organized and that Shakespeare intended that it be. The opening line is, "Who's there?" The question gets repeated throughout the play in various ways. Hamlet asks it of the Ghost—is it an "honest ghost"? Hamlet asks it of Claudius—is he guilty of the former king's murder? Claudius asks it of Hamlet—what is wrong with him? Hamlet asks it of the Polonius he has just stabbed—"Is it the king?" Hamlet asks it of Ophelia—"Are you honest?" and later, "Who is this they follow?" "The Murder of Gonzago" interrogates both Hamlet *and* Claudius. Hamlet forgets that the power of drama may affect him as well as the king. The questions about identity are ubiquitous. I would suggest that those questions are the playwright's intention. The play asks us who *we* are—who *I* am—as we respond to it. Anything we say about *Hamlet* or Hamlet is likely to be also about ourselves. Who's there? A director, editing the play for performance, might wish to keep that question riding through the production, probing at the characters inside the play as it probes at us out there in the audience.

A "modernization" of *Hamlet* can develop the competing detective stories and can explore the issue of identity. It will encounter trouble in recreating a world in which "eucharistic anxiety," as Stephen Greenblatt calls it,[5] reflects itself in so much ritual disturbance. The play creates for its audience an objectification of its own unconscious fears. For a modern or postmodern audience, a production can recreate the world of *Hamlet* and thus give the spectator some sense of the original experience. John Caird's stage production (Boston, Mass., 2000) did precisely that. It showed us a world in which the rituals were disturbingly awry. Ophelia's "funeral" for Polonius—in which she played the part of her father's corpse for a moment ("They lay him barefac'd in the bier")—was a shocking and profound aspect of this production. Simon Russell Beale's "inverse" Hamlet, where Hamlet's "natural self" emerged through the "antic disposition," was central to Caird's concept. This, of course, was a *Hamlet* set in some time other than our own. It educated us to its world and the processes of that world—as science fiction does and as fantasy does and as Shakespeare's plays can do. Critics complained that the depth of the production's exploration of the "religious" element left no room for the political dimension.[6] Fortinbras was erased. That aspect—the system's corruption—can be developed in contemporary productions. To educate an audience to "eucharistic anxiety" is more possible when the audience suspends its disbelief, as it is asked to do for a stage production, and is not asked to do on film (unless the film establishes the criteria for such suspension) and almost never does on TV, except for Saturday morning cartoons and presidential news conferences. But that education can only occur when the production provides a context where such anxiety is a possible product of the world of the production.

Hamlet as full-length film goes back to 1920, when the great Danish star Asta Neilsen played Hamlet as a woman disguised as a man for political reasons. She, of course, falls in love with Horatio, who falls in love with Ophelia. It is a moving and superbly photographed film. The Olivier version of 1949 is "the story of a man who could not make up his mind," as the voiceover tells us. It eliminates Rosencrantz and Guildenstern, and Fortinbras. Hamlet is king, very briefly, at the end. It is a black-and-white film with deep-field camerawork, featuring parapets and twisting staircases. Although a "Hamlet-centric" film (Olivier stars and directs), it includes the lovely blonde Jean Simmons as Ophelia and the scene borrowed from the painter Millais of Ophelia cruising down the river to muddy death. The camera watches her float by, pauses on the surface of the flower-strewn river, then pans downstream. She has disappeared. At one point, Hamlet puts a blonde wig on a boy actor. With the wig, he looks just like Ophelia. The Olivier film is intense and powerful. The Richardson (1970) gives us a quirky Hamlet in Nicol Williamson and a brilliant Ophelia in Marianne Faithfull, who is played as a subversive force undermining the smooth regime of Anthony Hopkins's Claudius. Clearly, this Ophelia and Laertes (Michael Pennington) have been having an incestuous affair, an outgrowth of the incest occurring between Claudius and his brother's wife, Gertrude (Judy Parfitt). Rodney Bennett's BBC-TV production (1980) gives us a bitingly ironic Hamlet in Derek Jacobi and Patrick Stewart's suave Claudius. It is a television production and thus lacks any sense of space or distance. It makes Denmark a claustrophobic space. The Ragnar Lyth (1984) stars the great Swedish actor, Stellan Scarsgaard, who plays Hamlet like a spoiled rock or tennis star. Here, Hamlet makes a puppet of Yorick's skull in the most powerful graveyard scene ever filmed. Pernilla Walgren's Ophelia is a political danger (as scripted) and breaks in on an official reception, destroying the function with her search for "the beauteous majesty of

Denmark." The Zeffirelli (1990) gives us an active and attractive Hamlet in Mel Gibson and another superb graveyard scene, in which Trevor Peacock's Gravedigger crosses himself on "rest her soul, she's dead," and Hamlet loses himself for a moment in the past as he gazes at Yorick's skull. Zeffirelli consistently contrasts the frailty of human flesh against the hard stones of Elsinore's architecture. This film is a bright and energetic contrast to the Olivier version. Kenneth Branagh's complete version gets all the words in and should be viewed for the wonderful Claudius and Gertrude of Derek Jacobi and Julie Christie. It has probably too many Hollywood hijinks and a lugubrious musical score, but it includes lines that even the long BBC-TV version edits out, and is therefore fascinating in that we get to see and hear, for the first time in any medium, how these lines fit into production, indeed how the words sound when spoken by an actor attempting to make them mean something in a dramatic context.

The Almereyda production (2000) suffers from its low budget. It is a tawdry affair, based on the ubiquitous surveillance one encounters in the big city. It was very favorably reviewed, however, except, it seems, by me.[7] I found it a "Holden Caulfield worries about where the ducks in Central Park go in the winter" *Hamlet*. Douglas Lanier defends it as "neo-*noir*," an "act of resistance," and a "means whereby film Shakespeare can recover something of its traditional oppositional edge."[8] Much as I sympathize with Lanier's assessment, I found Hamlet's "act of resistance"—the film-within-a-film "Mousetrap"—incoherent, and the film hardly a revelation, given the depth of corporate criminality rampant in the so-called "real world." I agree with what the film says about that world. What is it saying about *Hamlet*? I am not sure what films Lanier would call "oppositional." Surely not Olivier's *Henry V* or Branagh's *Love's Labour's Lost*. Perhaps Welles's *Chimes at Midnight*? Probably Brook's *King Lear*. More important, Lanier argues, is that Almereyda's film demonstrates "how fully media technology has become the instrument of corporate dominance."[9] The film, of course, must equate the corporation with the state, an easy enough analogy these days when governmental policies can be bought and sold. Certainly Claudius's Elsinore is a zone subject to surveillance. To make that fact "the world of the play," however, is to reduce the issues of the play to a merely modern or postmodern context. Evil becomes a disgraced admiral named Poindexter. The destiny of human life is a data bank. The issues of the inherited script ramify against the dimensions of eternity. We live in a much smaller world, as the Almereyda film reminds us.

Hamlet in and out of context is perhaps as ubiquitous as *Romeo and Juliet*. "Angels and ministers of grace defend us!" exclaims Sir John Ashwood (Alan Marshall) in *The White Cliffs of Dover* (1944, directed by Clarence Brown) as he realizes he has understandably picked up the wrong girl (Irene Dunne) at a party. In *Phantom Lady* (1944, directed by Robert Siodmak), an actor (Cyril Delevanti), wandering by in a backstage scene, says "Barrymore once told me that I was the greatest Polonius of my generation." A female companion (Georgia Davis), impressed, says "Really?"

"Alas, poor Yorick" emerges inevitably from the world of *The* (appalling) *Avengers* (1998). The film deals with the "Prospero Project," which has been stolen by an evil genius (Sean Connery). Like Prospero, the project threatens to control the weather, but the only reason for watching the film would be to escape even worse weather outside the theater. In a skit that mocks Shakespeare, Robin Williams holds a skull up and says, "I think we have a malpractice suit here." On SciFi Channel, the foregrounded cartoon characters relentlessly sneer at the awkwardly dubbed *Hamlet* that appeared on Austrian Television with Maximilian Schell in 1960. In episode 72 (3 October 1966) of *Gilligan's Island*, a musical *Hamlet* is delivered to the songs of Bizet. "Neither a borrower or a lender be" comes via "The Toreador Song." "Stay out of debt. Stay out of debt." Ophelia (Dawn Wells) is warned by Gilligan (Bob Denver) not to "go near the water"—difficult to avoid on an island. In *LA Story* (1991), Steve Martin leads Victoria Tennant into a cemetery where "the great Blunderman" is buried. "I knew him!" Steve says.[10] Arnold Schwarzeneger's *Last Action Hero* (1993) brilliantly recreates the deep-field black-and-white photography of Olivier's film. Arnold tosses Claudius through a window so that his heels kick at heaven. "Not to be," Arnold says, blowing up Elsinore. In an episode of *Law and Order* ("Seer": 23 April 2003), a defense attorney says "There are more things in heaven and earth, Mr. McCoy, than are dreamt of in your philosophy." McCoy (Sam Waterson) is not ruffled. "That would be excellent in a seminar on Shakespeare, counselor, but it won't fly in a court of law." Since the defense attorney is talking about a man claiming to be a psychic who has a vision of a murder, but whom everyone believes to be the murderer, the allusion to *Hamlet* raises the issue of what constitutes reality. It turns out that the man has repressed his actual witnessing of the murder and placed a visionary screen in front of what he did not and does not wish to see. The allusion points at television's inevitable tendency to psychologize the supernatural.

Strange Illusion (1945) has gone unremarked over the years, perhaps because James Lydon brings much more of Henry Aldrich to his role than Prince of Denmark. Lydon had played Henry for Paramount since 1940 and he had yet to grow out of it. He reads his lines as if on radio, as if he had to do everything with the spoken word. The film does have an echo of Henry's croaking reply to the voice calling him: "Coming, Mother." Another problem is that the director, the king of low-budget films, Edgar G. Ulmer, had $25,000 and a six day shooting schedule at his disposal. Despite its limitations, it isn't bad. Ulmer's emphasis on a shadowy and misty *noir* atmosphere permits the film to look better than it cost. It does not have the out-at-elbows feeling of the Almereyda film, for example. Ulmer also builds in the competing detective stories format of his source.

Paul Cartwright (Lydon) has a nightmare. In it, his mother, Virginia (Sally Eilers) is with a man other than her husband (or Paul's father, as Paul protests). "I am your father now," says the stranger. Paul's sister (Jayne Hazard) shows Paul "this beautiful bracelet he gave me." As the car that Paul's father is driving is hit by a train, Paul wakes up. The music accompanying the dream, Paul realizes, is Robert Schumann's piano concerto—his father's favorite. The concerto was written after Schumann married Clara Wieck (a Romeo and Juliet relationship, since Clara's father objected), and reinforces the dream. It signals a happy time in Schumann's life—"a year of song"—that was merely a prelude to his mental decline and death.

Paul receives a posthumous letter from his father—an arrangement they had worked out previously—a device that, like the premonitory dream, substitutes for the appearance of an actual ghost. "Your responsibility is to protect your mother and sister, be constantly vigilant of their associates and watch out for unscrupulous imposters." That admonition becomes more than a self-fulfilling prophecy. When Paul learns that a man is seeing his mother, Paul asks "Who's the Romeo?" He notices that the portrait of his father, the Judge, has been moved from above the fireplace in the living room to an upstairs study. (The study features a bust of Shakespeare.)

"The dream is beginning to happen," Paul says when his sister gets that bracelet from the suave newcomer, Brett Curtis (Warren William). Paul becomes increasingly obsessed with Curtis. "Are you deliberately trying to avoid me?" asks Paul's girlfriend, Lydia (Mary McLeod), in a brief allusion to the Ophelia story. Directed by the powerful eyes of the portrait, Paul goes to the Barrington file in his father's study. It tells of a wealthy young widow drowned within six months of her marriage. This remains an unsolved case.

As other aspects of Paul's dream are repeated in his waking world, Curtis complains that his relationship with Paul's mother is suffering: "Then Paul came home and you began to change." No opportunity exists, it seems, to send Paul back to his Wittenberg. Curtis invites his friend Professor Muhlbach to talk to Paul. Charles Arnt plays Muhlbach with supreme unctuousness. The walks grow slippery as he passes by. "I have been most successful with juvenile neurosis," Muhlbach says. "Filial devotion to a mother that goes beyond the bounds of normalcy can produce hallucinations." This deviation from normality, he suggests, should "be corrected immediately." Another hypothesis is that Paul suffers "from overwork at school." He is depicted as "remarkably intelligent for his age," but little about Lydon's characterization suggests an intellectual or a bookish bent. He does, though, agree to go to Restview, Muhlbach's sanitarium, so that he can investigate further. "Maybe I am going wacky." But even if his antic disposition is not particularly profound, it is "a good way to stall for time" and "I may find something out up there." So Paul assumes some of Hamlet's protective coloration. Paul is told that he is a guest at Restview, though the place is barred ("a prison") and though, as he quickly learns, his room is bugged and observable through a two-way mirror. Paul, though, spies from the rooftop one of the sites of the plot against his father. His dream is becoming more and more objectified in the world around him. He calls his girlfriend Lydia. "Are you missin' my kissin'?" Muhlbach professes bewilderment. "Young love in the modern manner," explains his nurse (the sinister Sonia Sorel). The moment captures a fragment of Polonius and Claudius eavesdropping on Hamlet and Ophelia, an encounter that puzzles Claudius even as he rejects the love thesis.

Paul and his friend Dr. Vincent (Regis Toomey) are able to forestall the "hasty marriage" of Curtis and Virginia and the dream turns positive. The mist clears. "Look, mother, we can see ahead!" Paul exclaims. Dr. Vincent—a father substitute, as he has been for Paul from the film's opening—steps in to take his mother's arm.

Both Warren William and Sally Eilers, at the end of their careers, are very good, as is Arnt. Furthermore, the theme of father–son relationships, certainly deeply embedded in *Hamlet,* is nicely developed here. That Dr. Vincent should step into the happy dream at the end has been prepared for by Vincent's close relationship with Paul. Vincent might have had a bit more to do with Virginia Cartwright during the film, but the ending is not just an imposed tidying up. At least Vincent clears the screen of overt oedipal implications.

Robert F. Willson, Jr. effectively places *My Darling Clementine* (1946, directed by John Ford) in the context that André Bazin outlines for the generic western film.[11] Willson suggests that "both of Ford's heroes are types of Hamlet, struggling with dilemmas tied to duty and revenge."[12] Both Wyatt Earp (Henry Fonda) and Doc Holliday (Victor Mature) participate in the final showdown at the O.K. Corral, a version of the final bloodbath in *Hamlet*, where good, evil, and moral relativity are indiscriminately struck down. I would suggest that Mature is more the Hamlet figure—he is full of self-loathing after Chiquaqua dies. He had been lifted into a momentary zone of self-esteem after his seemingly successful operation on her gunshot wound. Earlier, Mature and Fonda search for a missing actor, Granville Thorndyke (Alan Mowbray) and find him in a bar, goaded by sadistic Ike Clanton (Grant Withers), who refers to Thorndyke as "Yorick." Mature continues Hamlet's soliloquy once the drunken Thorndyke forgets his lines after "a weary life." Mature picks up with "But that the dread of something after death" and continues to "makes cowards of us all" until a coughing fit sends him out for air. Both Hamlets have been accompanied by a lugubrious piano obbligato. Mowbray is in a Hamlet outfit—medallion and dagger—in spite of the featured show at the local theater, which is the "Blood Chilling Drama," *The Convict's Oath*. Mowbray is histrionic. He gives a recitation. Mature reads the words meditatively—toward his own approaching death. The two styles define two theatrical traditions—the 19th century recitation-of-famous-lines declamatory style and the more personal approach that makes the words the thinking of a specific Hamlet defined by a specific actor. Chiquaqua is the Ophelia figure here, doomed by her lover, although it should be Clementine, of course, since the miner's daughter of the song drowns—though that lyric is not used in the song sung behind the opening credits.

As Thorndyke leaves town the morning after, he says goodbye to the old Civil War veteran (Francis Ford) who has been his silent companion and utters a couplet that I cannot identify:

> Great souls by instinct to each other turn,
> demand allegiance and in friendship burn.

"Goodnight sweet prince," he says, then calls to some ladies waving from a balcony, "Parting is such sweet sorrow," and rides off into the dust.

The film captures the approach of "civilization" that Crane satirizes in *The Bride Comes to Yellow Sky* and that Twain foreshadows at the end of *Huckleberry Finn*. In Thorndyke, we get a serious version of the rapscallion actors that Huck and Jim encounter.

Shakespeare's intrusion into the West is also depicted via Richard Burton's Richard III before a group of miners in *Prince of Players* (1955, directed by Philip Dunne). Burton, of course, plays Edwin Booth. His father, Junius Brutus Booth (Raymond Massey) has just handed him the prop crown and insisted that Edwin go on as Richard. With the addition of a nose-piece, Burton, spidering onto the stage, looks startlingly like Olivier.

Prince of Players is a dark precursor of *Shakespeare in Love*. The lines of *Romeo and Juliet* thread through the film, from Booth's first encounter with his Juliet, Mary Devlin (Maggie McNamara), soon to be his wife, to his quoting Juliet's lines ("Parting is such sweet sorrow ...") at the end as he gazes up at the empty theater box where she once sat. In the first of these scenes, set in New Orleans, Mary seeks Booth in a bar and finds him drunk in a brothel. They play a reverse balcony scene, she in the courtyard, he on the brothel's wrought-iron second-floor porch. They do most of the scene, which is, of course, greatly condensed, from "Speak again, bright angel" to "That I shall say goodnight till it be morrow." It is a moving scene, particularly as we watch two doomed young creatures, Burton and McNamara, playing it. On "this place," Mary indicates the garden of the brothel. Edwin pauses before he says "Love." As in *Shakespeare in Love*, a crowd gathers spontaneously to listen—the madam (Eleanor Audley) on the balcony and the denizens of the barroom on the other side. The scene shifts to the theater, where the two play the tomb scene. The play ends on Juliet's "There rest, and let me die." Before the two actors can kiss as two people, they must emerge for their curtain call. Booth repeats "Speak again, bright angel" as he looks down at Mary dead, and continues with "Death, that hath sucked the honey of thy breath, / Hath had no power yet upon thy beauty."

The film necessarily condenses and compresses the Eleanor Ruggles book on which it is based, creating a single character in David Prescott (Charles Bickford) for Booth's many male friends (Joe Jefferson and Lawrence Barrett, particularly), turning Booth's sister Asia (Elizabeth

Sellars) into his helper after Mary Devlin's death, replacing Mrs. Junius Brutus Booth's love for John Wilkes with Asia's fearful caring. Asia anticipates John Wilkes's final words when she calls his activities for the Confederacy "Useless! Useless!" The film ends shortly after the Lincoln assassination. Edwin Booth sits alone on stage as Hamlet, getting pelted with vegetables thrown by an angry crowd until they grow quiet. Finally, one man (John Doucette, also a citizen in the 1953 *Julius Caesar*) begins to applaud and gradually the rest join in. Booth looks up at the empty box where Mary should be. Other conflations include the film's depiction of Booth's immediate triumph in London (his initial reception was tepid). The rivalry with Henry Irving is eliminated, as is the murder of Polonius in Hamlet's fine Closet Scene with Eva LeGallienne's Gertrude. Hamlet, of course, was Booth's signature role, and the film provides a complete "To be or not to be" shot from stage left during an ostensibly live performance. We also get Booth rehearsing for his London debut ("I have heard of your paintings too, well enough ..."). Burton delivers the lines with his characteristic scorn, but they are a strange inclusion, since his relationship with Mary Devlin is depicted as love at first sight (as they recite *Romeo and Juliet*) and since the film credits Mary with curing Edwin of the "taint" that infects the Booths. Booth's second wife, Mary McVicker, is excised from the film.[13]

In a scene to be replicated in *My Darling Clementine*, Young Ned (Christopher Cook) finds his father drunk and reciting Falstaff ("Peace, good pint pot; peace, good tickle-brain") in the tavern. Ned becomes the Chief Justice, absorbing Falstaff's chiding. Finally, Junius takes the stage as Lear. Ned studies by candlelight below, but abandons his book and recites the lines his father is thundering to the storm. This is Edwin Booth's apprenticeship. Back at home, young John (Louis Alexander), the favorite, gets to play Ariel to Junius's Prospero. A needlepoint framed on the wall says, "The Play's the Thing." As Junius hands the prop crown to Edwin, who is about to take the former's place as Richard III, Junius recites Prospero's "Revels" speech. Later, while being prompted by Mary on Henry V's wooing of Katherine, Booth breaks into extemporaneous expressions of love that, as she says, are "not in the script."

John Derek's dashing John Wilkes is limited to a snippet of Petruchio's opening speech. The film hovers, of course, under the tension of an assassination we know will come. Asia attributes John's allegiance to the South to his jealousy of Edwin's treatment by the

Northern critics. The South loves John Wilkes in Shakespearean roles. The Northern critics compare John unfavorably with Edwin. "How small the stage he acts upon seems these days," John says, after becoming a courier for the Confederacy. Edwin does taunt John with the latter's unearned stage success. Edwin, after all, had been his father's keeper for years and has learned, as he says, how to do "Richard III in a barroom."

Prince of Players contains a good "final scene" of *Hamlet*. Burton gives a portion of Hamlet's request that Horatio (Ben Wright) tell his story. Burton's eyes roll up to the whites as Burton displays his uncanny ability to create that effect. It is pure Burton, of course. Booth stopped drinking after his first wife, Mary Devlin, died in 1864. The scene depicts a detailed proscenium format of the gaslight era and thus contrasts with more recent Shakespearean staging. The set in the film, however, is hardly as ornate or detailed as those designed for Booth by Charles W. Witham, as shown in Witham's drawings at the Museum of the City of New York. In fact, predictably, the film's set looks very much like the sets for *Hamlet* typical of proscenium productions of the 1950s. It is a set of battleship gray, a space for thrones upcenter, steps stage left up to a battlement, with mountains beyond. The same set is used for productions ostensibly occurring in London and New York at different moments in Booth's career. The film version of the scene ends with Horatio's eulogy and Hamlet's exit on two shields held on the shoulders of the guards. It is a "soldier's funeral," though not ordered by Fortinbras. The scene contrasts with Burton's performance in the Warner Electronovision version (1964), a live proscenium production from the Lunt-Fontanne Theater. There, Burton looked down at Claudius (Alfred Drake, *Oklahoma*'s original Curley), laughed, said "The rest is silence," and collapsed to the throne from which Claudius had fallen. The camerawork in the Electronovision production is capricious and the values are murky. The production never finds a balance between the microphone and projection necessary in a large auditorium. *Prince of Players* was produced in Cinemascope, at a time when the movies were demonstrating that they could be much bigger than television.

Alfred Hitchcock's great film *Vertigo* (1958) has an "Ophelia" moment. Scottie Ferguson (Cary Grant) is hired by Gavin Elster (Tom Helmore) to observe his wife Madeleine (Kim Novak). She is supposedly haunted by the ghost of her grandmother—in this case a spurious ghost that must, in a sense, be exorcised, as opposed to tested and believed. Scottie follows Madeleine to a park below the Golden Gate Bridge. She strews flowers into San Francisco Bay, then suddenly plunges in. Scotty yanks off his coat and follows. Madeleine floats for a moment, face up, arms extended in the classic Millais pose and then Scottie pulls her ashore. The moment signals Scottie's movement from acrophobia to a version of psychic vertigo. He has had a terrible experience earlier, as he watched a policeman plunge several stories to his death. Acrophobia is caused by the line that links the observer to the ground. It cannot happen in airplanes, for example, unless one looks down the lower wing of a steeply banking aircraft toward the ground. Vertigo results from a disparity between what the senses perceive and what they can process. If I am a wingman in a two-ship formation at night and my flight leader does slow rolls past the stars and through the lights of a city below, I must concentrate on his aircraft, even though I cannot help but take in the other sensory data. But I cannot process that data. It has not been translated into information that my inner ear can accommodate. Vertigo, an eerie feeling of disorientation far beyond the mere dizziness that a head cold can promote, results from the discrepancy of which I have given an example. The cure is for the pilot to snap onto his artificial horizon, a gyro instrument that depicts the attitude of the aircraft relative to the ground. One can feel the sensation spinning back into the Earth's rotation again as one settles into a normal relationship with gravity and the comforting electrodynamic forces that hold skin and bones together. This process is akin to what Scottie suffers in the film. One of Hitchcock's ways of showing Scottie's version of vertigo is to permit no one else in the frame except Madeleine. Buildings are deserted, streets are empty. They are the only ones in the park on a sunny day. The problem for the film, though, is that—unlike stage—it cannot ask us to suspend our disbelief. Much of *Vertigo* strains credulity. After Madeleine's apparent death, Scottie spots a shopgirl who reminds him of her. It is she, of course, and Scottie insists that she dress like Madeleine, wear her hair like Madeleine, *become* Madeleine (as she is, of course). She is transformed into the false persona she was at the outset, so we get a strange take on "god hath given you one face, and you make yourselves another." Scottie is Hamlet-like, in that he drives the issue of who is who, and, to some extent, controls point of view in his self-dictated compulsion, insisting that the devil "assume a pleasing shape"; in this case; the same pleasing shape that was used earlier to deceive Scottie but with which he fell in love. He suggests a way of looking at *Hamlet*, as well. Characters—not only Hamlet—look at surfaces but cannot penetrate to the truth behind the surfaces (as they are often aware). The truth—Ophelia is a decoy for Claudius and Polonius, Hamlet is not mad, but dangerous, the Ghost is veracious in his account of his death, Polonius is behind the arras, not Claudius, Ophelia's is the corpse they follow—erases vertigo but merely introduces further conflict between what the senses perceive and what they also process involuntarily. In *Vertigo*, Madeleine finally becomes the woman she was pretending to be, even in plunging from the same bell tower, and Scottie's acrophobia *and* vertigo erase themselves with her descent.

Of the "Shakespeare" films of Kurosawa, *The Bad Sleep Well* (1960), has been neglected. *Throne of Blood*, with its fog of confusion at the outset and the terrible stasis of evil intention represented by Lady Asaji, and *Ran*, with its powerful substitution of fire for storm as emblem of chaos, have been well documented.[14] Of Kurosawa's three "Shakespeare films," *The Bad Sleep Well* is the only *gendai-mono*, or modern story film. Robert Hapgood suggests that *The Bad Sleep Well* "is half over before the connections with *Hamlet* begin to present themselves."[15] The film begins with a wedding reception. But this post ritual ceremony is itself a "maimed rite." The bride Yoshiko (Kyoko Kagawa) is partially crippled, walking awkwardly on a platform shoe and stumbling as she goes. The reception staff bow as an elevator door opens, but instead of dignitaries, out rush a gaggle of reporters and cameramen, who comment cynically on the proceedings. "A beautiful heiress before she walks," one says. "Best one-act play I've ever seen," says another. "This is only the prologue," another says. The reporters become a cynical *benshi*, or narrator. The bride's brother (Tatsuya Mihashi) threatens to kill the groom if he is unkind to her. A rival wedding cake wheels out in the shape of a building. A rose leans out from a seventh floor window—the window from which a former executive of the company run by the bride's father apparently committed suicide. The master of ceremonies Mr. Shirai (Ko Nishimura) is stunned and cannot continue. The rival cake is a version of "Mousetrap." One of the company's executives, Mr. Wada (Kamatari Fujiwara), is arrested and hustled from the scene. An honored guest (Ken Mitsuda) rises to claim that he has no connection to anyone in the room. Later, we learn that the bridegroom, Nishi (Toshiro Mifune) has taken on another's identity (Itakura, played by Takeshi Kato) and is really the son of the executive who had supposedly committed suicide by jumping from that seventh-floor window. The man called Nishi, like Hieronimo, Hamlet, Altofronto, Vendice, and other revengers, does not present himself bare-faced to his enemies. That retrospective insight is hardly necessary, however, to sense all kinds of ceremonial disruption in the film's opening scene, as in *Hamlet*, where the second scene represents a coronation and marriage shadowed by a recent royal funeral. "The funeral bak'd meats did coldly furnish forth the marriage tables." Right away, then, we have images of authority attempting to establish themselves against subversive challenges from the out-of-power underdogs. The film will be punctuated by the news conferences with which Iwabachi (Masayoki Mori) explains away the terrible events we witness, putting upon them the smooth explanations that a Claudius or an Ari Fleischer or Scott McKellan expounds.

Hapgood notes the film's "constant pull toward the graphic, the immediate, the concrete, the simple, the extreme."[16] The extreme is often in the reaction of Nishi's victims, particularly Shirai to whom Nishi shows a photo of the man Shirai helped murder, a version of Hamlet's showing Gertrude a miniature of King Hamlet, as Kenneth S. Rothwell notes.[17] Rothwell adds that the smoke of *The Bad Sleep Well* suggests "the battlements of Elsinore."[18] In addition, Kurosawa uses long shots like the passageway along which the bride limps as she moves to the strange wedding reception at the outset, passageways that seem to have no ending, like the one the nightwatchmen patrol in the building from which Furuya was forced to jump and the one in which Nishi and Yoshiko reconcile, and the misty alley leading to Wada's home, where he plays ghost to Shirai. The effect is of a nightmare—an infinite perspective that stretches out from every step.

The film's surreal quality is reinforced by its recurrent theme music, capable of either ominous or joyous rendition. As Nishi and Wada discuss Yoshiko, cello and bass play the film's theme. Earlier, Nishi had whistled it, and he does so later, enthusiastically, as he contemplates a union with Yoshiko, with whom he has yet to consummate his marriage. But it is not "Yoshiko's Theme." It also sounds, in somber tones, as Moriyama (Takashi Shimiura) is threatened and imprisoned unless he reveals the whereabouts of the evidence that will prove the corruption case against the Dairyu Company. The music, then, is ambivalent, simultaneously signaling two opposite outcomes and holding us between the possibilities. We are, of course, hoping that the deprived Yoshiko will reconcile happily with Nishi.

Hamlet does not examine the ethic of revenge. He asks Horatio, rhetorically, whether it is "not perfect conscience" to dispatch Claudius. Laertes comes closer perhaps when he says, "Yet, 'tis almost 'gainst my conscience" as he prepares to strike at Hamlet. The lack of introspection on this issue—for all of the play's introspective qualities, as exemplified by both Hamlet and Claudius—is one element in the play's continuing mystery. A major question is never asked by the protagonist and therefore must be asked by the spectator. The film permits Nishi to contemplate the nature of his actions. "I don't hate enough," he complains. "It's hard to be evil. I must hate and become bad myself." He has not consummated his marriage with Yoshiko because she has been part of his plan, but he finds that he has fallen in love with her. "I wanted to punish people who prey on those who cannot fight back," he says, realizing that his wife is now a victim of his naive formula. His cleverness in confusing and implicating his enemies has made him an Iago. Tony Howard compares Nishi to Vendice in *The Revenger's Tragedy*.[19] Having made his decision to love Yoshiko, Nishi arrives with flowers bought as the theme music sounds—flowers for "a real wedding night ... for the bridal suite." Coming up the walkway, he whistles the theme. But, as a result of a counter investigation—the competing detective story—into Nishi's identity, Moriyama has uncovered Nishi's secret and he must flee.

Wada is an interesting background figure in the film, much more than the "Rosencrantz" that Rothwell makes of him in pursuing parallels too curiously.[20] Wada is arrested at the wedding reception and kept by the police for days. Like Miura (Gen Shimizu), he is released. Faced with rearrest, Miura runs in front of a truck. Wada scrambles up to the top of a giant slag heap, leaves a note, and is yanked from the abyss by Nishi. As for the suicide of Miura and the apparent suicide of Wada, Iwbuchi says at his press conference, "Ask the authorities." They, after all, incarcerated and hounded the suicides. "Your devoted superiors are celebrating," Nishi tells Wada, as Nishi forces Wada to witness his own funeral. The observer of one's own funeral goes back at least as far as *Our Town*, which borrows the motif from *A Christmas Carol*. Ingmar Bergman's Ophelia observed her maimed rites in the 1987–88 production. Nishi also plays a tape for Wada, on which one of Wada's bosses picks out a young woman for his pleasure after Miura and Wada have loyally erased the case against the Dairyu Company. "Don't you want revenge?" Nishi asks. Wada appears at the end of an alley as his own ghost to terrify his superior

Shirai, who ultimately goes mad. Having been Nishi's puppet, Wada begins to function as Nishi's conscience, and tries to facilitate a reconciliation between Nishi and Yoshiko, who do share a few tender moments before Yoshiko is tricked by her treacherous father into betraying Nishi's hiding place. Wada is a peacemaker who fails. Officially "dead," he is apparently killed at the end by the Dairyu powers. They march on. The film ends with a locomotive chugging past the place by the side of the tracks where Nishi's smashed Studebaker rests. If *Hamlet* deals in many ways with who controls the narrative, Dairyu is completely in command of the story it wants to tell as it rolls down the tracks past the wreckage of those who would contradict it.

At the end, Iwabuchi's children reject him. Yoshiko seems on the verge of insanity. Iwabuchi is left to bow to the telephone and the voice at the other end that commands him to go away for awhile, until whatever aftermath there may be has died down, and Dairyu can continue its corrupt expansion unopposed. Soon, we assume, the site where Nishi had hidden will be a bustling industrial or housing development. And the executives will sleep as soundly as a Cheney or a Bush sleeps while the zodiac rolls unnoticed above their dreaming heads.

If "Denmark's a prison," the wasteland of Nishi's hiding place and Moriyama's imprisonment is the film's physical moral center. It is a bombed-out zone as yet to be reconstituted into the industrial complex that is reaching for it. Howard calls it both "graveyard" and a "Wittenberg."[21] created by the firestorms of Curtis LeMay and his B-29s. But it is also where Nishi and Yoshiko enjoy a few moments of love together. It is the dead zone to which justice is driven and from which justice cannot emerge. Itakura's final despairing narrative tells us that the true story will never be told. It, like Nishi "is silence." One of the conflicts of the film, as in *Hamlet*, is that of competing stories. At the end, only Dairyu's narrative will be told. The play incorporates Horatio's account of the background to Denmark's military preparation, the Ghost's story, the Player's description of Priam and Hecuba, Gertrude's description of Ophelia's drowning, Hamlet's description of his escape from Claudius's commission and the pirates, and Hamlet's dying request that Horatio tell Hamlet's "story." Kurosawa's film also has its narratives that clarify and complicate what we have already experienced: the account of Furuya's death, one that tells how Nishi and Itakura changed identities, and, finally,

Itakura's despairing account of what has happened to Nishi, and the now-concealed evidence of Dairyu's criminal conspiracy. The winners write the narratives. At the end of the Lyth film, Horatio (Per Eggers) holds the evidence of Claudius's guilt and attempts to attract the attention of the survivors so that Horatio can "tell [Hamlet's] story." But the court is interested in the new king (Dag Norgaard). They follow him to another chamber, and the documents turn to fragments in Horatio's hands. The past has ceased to exist. Long live the king.

I was frustrated that Kurosawa did not pursue the revenge pattern, wherein the evildoers set up the mechanism of their own demise. At the end, though we are only told of his betrayal, Nishi seems naive and incompetent, hardly as he has been depicted throughout the film. Has he been blinded by love? It would seem that character is sacrificed to the thesis that evil triumphs. The bad sleep well.

In *Willie and Phil* (1980, directed by Paul Mazursky), Michael Ontkean's Willy is a schoolteacher in the South Bronx. Early in the film, a tomato splatters against the blackboard on which he has written 'Hamlet.' Later, he asks the class why Hamlet procrastinates, giving with his question a standard and possibly misleading reading of *Hamlet*. The answer he gets from Wilson (Laurence Fishburne) is that Hamlet doesn't drink, get high, or get laid. Willie asks Wilson whether he has read *Hamlet*. Wilson stands and recites Hamlet's "To be or not to be," moving around the class, low-fiving a friend on "there's the rub," and ending with "a bare bodkin." The performance surprises and delights Willie, of course. He is the earnest young teacher of the late 1960s–early 1970s, trying to do something socially significant. The sequence of clichés that is "To be or not to be" picks up energy from the student's pleasure in the language and in his satirizing of "British" acting (without overdoing it). This is a young man infatuated with Shakespeare.

"So," Willie rephrases, "if Hamlet had been sexually satisfied, he would have been able to make decisions?" Wilson looks at him for a moment and asks, "Wouldn't you?" The class laughs knowingly.

Fishburne disappears, and the film does little with his moment. A few allusions to sex with one's mother, a girl's question about incest (since the man she has made love with is a good friend of her sister and her sister's husband), an acid-induced journey away from whatever reality the characters think they are inhabiting, some sharply drawn generational conflicts, a fight between the two young men in love with the same woman are the only possible references to *Hamlet* that I can discern. At the end, Willie is back teaching. This time, it's *Macbeth*.

The film's triangle dissolves at the end. The '70s and their search for "authenticity" are over. The sobriety of the '80s has begun. Cole Porter's question—"What Is this Thing Called Love?" remains unanswered. This is a wandering and aimless film, with a voice-over for its jumpy transitions. The film repeats many of the clichés of the late 1960s and 1970s and does nothing interesting with them. It has none of the resonance of the Francois Truffaut film, *Jules et Jim* (1962, with Jeanne Moreau) with which this film opens and of which it is a remake. *Willie and Phil* does make an eerie and unintentional allusion when Natalie Wood walks past on the beach, in front of the water in which she will drown a year later.

Strange Brew (1983) is a piece of trash enlivened, but in no way redeemed, by one lucid moment. Claude (Paul Dooley—the Claudius figure) attempts to placate Pamela (Lynne Griffin, the Hamlet figure) as the family sits at a formal dinner. "I don't want you to think that your mother and I don't understand how you feel about losing your father," he says. He paraphrases Claudius: "It's easy to wallow in self-pity. The hard thing is to go on living." Gertrude (Jill Frappier) joins in with some sound philosophy. "The Colonel's dead, but we still enjoy his chicken." This stately event features a huge bucket of Colonel Sanders' best. The parallel is interesting, in that Sanders complained before he died of others having taken over his fried chicken empire. Pamela is not mollified. Claude and Gertrude, after all, had been married the day after Claude had killed the elder Elsinore brother. "Don't you think it's a little unusual to get married so soon after the funeral?" Claude changes the subject by offering Gertrude "some bean medley."

Outrageous Fortune (1987, directed by Arthur Hiller) depicts two would-be actors, one who wants to play Hamlet (Shelley Long) and another who is a fledgling porn queen (Bette Midler), pursuing a man (Peter Coyote) who has deceived them. Long auditions for a famous acting teacher (Robert Prosky) by doing Ophelia's mad scene, though we don't see it. Midler is asked to do Hamlet's soliloquy in mime, but cannot comply. She has not heard of Hamlet or *Hamlet*. Then they discover that Coyote has lied to them. Off they go in a wild chase that has some funny moments. At the end, after Long has used her dueling lessons to promote the villain's fall from a mocking finger of cliff, she is taking curtain calls in her Hamlet costume with her Ophelia (Midler) beside her. One might tease out some relationships between the picaresque story and Shakespeare's play, but any similarities would be purely coincidental.

Hamlet Goes Business (1987, directed by Aki Kaurismaki in Finland) is a parody filmed with the gritty realism of postwar Eastern bloc and Italian films. It inspired Michael Almereyda's threadbare version of 2000. In the Finnish film Hamlet tape-records meetings of Claus and his confederates. Hamlet and Polonius are captured on a surveillance video. Polonius is plugged through the mirror of a wardrobe closet. The film is also full of "accidental judgments." A maid pauses to go to the ladies' room and puts a poisoned chicken down as it is being delivered to Hamlet (Pirkka-Pekka Petelius). Gertrude (Elina Savo) happens by, munches on a chicken leg, and dies a few steps later. The Ophelia story is brilliantly depicted by a pouty Kati Outinen. She gives Hamlet's letters back, is told that he doesn't care for her, holds Hamlet's photo to her cheek then throws it aside, pops some pills as a sad song about unfulfilled dreams and hopes of meeting again plays in the background, then sinks back into her overflowing bathtub. This may be a parody of the pastoral that Gertrude creates in the play, but moves beyond parody simply because we have come to care for this Ophelia, and also, perhaps, because her madness has not been carried to the excruciating extreme that so many productions—the Branagh, with Kate Winslet, for example—inflict upon us. Another reason is that she seems to love this loutish Hamlet, in spite of his own lack of interest in her. The film seems random and slapdash, but is worth watching for its Ophelia. The other rewarding element is, strangely, the final credits. A banal song about the road of life and the brilliant day that could come tomorrow plays over images of machines—wheels spinning, turbines turning. It does not matter who is alive and who is dead. The machine will keep running. This is a Kottian ending, appropriate to the year that *Shakespeare, Our Contemporary* was published. The irresistible mechanism of history rolls on, oblivious to human agency and not at all placated by optimistic theories of the human experience.

The film, says Howard, "is a post-industrial epitaph for a dying system doomed indefinitely to repeat its tragedies as farce."[22] That may mean that "tragedy" can only be experienced by creating or recreating a world in which such "high events" can occur. In discussing Marlowe's *Dr. Faustus*, George Steiner speaks of "a medieval conception which retained its vitality in Elizabethan drama."[23] That it has little vitality today argues the inevitable failure of modernizations of those of Shakespeare's plays that partake of the concepts of heaven/hell, salvation/damnation.

Tom Stoppard's *Rosencrantz and Guildenstern Are Dead* (1990, with Gary Oldman and Tim Roth) does not try to recreate the worldview of the host play, and that is one element in its success. The film got lost in the flood of filmed Shakespeare in the 1990s, but it is a brilliant interrogation of *Hamlet* via modern philosophical tenets. The camera moves fluidly in and out of various planes of reality, insisting that we as the audience question the *level* of illusion at work during any given moment of what we know to be an illusion known as motion picture. At "Gonzago," a masked king and queen observe puppets. The King (Donald Sumpter) rises and looks back on masked players as a flash of recognition leaps back and erases all levels of fiction except that of film itself. The masks come off the players, and Hamlet believes that Claudius has also been unmasked. Perhaps he has—but for whom? Rosencrantz interprets the King's reaction in aesthetic terms. "It wasn't *that* bad," he says, as he and Guildenstern exit through the wreckage.

As Hamlet and Claudius vie to impose their contradictory interpretations upon Elsinore, the film addresses the question of art itself and its relationship to other modes of representation, even that of nature itself, as Rosencrantz brilliantly but fruitlessly experiments with it. His discoveries include gravity, the principle of harmonics, the law of acceleration, the aerodynamic application of Bernouilli's principle, steam power, the laws of equal and opposite reaction and of conservation of energy, and aspects of vector theory and convection. In addition, he sets a new record of 42 seconds for keeping a paper plane in the air, shattering the old record of 18.08 seconds set by Ken Blackburn. Rosencrantz is moving beyond the Baconian method of measurement and categorization, finding meanings a century before Newton. But he is a mute, inglorious Newton: as Elizabeth Wheeler says, "Perception both on an individual and a societal level is necessary for awareness of significance."[24] We, the latter-day audience, are the silent perceivers here. The problem is partly Guildenstern, of course, since he represents Thomas Kuhn's traditional scientist attached to inherited assumptions, and is thus incapable of validating what Rosencrantz observes. In fact, nature functions differently for Guildenstern, as shown when Rosencrantz attempts to demonstrate the law of equal and opposite reaction with the flowerpots. He demonstrates inertia instead. Since neither cultural perception nor repetition occurs, no reality pertains to anything that Rosencrantz discovers. To put it another way, Rosencrantz's observations do not translate to the two criteria that Stephen Hawking assigns to a scientific theory: description and prediction.[25] Furthermore, as Bohr and Heisenberg have shown us, observation changes what is observed, physically and in translation into language and reproducible modes. Here, the phenomena observed become alms for an oblivion to be shaped much later in a new physics that itself will move from Newton's static cosmos through Einstein's "cosmological constant" to Hubble's observation that the universe is expanding. In a sense, nature is like the Shakespearean script. The "meanings" are there, but the circumstances required for their articulation and formulation have not yet occurred. The script is expanding in ways that will come to be seen in retrospect to have been within the measurements of relativity and, as the changes occur, within the much smaller dimensions of quantum mechanics. Rosencrantz, even as he demolishes Aristotelian paradigms, cannot bring his insights to completion. His discoveries prove that probability *is* at work in his world, but the proof resides within a model yet to be defined. Stoppard's screenplay, of course, is an example of symbiosis.

Film is a more closed art form than theater. This one ends where it begins. The Player's wagon plies through the chalky cliffs—the "place without any visible character," as the stage directions to the play have it. Film can ask the question: *did* anything happen? The wagon from which the two characters stepped to Elsinore's throne room rumbles off through the stick-thin woods in the same direction it had been going. Did the wagon ever stop? Has it all been an instant within the Player's mind? Within the mind of some unknown playwright? Has it been one of those ideas that flick through a writer's mind, but are never put down in words? A dream forgotten at dawn? Certainly it seems to be as unrecorded as Rosencrantz's observations, as irrelevant as the hair and fingernails that continue to grow after death. *Hamlet* has occurred for them only as it included them. It has all been like the escape that the condemned man imagines in the eye-blink between the affixing of the noose and the drop in *An Occurrence at Owl Creek Bridge*. Like some versions of madness and all types of sanity, the film moves in and out of realities none of which is reality. The question is not posed in the adolescent mode—what *is* reality?—but how does art condition reality, transmit it though various frames, from artifice to imitation that verges on whatever the truth may be? What is true is that there never was a time when someone could have said no.

Rosencrantz's disquisition on being alive or dead in a box comes half true. Neither state is reached, since their existential bodies have been hanged, but their roles as characters remain inside the Player's wagon on the stage that can be lowered at a moment's notice. They are alive *and* dead. They are inside the play, thus potentially inside a fiction that is their only "life," that they will not recognize this time either. They are doomed to silence on rotting pages or to an endless repetition of the same questions without answers, a recurring nightmare. They may get a whiff of déjà vu now and then, but they are doomed to believe that each moment in this old and familiar play is always and forever the first and only time. They are in that script, their parts "written," as the Player says, as if the play were the book of fate. They are not dead exactly, but they can come alive only in the estranging world known as *Hamlet*. Guildenstern recognizes "Gonzago," but he does not recognize that "Gonzago" is a play-within-a-play or that he is within a play, both Shakespeare's and Stoppard's. The snippets of *Hamlet* that Stoppard includes in his play suggest that a fate *is* at work, but it is the specific scenario dictated by Shakespeare. They can come out of the script box (even if other characters mix up their names)—"Hey you, what's your name, come out of there!" as Rosencrantz demands—but it is a movement from stasis, suspended animation into an unfree, scripted environment, where, as Guildenstern says, "There's something they're not telling us."

Nothing can be real here because Stoppard insists on dual contexts, a fraction of Shakespeare's play, the limited awareness of his title characters, and the relationship between these two zones of misunderstanding. The master metaphor is symbiosis. Rosencrantz and Guildenstern exist within a play that provides them with their existence. The world of art exists within a world of natural phenomena that can no more be articulated than the "meaning" of *Hamlet* can be phrased. The independent verification of meaning on which science exists is never available to a work of art, so that art challenges science by occurring only once. To be science it would have to be capable of replication according to precise measurements. Rosencrantz and Guildenstern recur with great precision—depending on what text of *Hamlet* is used—but their "meaning" is unavailable to them and to us in that their replication is not susceptible to measurement. Does that make them meaningless? No, but their meaning will vary with the observer in ways well beyond any scientific principle of indeterminacy. The principle of symbiosis when applied to art introduces an infinite number of variables. It becomes nonscience, but in ways very different than what Rosencrantz observes. He can repeat his experiments for his own eyes, but he cannot articulate them.

When Hamlet escapes to the pirate ship, Guildenstern complains: "We need Hamlet for our release." What he means is that they need *Hamlet* for their release. Neither Rosencrantz nor Guildenstern recognizes the italicization that would explain to them their symbiotic relationship with the play in the Player's box. They live within a work of art, and are themselves fictions. Stoppard glances, of course, at the ways in which the "unknown citizen" (to borrow Auden's designation) is a puppet within scenarios constructed by politics and politicians. The two will not get Hamlet to England, but *Hamlet* will get them there and provide sudden closure. Hamlet has rewritten the commission, and *Hamlet* will not release them. That closure will occur in each production, though only reported, after they have struggled (we infer) through the same confusion that Stoppard depicts; that is, unless a director such as Olivier erases them altogether. There never was a moment when they could have said "no," nor will there be. They will never understand the play in which they participate. Nor will we, of course. The existential commentary rides out, making us much more like them than Hamlet, who at least motivates much of what *he* does not understand either.

Stoppard's Rosencrantz and Guildenstern predict in 1990 the future of the Shakespeare script, awaiting subjugation to a powerful and alien authority to which it has no countering voice.

Star Trek began to boldly steal lines from Shakespeare right away. Episode number 11 of the first season (1966) is called "A Dagger of the Mind." Episode number 13 (8 December 1966) is "The Conscience of the King." In it, a mass murderer, Kudos, is seeking his kudos as the actor-manager of a theatrical company disguised as Prince Hamlet.* *Star Trek VI: The Undiscovered Country* (1991), directed by Nicholas Meyer, is a story of espionage, political assassination, and disguise on a galactic scale. Made as the Cold War was ending, it is full of allusions to the departure of the tense years fabricated by both parties in the "war." The Klingon moon Praxis explodes. Klingon's enormous military expenditures have exhausted their ability to confront the crisis. The planet has about 50 years of oxygen left. Captain Kirk (William Shatner), against his will, is sent on a diplomatic mission to the Klingons. "Only Nixon could go to China," he is told. At the banquet aboard the Starship Enterprise, the Klingon Chancellor Gorkon (David Warner) proposes a toast: "The Undiscovered Country—the Future."

Since Hamlet's phrase apparently alludes to death and its kingdom, "the undiscovered country" may be said to embrace "the future." (Hamlet is reading a line from Seneca, obviously, at that point in his soliloquy. He's seen a "traveler return'd."). Spock (Leonard Nemoy) identifies the line as "*Hamlet*. Act three, scene one." The Chancellor tells Spock that "You have not experienced Shakespeare until you have read him in the original Klingon." And that would be a guttural and monosyllabic experience, punctuated occasionally by the low bark of Klingon laughter. General Chang (Christopher Plummer, like Warner, an actor who has played Hamlet) continues: "To be or not to be—that is the question that preoccupies our people. We need breathing room." Kirk nails that one: "Adolph Hitler. 1938." The Chancellor suggests that "If there is to be a brave new world, our generation will have the hardest time living in it." Chang bids farewell to Kirk with a double quotation: "Parting is such sweet sorrow. Have we not heard the chimes at midnight?"

The Klingon ship is mysteriously attacked and the Chancellor is killed. Kirk and McCoy (DeForest Kelley) are tried by the Klingons. Chang the prosecutor asks Kirk, "What would your favorite author say? 'Let's sit upon the ground and tell sad stories of the death of kings'? Tell us your sad story." Kirk and Scotty are condemned to the penal asteroid of Rua Penthe to work in the lithium mines. Martia (Iman) is a comaloid, or shapeshifter. She tells Kirk "I thought I would assume a pleasing shape." Kirk apparently senses Shakespeare and knows that those who speak it are dangerous. Martia assumes his shape, but Kirk convinces his captors that *he* is the real phony and so escapes with McCoy back to the safety of the Federation. Chang attacks. "No peace in our time," he says, playing Hitler to the Chamberlainian optimism of 1938. "Once more into the breach, dear friends. If you tickle us, do we not laugh? If you prick us, do we not bleed? If you wrong us, shall we not revenge? The game's afoot. Our revels now are ended. Cry 'Havoc!' and let slip the dogs of war. I am constant as the northern star." Kirk's missile heads in Chang's direction. "To be or not to be."

Kirk is ordered to put back to space dock to be decommissioned. He refuses. Like Tennyson's Ulysses he will boldly go where no one has gone before. But he does not adduce Tennyson or Shakespeare. "Second star to the right," he says, "and straight on until morning." The realities of age—of men and spaceships—are to be ignored. The

Cold War may be over, but Captain Hook awaits the lost boys and girls in some undiscovered galaxy.

A "version" of *Hamlet* likely to be neglected is "The Trial of Hamlet," which appeared on C-Span on 17 February 1994. Here, Hamlet's killing of Polonius is examined to determine whether Hamlet should stand trial. The hearing, then, is the equivalent of a grand jury. It occurs in the elegant West Conference Room of the Supreme Court building, with Justice Kennedy presiding and Justice Ginsburg in the jury. Abbe Lowell, Meyer Feldman, and Thomas Feldman appear for the defense, and Theodore Olson and Peter Wallison for the prosecution ("The Crown").

Justice Kennedy defines the case against Hamlet around a "narrow issue." Was Hamlet at the time he killed Polonius capable of understanding the criminality of his conduct or of conforming his conduct to the requirements of the law?

Hamlet has survived Laertes's apparently fatal thrust but "all questions of his accession to the throne of Denmark have been held in abeyance" until his criminal responsibility has been established. If he is found to have been insane when he killed Polonius, Hamlet will be confined to a mental institution. If the jury finds him sane, he will be tried for anything from involuntary manslaughter to first-degree murder. If the latter charge were to be brought, it would be based, one assumes, on Hamlet's soliloquy as he decides not to kill the apparently praying Claudius, and on his belief that the person behind the arras is Claudius ("I took thee for thy better"). Although premeditation could be argued, the sword seems to leap at Polonius almost of its own volition. Hamlet's "Up sword" as he spares Claudius a moment earlier has been very reluctant.

The jurors, Kennedy says, are the arbiters of fact. The judge merely interprets the law. The evidence is the conflated text of *Hamlet* (the Folger Edition) and the testimony of witnesses. Hamlet's killing of Polonius is not contested. His mental condition at the time of the killing, Kennedy says, is the jury's sole concern. The defense must show that the preponderance of evidence demonstrates that Hamlet was not criminally responsible when he killed Polonius. This means, Kennedy says, applying the less stringent standards that apply to a grand jury, "more probably than not," as opposed to "beyond a reasonable doubt."

The defense, as argued by Dr. Thomas Guttheil of Harvard, is that Hamlet shows no emotion as he kills Polonius—"how now, a rat?"—or any remorse afterwards. Those who know Hamlet best attest to his madness. "Mad as the sea," his mother says. Furthermore, Hamlet hallucinates, as demonstrated by his seeing a ghost in Gertrude's closet that she cannot see or hear. Hamlet suffers from what was once known as manic depression, but is now called bipolar disorder, in Hamlet's case of the rapid-cycling form. The victim swings between elation and depression. Its manic phase manifests itself in hypersexuality, babbling speech, episodes of inappropriate hostility, and a grandiose sense of mission. The depressive symptoms are suicidal anadonia, loss of pleasure, bad dreams, alienation from the environment, and a blurring of the sense of right and wrong. Hamlet is thus unable to understand that he has killed someone. He did not a) have the capacity to grasp his criminality, or b) have the ability to conform his actions to the law. Were a policeman standing next to Hamlet when he heard Polonius behind the curtain, Hamlet would have behaved the same way. To attempt to *fake* mental illness, the defense argues, is for the mentally ill person to claim mastery over his illness. The secondary gain of such fakery is that it achieves something for the practitioner. But Hamlet gains nothing, as proved by his inappropriate hostility to Ophelia. "To conclude that his conduct is sometimes inappropriate," says Abbe Lowell, "is like saying that his father died of earache."

The prosecution argues that Hamlet's "antic disposition" is a defense against a King who has killed Hamlet's father, and against Polonius and Rosencrantz and Guildenstern, and even Ophelia—all of whom are spying on Hamlet or involved in the process of spying. Hamlet is constantly aware of the precariousness of his situation. His feigning does not show diminution but enhanced capacity. It is a survival technique. What triggers his melancholia are actual events, and, according to Dr. Alan Stone, also of Harvard Yard, if someone did not respond as Hamlet had, "we *would* have a madman on our hands." Hamlet *is* spied upon and therefore cannot be called delusional. Since he *is* a prince, his visions are not grandiose ("O, cursed spite, that ever I was born to set [the time] right!"). That's his mission. As a student of philosophy, Hamlet is profound, not merely suicidal. Camus's statement on the ethics of suicide would be a modern example of Hamlet's exploration of the consequences of human action, including "self-slaughter." Hamlet does experience grief, complicated by his mother's behavior. Madness means that a person is trapped within himself—as *Ophelia* is—but Hamlet devises a "reality check," the play-within-a-play, and appoints an independent witness in Horatio, who agrees with Hamlet's interpretation of Claudius's reaction to "Gonzago." Hamlet shows a remarkable ability to *control* his impulses when he decides not to kill an apparently praying Claudius. Those who claim that Hamlet is mad, as Polonius does, are "mistaken and wrong-headed," says Dr. Stone. Ophelia's madness is a contrast, not a parallel, to Hamlet. The prosecution argues that to hold Hamlet responsible is to offer him his only chance at vindication—at a trial that could acquit him. The defense counters that Hamlet "is a sick boy who needs help."

The verdict is that Hamlet "is criminally responsible" for killing Polonius. The jury recommends to the prosecution that it "investigate whether Hamlet should be held criminally responsible for the destruction of Ophelia." That recommendation represents a knotty assignment, of course. Can someone be held accountable for another's suicide? And can a person as out of contact with rationality as Ophelia be said to have committed suicide? The jury's recommendation would seem to represent a feminist backlash against the "sweet prince."

The prosecution's case could be strengthened in several ways. That Dr. Stone believes in ghosts (as he says) does not mean that Hamlet is *not* hallucinating the Ghost in Gertrude's closet. But since the Ghost has spoken lines in the inherited script, that hallucination represents a remarkable feat of ventriloquism on Hamlet's part. The voice he projects is *also* heard by the audience, and that gives the Ghost an objective reality, even if an actor like Jonathan Price suggests that the voice is coming from Hamlet. "It is not possible," says Dr. Guttheil, "for a hallucination to tell you something you don't know. It's your mind." While it could be argued that the Ghost represents a creature emerging from Hamlet's "prophetic soul" and, later, his awareness of a "blunted purpose," the Ghost does provide details about the murder that Hamlet could not have known. Guttheil, I think, would be on stronger ground were he to argue the theory that dreams can also come from sources beyond the metaphysical boundaries of any individual. In the John Barton production of 1980, Gertrude *did* see the Ghost, but repressed that horrifying vision. Suffice it that a key element of the insanity plea—that the hearing of voices is an element in bipolar disorder—can be refuted by the evidence.

Dr. Stone counters defense's argument that Hamlet accosts Gertrude on her bed. The bed does not appear until Gielgud's production in the 1930s. In the illustration for Rowe's 1709 edition, based on an admittedly Restoration stage version of the play, the Ghost appears in a sitting room. There, Michael Kahn, Shakespeare Theater director, under whose auspices this trial is conducted, might have been helpful. Furthermore the prosecution could have produced precedents for protective "madness"—Junius Brutus and Marston's Malevole. The defense could have countered with Hieronimo. The prosecution could have adduced actors like Forbes-Robertson, who do not believe Hamlet is mad. The defense could have shown Derek Jacobi saying, "It *hath* made me mad!"—though does not an awareness that one is mad argue sanity? Furthermore, Hamlet does say of Polonius, "For this same lord, I do repent me." Claudius says that "what [Hamlet] spoke ... was not like madness." He goes on to say, though, that the *official* view is that "madness in great ones must not unwatch'd go." It may be, as Dover Wilson argues,[26] and Olivier's film shows, Hamlet knows that Claudius and Polonius are eavesdropping on his meeting with Ophelia and that knowledge motivates Hamlet's behavior, and, further, that Hamlet's knowledge of Ophelia's complicity dictates some of his salaciousness at the play. Furthermore, his "hypersexuality" can be explained as an aspect of his antic disposition. And it is not at all clear that Horatio's comments after "Gonzago" signal agreement with Hamlet's interpretation of Claudius's reaction to the play.

In the hubbub after Kennedy gavels the trial to a close, the actor playing Hamlet is heard telling Kennedy that he had "a great time!" He was not called, however, to testify in his own defense. Instead, lawyers and psychiatrists do with *Hamlet* what literary critics have done for years—take the same evidence and reach diametrically different conclusions with it.

Since this trial is very much an anachronism, applying recent psychiatric and legal theory to an early 17th-century killing, it would have been helpful for someone to provide some background, giving us a sense of how the law, as Justice Kennedy says, "was beginning to change when Shakespeare wrote." Early modern England was here, as elsewhere, a testing ground for the new or evolving concepts that so deeply inform Shakespeare's plays. I would have been grateful for an outline of the "insanity defense," beginning with Henry de Bracton in the 1400s on the legal consequences of mental disorder, moving on to Lord Hale's "child of 14" test, and Justice Tracy's "wild beast test," which stems from Bracton. Perhaps the first real insanity defense was in the Hadfield Case (1800), where Thomas Erskine put forward the concept of "delusion" as "the true character of insanity," and convinced the court. The McNaghten Rules, formulated in 1843, became the subject of subsequent jurisprudence. They say that "the party accused ... was laboring under such a defect of reason, from disease of mind, as not to know that nature and quality of the act he was doing, or if he did know it, that he did not know he was doing wrong." The issue is the condition of the defendant at the time of the crime, and the debate has diverged: in the United States "morality" has tended to be the definition of "wrong," while in Great Britain it has been "contrary to the law." Critics point out that the problem with the McNaghten Rules is that they rest on the concept of "rationality" and present an old-fashioned model of how mind and psyche work. One of the first "modern" insanity defenses was Darrow's of Loeb and Leopold in 1925. Darrow argued that they murdered Bobby Franks "as they might kill a spider or a fly."[27] In the United States the "irresistible impulse test" emerged out of dissatisfaction with the McNaghten Rules. "Partial insanity" or "diminished responsibility" can affect the element of premeditation, a factor of great importance in capital cases. Wendy Kaminer says, "Generally, the insanity defense protects the psychotic—people who are certifiably mentally ill—not the psychopathic (although temporary insanity defense, like the one proffered by Lorena Bobbitt, can involve such fuzzy concepts as posttraumatic stress disorders). In most cases the legal line we draw between sanity and insanity reflects the belief that psychopaths, or sociopaths, like Ted Bundy or John Wayne Gacy, act out of choice, not compulsion."[28]

The trial of Hamlet occurred when actual murder trials were being conducted, and even televised by Court TV—Pamela Smart, the Menendez brothers, and O.J.—as opposed to the more contemporary proceedings against corporate thugs or the felony trials of basketball players.

Of *The Lion King* (1994), Daniel Rosenthal says, "Shakespeare's ending might prove a surprise" to "millions of children" informed of *Hamlet* by this film.[29] As Doug Stenberg demonstrates, however, the film emerges from *Henry IV* and *Macbeth*, as well as *Hamlet*.[30] The film's "message" is hierarchy. The "gene pool" has been unkind to Scar, but life is not fair either to the mouse with which he toys, the hyenas at the bottom of the food chain, or the unoffending grubs on which Pumbaa and Timon gorge. According to Carolyn Newberger, the film's stereotypes include hyenas disguised as ghetto dwellers and Scar as homosexual, an attribution reinforced by his apparent lack of interest in any of the many lionesses in a male-deprived pride.[31]

The film opens as all animals bow to the figures atop Pride Rock, as Rafiki holds up the newborn heir, Simba. King Mufasa shows Simba around the kingdom, saying that all is "a delicate balance. We are all connected in the great circle of life."

"Don't we eat the antelope?" Simba asks (he later admits to munching on zebra and hippo). "When we die," Mufasa explains, "our bodies become the grass, and the antelope eat the grass." While this explanation may support a Coleridgean thesis that "We are all one life," it hardly refutes the much stronger and more visual hierarchical emphasis. A thesis of a cycle of life does not exclude powerful carnivores, and some hyenas are less equal than others. Stenberg demonstrates the film's reliance on "chain of being" concepts. The film is very uneasy in its conflation of medieval and romantic doctrines. While all nature may participate in a circle of life, "Vultures are sure someone's not coming back from lunch."

"Long live the king!" Scar says to Mufasa, letting the latter drop to his death. Scar's coronation is Nazi-like, with hordes of hyenas goose-stepping past his elevated perch. Scar's exhortation to his followers is a perversion or perhaps a logical extension of the Boy Scout motto: "Be Prepared!" Like Hitler, Scar empowers the worst of his society, again suggesting the chain of being as opposed to the circle of life agenda, but perverting it, as Macbeth does. We hear Macbeth's claim that we must "wail his fall / Whom I myself struck down" in Scar's "Mufasa's death is a terrible tragedy, but to lose Simba, who had just begun to live, for me it is a deep personal loss." Claudius's "that we with wisest sorrow think on [Hamlet] / Together with remembrance of ourselves" recurs in Scar's "Yet out of the ashes of this tragedy we shall rise to greet the dawning of a new era, in which lion and hyena come together in a great and glorious future." But since Scar takes no new (or old) wife, the pride is doomed to extinction. Ecological disaster, though, becomes a more immediate emergency than the lack of an heir.

Scar convinces Simba that he is responsible for Mufasa's death, and Simba runs away. Nala, Simba's childhood playmate, finds him in a far country, and tries to get him to return to be king. Simba's guilt is unconvincing, but the play must be kept going. It is as if the writers had read E. E. Stoll on why *Hamlet* is so long. Simba follows Rafiki down into a cavern—a symbolic trip to the underworld—where Simba sees his reflection. But it is Mufasa, all the zodiac behind him, insisting that Simba "Remember me!" This is not a call for mere revenge, though, it is a summons to kingship. "If I don't fight for it, who will?" Simba asks. He forces Scar to admit that Scar is guilty of Mufasa's death. It is the public admission that Hamlet does not get from Claudius that would have been a precondition for Hamlet's ascending the throne. Simba tosses Scar to the hyenas, whom Scar has betrayed.

"It is time," Rafiki says. Rain falls. The skull of a wildebeeste—the animals who had killed Mufasa in the stampede—washes away. The terrible wasteland that Scar and his hyenas had permitted to develop is green again as the sun returns. Paradise Lost. Paradise Regained.

At the end, Rafiki the baboon, who is a combination wise Polonius and witch doctor, holds up yet another lion cub to the adoring mass of animals below Pride Rock. Royal continuity has been restored, after Scar's temporary interruption. The parallel here is to the end of *Macbeth*, where Malcolm's followers proclaim him "King of Scotland" (not "King of Scots"), confirming Duncan's effort to establish an hereditary kingdom. As Stenberg points out, Scar has made of wasteland of the kingdom—"in which lion and hyena come together," as Scar says—turning the world upside down, as Macbeth does. Darkness prevails when the sun should be shining. Mousing owls rise to down falcons. Horses, man's servants and transport into battle, issue forth to make war on mankind. "Measure, time, and place" have been overturned. Now, order has been restored. It is not a circle of life that has been reinstituted, however. It is a dynasty within the inexorable movement of history. Thus the ending is more like that of *Macbeth*, where the orderly progress of James to the throne of England has merely been interrupted by a terrible nightmare that Shakespeare recreates in playform, than of *Hamlet*, where a foreign prince marches briskly in and takes over.

In *Renaissance Man* (1994), out-of-work Detroit ad-man Bill Rago (Danny De Vito) is sent to teach the awkward squad at an Army base. The class focuses on *Hamlet*, which Bill Rago just happens to be reading. He uses *Romeo and Juliet*, however, for his example of oxymoron ("parting is such sweet sorrow") and Juliet's speech to Romeo (II.ii "Or, if thou thinkst I am too quickly won...") as his example of a boy actor playing a woman. One morning, Rago asks the drill sergeant (Gregory Hines) to "cut some slack" for a couple of his students who have been a minute late to formation. Later, after his class of misfits believes that he has deserted them, Rago performs on the "Victory Tower" to prove that he gives a damn. No supervisor would have permitted a civilian near the place. The film attempts to "humanize" the infantry, but Shakespeare has always had it right. It is "action of the tiger" that counts in wartime. The scriptwriters seem to sense this. The play that Rago takes his soldiers to see is *Henry V* in Stratford, Canada. The big scene is Henry's exhortation of his troops before Harfluer. The troops respond to Don Rielly's Henry, though one, a drummer, responds to the kettledrummers. That moment provides a glimpse of the truth of the experience of live theater. Bill Rago has told them that "plays [are] TV without the box," thus falsifying what live theater can be. As an adman, he might have said, TV without the commercials. Later, on bivouac, one of the men (Lillo Brancato) must recite Henry's "band of brothers" speech for the drill sergeant in a driving rain. At the final review, the young soldier (Peter Simmons) who has claimed that his father was a hero in Vietnam receives his father's Silver Star posthumously. The company gives Rago an "eyes left" and a collective smile. This is a sentimental and unconvincing film. The Army may have come up with the slogan "An Army of One" in order to lure young men into the infantry, but George Patton knew much more when he said, "An army is a team. All this individuality stuff is a bunch of nonsense." (That of course from a notorious individualist!) Most of the film is nonsense.

Rago's soldiers do hit an effective moment, though. Their rap version of *Hamlet* goes like this:

> Hamlet's mother—she's the queen –
> Buys it in the final scene.
> Drinks a glass of funky wine.
> Now she's Satan's Valentine.

The "modernized" *Hamlet* makes the issues of the play appropriately eschatological. The verse takes over the narrative at a point where it stops; "Follow my mother." Valentine's Day, a celebration of physical love, took over from the *agape* demonstrated by either of the Christian martyrs who may have been Saint Valentine. Since Valentine's Day may emerge from Lupercal, the pagan allusion in the soldiers' song works in ways perhaps not anticipated by the lyricists.

Kenneth Branagh's *A Midwinter's Tale* (1996: aka for non-United States consumption as *In the Bleak Midwinter*) trades on clichés: a threadbare group of actors going to a town called Hope to do *Hamlet* in a run-down church at Christmas; the director who threatens suicide in front of his company, and almost has to go through with it, since the counter-thesis is a long time in announcing itself; the cynical older actor who has never played Shakespeare; the ingenue who calls this ragtag group her "family"; the actor who cannot remember his lines; the designer whose "concept" is "space," then "smoke"; the agent who would pull her client out of the play for a three-film Hollywood contract; the Ophelia who actually slaps Hamlet during a performance. Some of the configurations go back to the backstage dramas of the 1930s. Add to the stereotypical characters and situations, that the actor who cannot remember his lines also drinks to forget the rest of his life (he drinks so much that he is likely to influence the next harvest, as one of his colleagues warns); that the ingenue is virtually blind but won't wear glasses and thus makes entrances that are bone-threatening crashes; and that the director will spend precious moments with Francisco to find the most frightening moment of his life, so that "Who's there?" will project the fullness of fear to the audience; and that the actor's subtext is changing a tire on a busy motorway, which he mimes before Bernardo's entrance, and you have unpromising material indeed. Then consider that the production of *Hamlet*—which does occur—brings a son to his father, a mother to her son, a father to his daughter, two lovers (Hamlet and Ophelia) together, Hollywood contracts to two minor actors (the male a wicked parody of the great Patrick Stewart), and Christmas bells sprinkling like crystal over the depressed village, and you cry, "Hold, enough!"

But out of this comes a funny and moving film that transforms the bleak midwinter into a Christmas card. The film is caviar to the general, almost all subtext, some of it having to do with the history of British theater, some with the play *Hamlet*. The film is superbly edited and timed, insisting in a Capotesque way that we overhear the lines as one sequence dissolve into the next. Nicholas Farrell develops a subtextual foxiness for his Reynaldo. Gerald Horan delivers his "And let him play his music!" as if he were Coriolanus haranguing the Roman mob. The church in which the play is to occur is also the "digs" for the actors. Two sleep in the crypt—"cryptic actors," as one of them says. A cardboard Shakespeare watches the performance, and a cutout American Indian also observes, stonily absorbing the political incorrectness that Mickey and Judy are perpetrating with their extravaganza. But what begins as murder in the cathedral ends as a community of the spirit, as the setting gradually exchanges its irony for its sacramental values.

A Daziel-Pascoe film of 1997, "A Killing Kindness," deriving from the novel by Reginald Hill and directed by Edward Bennett, features a murderer who leaves quotations from *Hamlet* as clues. "I must be cruel only to be kind"; "Why wouldst thou be a breeder of sinners?"; and "I say we will have no more marriages"—these lines are phoned in after the murders of three young women. A medium, hired by one of the mothers, describes an Ophelia-like ending: "Green all over me. Children's faces peering down at me. The sun shining like a lemon. Wings, white as a windmill's sails." The problem is that this victim had been found in a canal at night. Suspicion points at a local drama teacher. We see two scenes from the play: one in which Hamlet accosts Gertrude in her closet, in which the director shows how to kill Polonius with conviction, and Gertrude's speech about Ophelia's drowning. Since the director, Mark Wildgoose (Richard Hawley), is having an extramarital affair with his Gertrude (Julie Graham), the sexual impropriety makes him a suspect, along with his knowledge of the play. "We wait upon the law's delay," he says, explaining that he is not yet divorced. "Loonies," as Dalziel (Warren Clarke) calls them, phone in with more famous lines: "Now, get you to my lady's chamber. Tell her, let her paint an inch thick. To this favor she must come"; "That one may smile and smile and be a villain"; "The time is out of joint. O cursed spite that ever I was born to set it right." But when one of the other characters, Austin Greenall (Paul Goodwin), proprietor of the local gliding school, talks about counting himself "king of infinite space," those of us who have read the play suddenly look upon the face of murder. It is then just a question of who will be another victim. Wildgoose is killed and his body dragged into a greenhouse. "I'll lug the guts into a neighbor room," quotes Pascoe (Colin Buchanan). Greenall finally confesses that his killings have been to prevent other people from marrying disastrously as he has done, Pascoe explains, "Yes, get thee to a nunnery." It turns out that the body found in a canal had actually fallen into a pond during the day at a site near the gliding school, so the medium's reading of the mind of the dying young woman turns out to have been accurate. Dalziel has misquoted the play himself: "Alas, poor Horatio. I knew him well!" He ends up being godfather to the Pascoe's daughter and must renounce the sins of the flesh in her name. While he objects to this declaration as unsuited to his persona, the drama is finally reenclosed within proper ritual boundaries, as *Hamlet* may be once Fortinbras uses Hamlet's body-politic ("most royal... had he been put on") to reinforce the "rights of memory" that make him Denmark's king.

This made-for-TV film does have a few thematic links with *Hamlet*. It also has, as murder mysteries will, a lot of false leads. I don't think that—in spite of the British schoolboy's knowledge of the "set" play that the script assumes—the Arts & Entertainment audience of 1998 was meant to recognize the "king of infinite space" reference that tells us who the murderer is. A lot of productions, this one less brutally than many, punish a knowledge of Shakespeare.

A production I saw years ago at the Arena Stage in Washington, D.C., was set in Bismarkian Germany. This context lent remarkable power to the Ghost, an emanation of the concept of 'fatherland.' The graveyard scene, though, was largely gone, perhaps because Elizabethan burial practices did not sort well with the historical setting. And no "eucharistic anxiety" could really emerge. I assigned the character's crossing of themselves to a fear of rampant Darwinism. The production did, though, show ceremony interrupted. The ceremonies, however, were those of a modern aristocratic world. Ophelia's madness was an embarrassing interruption of a state dinner, for example. That single element—the discord deep at the heart of Elsinore, deeper than any group of characters imitating an action—cannot emerge in worlds that are close to our own in time. Or, if it can, I have not seen it yet. For all the aspects of *Hamlet* that can find analogies in a contemporary world, we must be educated in production to something that was profound in Shakespeare's time and is profoundly anachronistic today: a spiritual out-of-jointedness that touches every aspect of the world of the play.‡

Another example of *Hamlet*'s reduction to a commercial imperative occurred on 21 May 2004, when Cynthia Olick began her news report on CNBC with "To be or not to be." The report dealt with the company making the number "2" for signs at gas stations. "In this brave new world," said Olick, the number is in short supply.

Notes

* These episodes are mentioned by Lt. "Bud" Roberts of *JAG* as he returns some Shakespeare books to their owner (Episode 167, "When the Bough Breaks," 19 November 2002). In "'Conscience of the King,'" Roberts says, "Kirk plays Hamlet to Kudos's Claudius."
‡ The tendency of Shakespeare to appear in the mouths of bad men is countered by *My Darling Clementine* (1946).

‡ On Claude Chabrol's *Ophelia*, which I have not seen, see Kenneth S. Rothwell. *A History of Shakespeare on Screen*. Cambridge: Cambridge University Press, 1999, pp. 176–178 and "Chabrol's *Ophelia*." *Shakespeare on Film Newsletter* 3/1 (December 1978): 1 & 8.

Chapter 3
Othello

Othello is a "domestic tragedy." That means that it does not contain ghostly emissaries from some region of the afterworld, does not smash its crime against the clouds through which peer the eyes of God, and does not interrogate the cosmos, asking where justice is, if it exists at all. No worlds tumble as Othello falls. Instead, *Othello* narrows down to what A. C. Bradley calls "a close-shut, murderous room."[1] The play raises the issue of human evil more profoundly through Iago than through any figure other than the historical Hitler or Stalin. Shakespeare wants no irrelevancy, like a ghost or voices crying "Sleep no more!" or issues like the unjust death of Cordelia to interfere with the question he raises. We know why Desdemona dies, but what or who is Iago? That we never learn, and that is why the play continues to intrigue us. The recent case of O. J. Simpson and his murder of Nicole Brown Simpson created some superficial likenesses between Shakespeare's play and "real life," in that the murderer was a black man, the murdered person a white woman, but the O.J. case suggests only that Shakespeare was aware of the potential explosiveness inherent in race, particularly when the issue of race impinges on the question of sex. African American writing—*Native Son, The Autobiography of Malcolm X,* and *Soul on Ice,* for example—helps to explain Iago, as does John Howard Griffin, who changed himself into a black man by putting chemicals on his skin, and describes in *Black Like Me* his racist response as he looked into a mirror. As a white man, he hated the black man he saw there. Is it a satisfactory answer, however, to say that Iago is a racist? Is it satisfactory to say that Hitler and the Nazis were antisemitic? The murder of Desdemona and the death camps argue something beyond the definition and scope of even the most vicious of categories.

The world of *Othello* is a Christian world, but unless we speculate that Iago is a devil or *the* devil (as some critics have done, and as

Othello does at the end), no evidence exists for any divine or malign intervention in the affairs of its characters. The world of Venice, where the play begins, is a world of go-betweens.[2] No one goes directly to anyone else. Great ones beg Othello with doffed caps to make Iago his Lieutenant. Cassio, we learn, was an emissary between Othello and Desdemona. To employ a go-between, however, is to empower the messenger. Iago can pose as the honest man in the middle who can interpret Venice for the outsider, Othello. Othello is a *convert* to Christianity—meaning that another religious system lurks below the surface of his conversion—and Othello is not a native of Venice. While some debate about what Othello "looks like," the play suggests that he is an African, not a Moor, but a *Black*amoor. Venice needs him because he is a great general and thus a marvelous, necessary man to have against the Turkish threat. Lincoln needed Ulysses S. Grant and the United States of the late thirties needed Joe Louis. After he had kayoed Max Schmeling in 1938 and said his piece for the war effort a few years later, Louis was abandoned to the mercies of the Internal Revenue Service.

Cyprus is an island under martial law. Cyprus is "a town of war, / Yet wild, the people's hearts brimful of fear." The context is confusing: the Turks have only just sunk in the storm as Othello announces his wedding celebration. The night subtly introduces the conflict between a foreign, unbelieving, pagan infidel and a Christian sacrament. That Cyprus is under martial law means that Cassio's getting drunk while captain of the guard should merit more than just dismissal as a punishment.

The moment at which Othello learns of the origins of the brawl—from Iago, of course—is worth some attention. "Who began this?" Othello demands. "I do not know," Iago replies. "Friends all but now, even now, / In quarter and in terms like bride and groom / Devesting them for bed." With a perfectly innocent simile, Iago describes what Othello has just been doing! And it is *Cassio* who is guilty of interrupting the consummation of Othello's marriage. Before he introduces jealousy, Iago has begun to disturb Othello in the area of his sexuality.

Before we can cede the play to Iago, however, we must ask what in Othello makes him in any way susceptible to Iago's manipulations and insinuations? The answer is Othello's *hubris*, or overwhelming pride. In the pagan world, human pride is likely to evoke retaliation from the gods. In the Christian world, it is the chiefest of the seven deadly sins. Othello has borne himself humbly before the Venetian Senate, although, as Olivier shows, he must enjoy the effect his exotic tales and fabulous language have on this group of merchants and legalists. As he lands on Cyprus, however, he makes himself a pagan god. The storm is past, the Turks are drowned (perhaps a few swarthy bodies bob in the chafing surf) and there, against the clearing green of the sky, stands Desdemona. Othello has made it! He should kneel and thank God for his deliverance and that of Cyprus. Instead, he says,

> If it were now to die,
> 'Twere now to be most happy; for I fear
> My soul hath her content so absolute
> That not another comfort like to this
> Succeeds in unknown fate.

Desdemona remonstrates: "The heavens forbid / But that our loves and comforts should increase, / Even as our days do grow." She enunciates the Christian concept of growth and development within the context of matrimony. Othello, however, has said, It doesn't get any better than this! It won't. For a human to assert perfection is to insist on an inevitable gravity, indeed to surrender to the "fate" that Othello mentions. It is a "known fate," however. No gods are listening, but Iago is. He sneers, "O, you are well tun'd now! / But I'll set down the pegs that make this music, / As honest as I am." Iago will slacken the strings, he tells us. He is telling us the truth, he says, and implying that it is his reputed honesty that will permit him to change Othello's tune. He is a retailer of aphorisms (compare his words on "reputation": it is for one audience, Othello, the most valuable thing a person can have, and for another, Cassio, an intangible worth nothing). Against that stock of clichés is Othello's majesty, couched in his newly acquired language, which he turns into a great organ, full of the modification that he piles up in front of his nouns. Within hours of Othello's grandiloquent arrival on the shores of Cyprus, Iago has fomented a fight that snorts and snarls under Othello's wedding chamber. The climax of the play, however, has been Othello's speech on landing. He has handed himself over to Iago, who only has to show the least hint of imperfection for Othello's grand structure to begin to collapse.

Othello has given Desdemona a handkerchief, his "first gift"—the object of transition from a pagan past to a Christian marriage. Desdemona loses it trying to bind Othello's head, after he has complained of a headache (an allusion to his fear that he has been cuckolded). Emilia gives it to Iago. The handkerchief becomes the object that pushes Othello back into his pagan past. At the end of the long scene in which Iago convinces him that Desdemona has been unfaithful, Othello and Iago kneel and exchange vows.

> Othello. Now, by yond marble heaven,
> In the due reverence of a sacred vow
> I hear engage my words. [Kneels]
> Iago. Do not rise yet. [Kneels]
> Witness you ever burning lights above,
> You elements that clip us round about,
> Witness that here Iago doth give up
> The execution of his wit, hands, heart,
> To wrong'd Othello's service. Let him command,
> And to obey shall be in me remorse,
> What bloody business ever. [They rise]
> Othello. I greet thy love,
> Not with vain thanks, but with acceptance bounteous...
> Now art thou my Lieutenant.
> Iago. I am your own forever.

What we witness here is a perversion of Christian marriage, in which the two kneel and exchange vows, and wherein Iago gains command over his supposed master. And, unwittingly, Othello has completed a version of Faustian bargain.

It soon becomes clear that what Brabantio, Desdemona's father, believed ("He thought 'twas witchcraft") was *true*. The handkerchief had "magic in the web." It was woven of the silk of "hallowed" worms by a "sibyl" and designed to make the woman who had it "amiable." To lose it, or make a gift of it, is to force her husband to "hold her loathed" and to "hunt / After new fancies." Othello is back in that pagan past of things forbidden to the Christian dispensation: witchcraft, charms, talismans, and black magic. Desdemona, of course, is pleading for the reinstatement of Cassio, not knowing that he has been named as her lover, so that as Othello demands the handkerchief, she insists on Cassio's suit. The two are at terrifying cross-purposes. It is a classic "anima-animus conflict."

As Romeo looks at Juliet in the Capulet tomb, she seems almost alive to him. If he would only pause for a moment, she *would* be alive. As Othello looks at Desdemona sleeping, she seems to be a "rose," pure and innocent, with skin "whiter ... than snow." Her "balmy breath ... dost almost persuade / Justice to break her sword." If Othello would trust his senses ... but by this time he has convinced himself that he is killing Desdemona for "the cause": the principle that adulterers (particularly if they are women) must die, "else she'll betray more men." Othello's awareness of her chastity comes only after he has killed her. After the murder, back in the Christian world he had temporarily abandoned, he talks of Judgment Day, typically casting himself in the role of hero, this time as an echo of the fallen Lucifer, who took on God "in dubious battle" and was thrown out of Heaven:

> When we shall meet at compt
> This look of thine will hurl my soul from heaven
> And fiends will snatch at it.

At the end, he recognizes what has happened to him. He talks of a "malignant and a turban'd Turk." The Turks sank in the storm, but the "Turk" surfaced in Othello, up from the "Pontic" (or Black) Sea, the pagan past he had repressed. He became the enemy he had been dispatched to Cyprus to defeat. Here, he kills himself, the commander executing a traitor. It is a superb moment in which the conflicting roles coalesce. Othello validates the heroism that has been attributed to him but that we have never seen until this last moment. He deserves to be at the center of this narrative, because, even if it is couched in the "Othello music," it speaks truth of him and makes of him at last, by awareness and action, the great man he has believed himself to be all along. He has compared himself to a "base Indian [who] threw a pearl away / Richer than all his tribe," according to the Quarto version of the play. The Folio, published in 1623, seven years after Shakspeare's death, reads "Judean." Within the "Christian" reading, this makes better sense, particularly when we consider Othello's "I kiss'd thee, ere I kill'd thee," which like "Judean," points at the archbetrayer, Judas, the first to be damned within the Christian epoch.

Othello attempts to kill Iago, but says that if Iago is "a devil, I cannot kill thee." Whatever Iago is, he will not explain why he has fomented this evil. "From this time forth, I never will speak word." His silence resonates out from the play. Within that silence resides the mystery of human evil.

Inevitably, *Othello* is seen as a play about race. It has to be a play about race today, but an exclusive focus on that aspect of the script will blur other elements. To try to avoid race, as Jonathan Miller did in his BBC version (1981), is to create a strange production, in which Othello (Anthony Hopkins) is the best-looking and best-spoken of all the characters.[3] What can Brabantio (Geoffrey Chater) find wrong in this exemplary son-in-law? Iago (Bob Hoskins) has no place to go but into the realm of psychopathology. That is a comfortable zone for

Hoskins, but it explains evil as an a priori absence, rather than exploring it as a developing presence.

Some offshoots of *Othello* are worth mentioning in brief. *A Double Life* (Universal International, 1947) won an Oscar for Ronald Colman as Anthony John, an actor who falls under the spell of the role he is playing, in this case, Othello. He murders a waitress he has met—Shelley Winters, in her first film role—with the "kiss of death" he has been using on stage opposite the Desdemona of Signe Hasso. This *noir* was directed by George Cukor and written by Ruth Gordon and Garson Kanin. One of the film's virtues is that it shows the proscenium format in which a Shakespeare play would have been produced on Broadway in the 1940s. Robert F. Willson, Jr., places the film in its historical context—films like *Double Indemnity*, *The Postman Always Rings Twice*, and *The Snakepit*.[4] The role of Othello, Willson suggests, is Anthony John's Iago.[5] *Jubal* (Columbia, 1956) is a western *Othello*. The film does not incorporate a racial element, but director Delmer Daves gets strong performances from Ernest Borgnine (the Othello figure), Glenn Ford (a Cassio greatly expanded) and Rod Steiger (the film's Iago).[6] Shakespeare has, of course, encouraged other art, including Verdi's superb *Otello*. For Shakespeare's influence on other artists, I recommend the version made at La Scala in 1986, featuring a splendid opening storm, along with Placido Domingo in the tenor role of Otello and Justino Diaz as the baritone Iago.

In *The Comedians* (1967, directed by Peter Glenville), Brown (Richard Burton) needlessly jealous of Martha (Elizabeth Taylor) says, "Othello caught Desdemona with his tales of adventure." The film is based on the novel by Graham Greene and hinges on issues of trust and commitment. Although set in Duvalier's Haiti, neither novel nor film deals with race. Major Jones (Alec Guiness) is a phony adventurer and, for all of his boasting, a strikeout with women. Brown is a nihilist who becomes an existentialist, or at least someone who is willing to die for nothing as opposed to living for nothing. Hemingway's short stories anticipate much of this, as does, in a way *For Whom the Bell Tolls*.

"Homicidal Ham," which aired on 27 October 1983, was number 26 in the *Cheers* series. Written by David Lloyd, it featured a paroled murderer, Andy (Derek McGrath), who convinces Diane (Shelley Long) that he could make it on the outside if only he were to be allowed to act. She convinces him that she'll introduce him to directors on Cape Cod if he auditions successfully before her former drama coach,

Professor DeWitt (Seven Darden). DeWitt arrives at Cheers and says to Diane, "I never pictured you as a waitress." "But I played a waitress in your production of *Bus Stop*!" she replies. "That's what I meant," he says. After that, all goes well. Andy and Diane exchange "I love yous"—his romantic, hers in the mode of "good friends." Then Andy observes Diane kissing her boyfriend, Sam (Ted Danson). He gets instantly jealous and says "Put out the light" very meaningfully as he goes on stage. Diane, aware that she is in danger, tries to end the scene prematurely but is egged on by her audience. As in *A Double Life*, some members of the audience grow uneasy, but Professor DeWitt is totally convinced by Andy's performance. It continues until Diane is able to shout, "Help! He's trying to kill me!" Coach (Nicholas Colasanto) responds: "That's the first line of Shakespeare I've ever understood!" Finally, Sam pulls Andy away and Diane is saved. Like Colman's Anthony John, Andy has become Othello. But Colman's psyche has become saturated with the role he is playing. For Andy the role is a medium for his sudden jealousy.

The latter emotion and motive are necessitated by the pressures of a 24-minute script.

Laurie E. Osborne says that the animated films that appeared on HBO in the early 1990s "underscore the mechanics of film, particularly as it brings Shakespeare's poetry into illusory motion. In fact, they prepare their audience to understand the plays cinematically rather than theatrically or literally."[7] Osborne deals with the animated Shakespeare films definitively, and I have also looked at them.[8] I will mention *Othello* here, though, since it is likely to be overlooked. The animated *Othello* is inconsistent and at times disjointed but remarkably powerful for cel animation, rarely a medium for tragedy. The pictures themselves are consistently made up of grays, browns, and blacks, with each of those colors or noncolors finding itself in Othello's face, as if his skin pigmentation keeps changing. The idea, of course, is that he is not "constant." His black eyes roll like eight balls against the whites. Desdemona is a pale and diaphanous Ophelia-like creature who tends to float, in contrast to the heavy, earthbound Othello. That vivid colors are *not* employed mutes the "cartoon" feeling of this production, appropriately for this script.

The production opens with the title *Othello* standing against a rolling surf. The surf finally obliterates the letters. A narrator tells us that Othello and Desdemona have been married. The first words from the play are Iago's "I do hate him as I do hell pains." A montage shows Othello arriving by ship to a waiting Desdemona, who covers Othello's eyes with a handkerchief with one major strawberry in its center. This image suggests both her "deception" of Othello and the "happy ending," in which she produces that precise handkerchief on his demand (3.4.52). The two kiss against a background of flames. "You're well tuned now," Iago says. The flames suggest both passion and jealousy—here, Iago's. He will transfer his own "hell pains" to Othello. The lines to the awakened Brabantio about the "old black ram" and "the beast with the two backs" (and later "her body's lust," "With her, on her, what you will," and "whore") are retained, augmenting the case for Iago's sexual jealousy.

Visually, the production is fascinating. Othello's brief rendition of his previous career omits references to slavery, Cannibals, Anthropophagi, and men whose heads do grow beneath their shoulders, but behind his words are Uccello-like images of combat, sieges, and sea battles between giant galleys. This is the "tale" that would win the Duke's daughter. Another brilliant image—used only once—occurs when Othello shouts "Devil!" He looks up at the ceiling of a great cathedral, which cracks into fragments as if from an earthquake or the Crucifixion. Othello's high-arched and seemingly indestructible faith in Desdemona is shattered. Since he is a "man of high estate" in the Aristotelian sense, his own fate is "not a single doom," but reaches out to the architecture of the state itself, insignificant as Cyprus is in the play. The concept is briefly presented, not worked into the fabric of the production's visual and ideational texture. One instant that those who know Shakespeare films will recognize is Othello's undulating swing of his shoulders on "I'll tear her all to pieces," which is borrowed from Olivier's film version. The Iago in this production seems to have been modeled on Frank Finlay's cool and understated smirk of an Iago opposite Olivier. Even more obviously, the death of Desdemona's maid, Barbary, copies the scene in which Jean Simmons cruises down the river in the Olivier *Hamlet*. The links, of course, are her song "Willow" and the "willow" of which Gertrude speaks from which the hapless Ophelia tumbles into the water. Both women sing their requiems before they sink. Here, the Barbary episode arrives through Desdemona's hair, which becomes the willow tree. It is a kind of dream that reinforces Desdemona's dilemma by imaging and presaging the death of the hapless woman who loves a madman. The image of the drowning Barbary also foreshadows Desdemona's "passivity on her deathbed," as Osborne says.⁹ The powerful cross-purposes of the "Cassio ... Handkerchief" exchange between Desdemona and Othello are retained, and they help make her more of a protagonist than mere victim of male machination and misapprehension. At the end, Othello holds his hand in the torch illuminating Desdemona's chamber, quenches it, and reignites it. The image suggests his remarkable power and imperviousness to physical pain, as well as his claim that he has overcome his jealousy and is killing his wife for "the cause" (though that justification is not included here). Dying "upon a kiss," Othello pulls a curtain down. As it floats slowly in space, it captures Desdemona's precious frailty and, of course, the whisper of handkerchief that became such a heavy thing. The final scene combines images of power and vulnerability with enough of Othello's potent double epithets to suggest the linguistic premises of his self-conception, even as he sees himself standing on the far side of tragedy. I wished only for Othello's apostrophe to Desdemona, "when we shall meet at compt ... ." Surely Iago's earlier disquisition on wives, designed to heighten the tension in the time between the arrival of Desdemona on Cyprus and the coming of Othello's ship, could have been sacrificed for the sake of the later moment.

One of the advantages of the editing is that it avoids the issue of Othello's "peaking." On stage, the actor must balance on an uneasy equation between suspicion and certainty for a long time, from the middle of the long third scene of Act 3 to the illusory calm of "It is the cause ..." just before the murder of Desdemona. Not so here, where the rush of torches and the sudden flash of swords along streets breaking loose from martial law are vividly depicted. Any moments of introspection like "Othello's occupation gone" are sacrificed to the frantic pace of this production. The pressure of condensation seldom permits any rhythm other than "fast forward." But the condensation of a script almost as long as *Hamlet* into a powerful 26-minute sequence is itself a remarkable achievement.

These productions will serve as an introduction for younger students to Shakespeare and film and will challenge older students to examine issues like editing for film and interpretation of the script. A lot is lost, of course, but the films are more satisfying than many longer versions.†

One problem with the film *O* (1999, released in 2001) is that it pursues the curve of *Othello* so closely that at moments one is distracted by contemplating the parallels between what is happening on the screen and what happens in the play. A more basic problem is that the world of a prep school cannot approximate the vast dimensions of a Shakespearean tragedy, even a "domestic tragedy" like *Othello*.

The concept—a black ringer brought in to win a basketball championship for Palmetto Prep—breaks down almost immediately. As Glenn Kenny says "Leading a high school basketball team to the division championship is not even vaguely the same thing [as] defending Venice from the Turks."[10] It might help were "O" (Mekhi Phifer) an articulate contrast to his white mates, but he is just as mumbly and prone to the "f" word as universal modifier as his fellow preppies. More plausible is the poisoning of O's spirit by Hugo. Josh Hartnett is convincing for a few moments in the workout room as he says "White girls are snakes, bro." O is young and in an alien world. That "Desi" (Julia Stiles) loves him is wonderful, but that she is white is indisputable. The cynical man of the world, Hugo, knows the "disposition" of white girls. O does not. I think that the film could have built out from there and left its ur-play alone. It might have become very predictable but then so is the film that results from a rigid adherence to the *Othello* praxis. It was shelved after Columbine, of course, but I suspect that as uncomfortable as that parallel made the original distributor, Miramax, what Columbine did was to erase the intended allusion to O. J. Simpson. The young basketball star's name is "Odin James." He is, according to Owen Gleiberman, 'a junior O.J.'"[11] A massacre at a middle-class high school caused the film's release to be delayed. It was meant to capitalize on the murder of a white man and woman by a black man, apparently not as sensitive an issue to bourgeois moviegoers as the Columbine shootings.

Ironically, in at least five instances, Shakespeare's play would have helped the screenplay. Desdemona claims to see "Othello's visage in his mind." She has an intuitive grasp of the soul beneath the skin. Othello, of course, becomes alienated from that selfhood. Does Desi have a similar grasp of O's inner qualities? I think that Stiles could have shown that to us had she been given a chance. A couple of times, late in the film, her glance reveals puzzlement at O's strange behavior. But what is the quality from which he is estranged? As the passive Desi, Stiles, a superb Ophelia in the Almereyda *Hamlet*, is squandered here. She's "not much more than a winsome chickie."[12]

Desi's father, the Dean, objects to her relationship with O. Why? His response demonstrates no racism. Certainly Brabantio is a racist. Is the film trying to be politically correct here and to save its racial explosion for later? Perhaps. The Dean might have said, "You would have had to get her drunk!" to parallel Brabantio's charges about charms and potions. It might have helped had O said, "But you invited me to your house! You told me that you wanted me here at Palmetto Prep! You listened to stories of my background!" One problem, of course, is that O has no story. He is a cliché in the film. Or, if he has a past, he does not talk of it and lacks the verbal skills to utter as much as I write for him above.

The play moves from Venice to Cyprus. The former is "not a grange," as Brabantio says, but the latter is a zone across the waters still trembling with the close brush of the Turk, an island under martial law, a place that Iago can control more easily than he can a Venice in which a Duke and his Senators rule. In the film, although O makes a visit to Desi after hours and although some action at the end occurs along a dark, country road, the script is centered in one place. Its single location gives the film a static quality. Furthermore, the film's "setting is simply incapable of supporting the moral weight of the events that subsequently transpire."[13] And, while Shakespeare's tragedies almost always give us a sense of a specific past that conditions the present—*King Lear* being the exception—there's no past in this film. O comes from somewhere other than Palmetto Prep, just as Othello comes from places other than Venice. We learn something of those places from Othello, but nothing from O. And, of course, the teenage O has really not been anywhere.

Othello makes a god of himself as he lands at Cyprus, and treads the fatal carpet of his own rhetoric. He moves himself out of time. O does not fall from any real heights or from altitudes of self-conception. He just gets jealous. The film's version of Othello is bereft even of the ability to utter the teenage equivalent of "It don't get no better than this!" and thus to elicit a rejoinder from Desi that it will, it will!

Emilia's unmasking of Iago is public. Here, it is merely for O's benefit. It seems to be the Bianca figure who informs on Hugo. Emily, played by Rain Phoenix, offspring or cloudy adumbration, one assumes, of River, gets shot by Hugo. But how Emily makes any sense of the scene on the road where Roger (Elden Hansen) is dead and Mike (Andrew Keegan) is wounded is hard to determine. The ending, so cadenced and modulated in Shakespeare, as Iago sees in the dark and Othello blindly puts out lights, is a muddle here.

For a moment, the film does get close to a 1999 equivalent of the early 17th-century script. The character of Othello is a conscious construction that places a veneer of humility ("my most approv'd good masters") over a core of confident self-worth ("My parts, my title, and my perfect soul"). O in the film exists at a much earlier stage of language acquisition, but the contrast between façade and inner certainty is conveyed effectively as O says to Desi, in effect, "I can call myself 'nigger' because I am one. You cannot call me 'nigger' because you are white." This assertion of superiority lashes back at O when Hugo tells him that Desi and Mike "call you 'nigger.'" O's central premise about himself is shaken, and thus doubts about Desi are easy for Hugo to encourage. This moment between O and Hugo is perhaps the film's best because it derives from the prior communication between O and Desi and because it depends on race, as opposed to the "envy" that director Tim Blake Nelson says "drives the plot."[14] O's jealousy is further encouraged by Hugo's putting words into Michael's mouth: "He says that sometimes he just likes to lie with her without any clothes on." The line picks up Iago's maddening "Or to be naked with her friend in bed / An hour or more, not meaning any harm." At this moment the film touches the play's power because it allows us to experience the suggestion's invasion of O's consciousness and its pervasion of his being.

It may be that the imposition of envy upon the film script disturbs its sporadic focus on race. An African American community does exist near Palmetto Prep. O elicits drugs from it. But why does he suddenly need drugs? Are drugs an obligatory part of a black man's experience in 1999 as being "sold to slavery" is of Othello's? None of the tension that can exist between black students in a white school and the community around the school is developed here (as it is in Stiles's 2000 film, *Save the Last Dance*). Elvis Mitchell suggests that the film might have explored Isaiah Thomas's complaint that in 1988 "that black players were still thought of as instinctive while white players like Larry Bird were considered smart."[15] This film's camera is far too blatant to suggest the distinction, and its young basketball player far too oblivious to permit him to grasp it. Were he to do so, he would not be an easy prey for Hugo's insinuation of jealousy into his psyche. Something is to be said for Mitchell's suggestion, however, since O, as point guard, *would* be the smartest player on the floor. The film makes nothing of that and I suspect that the film's creators are innocent of competitive team sports.

The question of race emerges when O shatters a backboard and then, significantly, holds onto the ball and defies the white crowd. It is a conversion to savagery which, A. C. Bradley notwithstanding, also occurs within Othello. The emphasis would have been stronger had it been a *white* ballboy that O pushes away. The film borrows from Oliver Parker's version vividly when O, making love to Desi, suddenly sees the white Mike in the mirror doing the same thing. O begins to make hate, and Desi cries "Stop!" O does not. Desi complains to Emily, who primly responds "You said, 'Stop!'" One must ask, however, at what point invited sexuality becomes transgression? Depending on when the command is uttered, some things about "Stop!" may be hard to understand. This moment and its repetition in Desi's report places the racial–sexual nexus of *Othello* in a potentially powerful context that the film does not explore.

I felt that Hugo too easily goes too far. He does have motive. Hugo's father calls O a "son," and O calls Mike up to share the MVP trophy with him when Hugo is sure he is the co-MVP. But these reasons tend to undercut the radical evil he foments. I did not sense in Hugo "the motive-hunting of motiveless malignity." His motives are clear and therefore the issue of human iniquity that the play raises is not raised here, except as a kind of puzzle. Is this or that enough to cause him to do what he does? We are given at least two explanations to latch onto, although, as Mitchell says, "It is never clear if he was unjustly ignored or if he is deluded about his place on the team."[16] Perhaps that confusion is the film's effort at motivelessness but it seems more likely that the sources of envy have somehow been delineated, put on a level that the perceived teen audience will understand. According to Peter Rainer the "checklist" of motives includes "homoerotic attachment, drug-induced paranoia, racism, and just plain depravity."[17] This "audience," says Owen Gleiberman, "thinks *King Lear* is the name of Puffy Combs' jet."[18] Even this audience, though, is denied an experience of the power of evil by having evil explained to it, and by being given more than one explanation.

The film indulges in a lot of irrelevant symbolism about hawks and pigeons, suggesting the power of teenage aspiration, what director Nelson calls "the envy of adolescence, which combines the acute and unwieldy passion of childhood with the sinister ability to act that comes with adulthood."[19] But, since this is Hugo's fantasy and since Iago never wishes to be a hawk, the parallel just gets in the way here. Furthermore, Shakespeare does not place Iago between adolescence and adulthood. He is frightening at least partly because he *is* so mature in so many ways. One does sense in the film the eerie link with Columbine as Hugo lays out his plan to O. I could hear Hugo thinking

"Good wombs have borne bad sons." I suspect that director and writer are innocent of the kind of rough locker-room kidding around in which teenage athletes indulge. Hugo's "Man, that dude is hung!" would have suggested the sexual–racial nexus that boils under the Shakespeare script. It would have objectified envy.

Gleiberman complains that "unlike Othello, [O] withdraws, in his very vengeance, from the audience, and the movie, for all its feeling, recedes from tragedy."[17] That is true. The strangling of Desi occurs almost wordlessly and very quickly. We cannot be sure that she is dead until an ambulance attendant pulls the sheet over her head on the way out, an allusion to Desdemona's seemingly postmortem utterances. An inarticulate O, however, could hardly have been expected to simulate Othello's stream-of-consciousness meditations about lights, roses, and whiteness, although he might have thought, "Her skin is so f...ing white!" The conventions of this film, however, limit insight to what we see as opposed to what O says.

Does the film reward knowledge of *Othello*? Only at moments. At other times, it punishes those who know the play by reminding them of it, just as the film's own narrative begins to take hold. Will the film encourage students to read *Othello*? If they do, Iago is likely to confuse them. What's his motive? Othello's magnificent language may also be baffling. In the play, Othello is not merely jealous. He also talks too much, making of himself the center of his exotic narratives. That central trait in the film is found only in O's discussion of the "N" word with Desi. It may be, however, that students encountering Othello's language for the first time will find it as deeply compelling as I did on first reading Othello's final speech in 1949.

At the end of the film, the ambulances and news vans from Channel 2 imitate the ending of Luhrmann's *Romeo + Juliet* and remind us that *O* is seeking the same audience. Luhrmann powerfully captures the uncontrolled adolescent pace of the script. Fortunately, the action imitated needs little language to articulate it. Luhrmann's teenagers are totally lost when they try to speak the verse. One can argue that *Romeo and Juliet* demonstrates Romeo's growth from the artificial Petrarchan conventions to the mature voice he demonstrates as he gazes on the still-living Juliet in the tomb. *Othello*, however, makes language far more central to its tragic hero. Without the words and the magnificent arc of their overreaching, no tragedy exists. Without the contrast in linguistic techniques between Othello and Iago, our *understanding* of the tragedy is undercut. In *O*, the film achieves power when it touches the racial undercurrents of the script and of our own cultural moment. As I have argued elsewhere, our own national history and our own great African American literature make *Othello*, for us, inevitably a play about race.

The film is disturbing because it provides inevitability without any dignity. O's incoherent final speech does not touch on who he was, who he had been. How could it? He has been a tiny prep school basketball player, an Archibald or Bogues, among boys of average height. The camera shots—low angle or from above—disguise a diminutive star who, we are told, has attracted the interest of college scouts. Othello's language no doubt "builds him up," but his emphasized reputation has an emphatic past to build upon. At the end, Shakespeare's Othello proves he is who he said he was by executing an enemy of the state who happens to be himself. The film is disturbing as the news is, seldom as a work of art can be.

The PBS *Othello* (2002) is a "yarn" (as the publicity has it) about an ambitious subcommissioner of Scotland Yard (Christopher Eccleston) who elicits a racist remark from his boss, thus getting his superior canned, only to find a black subordinate (Eamonn Walker) jumping into the vacancy because London is seething with racial tension. Jago, then, must get rid of John Othello. In the script, of course, it is Othello who makes the choice of Cassio over Iago, and we should not underestimate the sting of merit spurned or the depth of Iago's grievance. In the PBS version, Dessie (Keeley Hawes), harassed by skinheads because she is married to a black man, is protected by Michael Cass (Richard Coyle), whom Jago has recommended for the job. That posting is improbable, but it makes things easy for Jago. Michael cooperates by making a pass at Dessie— gracefully put by—then by spilling wine on his shirt. As Dessie puts the shirt in the sink to soak, Michael dons the golden robe Dessie had given Othello. It had been her "first gift," of course, and has gathered talismanic value unto itself. Othello enters at this moment of apparent postcoital relaxation. Jago suggests that the robe be tested for the fluids of "A, B, and C" and reports positive results to Othello. When it is too late, Jago says that the lab got the results wrong. Lulu, played splendidly by Rachel Stirling, has little to do here other than to keep telling Jago that she knows nothing bad about her pal, Dessie. Lulu intuits Jago's responsibility for the tragic loading of the bed, but she says nothing. Jago, who greeted us at the outset by telling us that the story was about "love," tells us the same thing at the end. Now, however, he is the bemedaled Commissioner of Police. Did he not understand the events he just orchestrated, or is he talking about his own murderous narcissism? We are left to assume that "love" is the lie he is retailing within his world. But, since he addresses us directly on occasion, his stance of "unreliable narrator" at beginning and end is inconsistent and confusing. Cass disappears after a fistfight in a parking garage with Othello, once Cass has claimed that he did not recognize his assailant. The murder–suicide is ascribed by the male authorities to Dessie, who "was apparently quite a handful."

The production makes some effort to suggest the original. John Othello comes to Dessie after quelling a riot, a parallel to Othello's emergence on Cyprus after the storm to the vision of Desdemona standing there before him. In that Othello is leaving dangerous streets, Director Saxe also suggests the martial law that Othello abandons for his wedding night. John Othello talks about his past, but it is a past of slavery in tropical cane fields, hardly the fabulous adventures among alien plumage and monsters that Othello describes to the fascinated Venetian Senate, though Shakespeare's Othello does include slavery as a segment of his background. The production suggests Venice by putting Othello and Dessie's trendy flat on a canal off the Thames, in what had been the dockyard past which Conrad's "Narcissis" chugged over a hundred years ago.

According to Daniel Rosenthal, the production's subplot "substitutes for the war between Venice and Turkey."[20] Alan Roderick (Del Synott), the Roderigo figure, is supposed to testify against three fellow officers who murdered a black man (the episode is modeled on the Steven Lawrence murder in London in 1993). Jago bumps Roderick off, making it look like suicide, thereby fulfilling Jago's promise to look after the racist cops, and creating a humiliating moment for John Othello at the Old Bailey. He waits for the indictment to come down, but, of course, the witness does not show up. The three cops smile down at him. This subplot provides racist context, but it has little to do with Dessie, and certainly nothing to do with Venice and the Ottomites. In the script, it is Roderigo, of all people, who glimpses what Iago is up to. While Alan Roderick is a dupe more easily played upon, he refuses to merge with the violent and brutal culture of his fellow constables. This substitution obviously does not find any analogy in *Othello*.

The parallel is that Jago "socializes" John Othello into the lascivious culture of all women. Men may see them as "secret gardens," Jago says, but they view themselves as "envelopes" to be opened and resealed. "She slept around?" John asks. "No more than anyone else. Probably." Jago here resembles the Iago of the play, who makes Desdemona the stereotypic Venetian woman. Othello's descent into jealousy is effectively charted in a series of dissolves that suggests a passage of time that can be difficult on stage as the long third scene of Act three grinds remorselessly on. Cass "is enjoying his work just a little too much," Jago suggests. Jago convinces Othello of Dessie's wild past. She refuses to defend who she was before she met Othello. Her line, "I was like a blank sheet waiting for you to write your name on me" sounds, however, as if she's been rehearsing what she will say if asked what she was doing before he showed up. The stages of his obsession and her inevitably futile defense against it are compellingly delineated. These are the domestic misunderstandings to which soap operas with their predictable camera angles—close-up, two-shot, and reaction-shot—and perhaps our own lives have conditioned us. The sequence is well acted by Walker and Hawes, and neatly scaled to the medium of television.

Director Geoff Saxe borrows from Oliver Parker's version by permitting Jago to address us directly, as Kenneth Branagh's Iago does in the film. I am convinced that the mixed soliloquy convention is in the script. Iago searches our faces for the "he ... that says I play the villain," while Othello intones homilies to his "soul" or to the "chaste stars." In the Parker film, Kenneth Branagh is ingratiating and amusing, proving to us how plausible he is to those inside the frame. Christopher Eccleston is intrusive, his hawk nose, scowl, and pale blue eyes invading our space. Jago also gets some internal monologues that refute or perhaps reinforce his sneer of a smile. Steven Oxman puts it mildly when he accuses Eccleston of "a touch too much smarminess."[21] The problem with Jago may rest neither with his clearly articulated motive nor with Eccleston's acting, but with the medium. What can resonate as evil on stage, when we are inhabiting the same space as Iago, can arrive as mere nastiness within TV's inevitable diminution. Ian McKellen had Shakespeare's script available as a basis for a thoughtful TV Iago for Trevor Nunn. Film can be an ideal space for Iago, as Branagh shows, and as Frank Finlay demonstrated, opposite the bravura performance that Olivier imported to film from his Old Vic stage production. Film, we recall, was a powerful medium for Hitler. Could he have become a world-threatening figure via television? Or would television, that remarkably superficial medium, have (ironically) exposed him, as it tended to expose Richard Nixon?

Eccleston's Jago encourages Cass, Dessie's constant companion, by saying that "it's just a show marriage. He'd like to, but he can't. Treat that as background." This is one of the few places where the production hints at the artificial quality of the culture that permits Iago / Jago to function so effortlessly (as brilliantly analyzed by Michael Long). Less convincing is Dessie's role as postmodernist woman. She has nothing to do but jog? Joss Ackland as Brabant, Dessie's father, is tame compared to the furious Brabantio: "I'll be honest with you. I am not happy about this." In civilized present-day London, overt racism inhabits only the hoodlum cops. Also unconvincing is Jago's "I'm almost sorry I started this. It is out of my control." But it is not! Jago has yet to confirm that Cass's secretions have somehow adhered to the fibers of the golden robe. At one weird moment, Jago embraces one of the racist cops he has been interrogating. A white halo surrounds them as the camera cuts to a shot from the bottom of a pool with Othello swimming. The sequence transmits a strange mixed message about purification and pollution and signals incoherence at the heart of the production.

Saxe also borrows from Parker in having Othello hallucinate the mutual nakedness of Cass and Dessie, and from the Scottish play. Cass makes an unscheduled appearance at an intimate dinner party—a physical manifestation of the fear that is haunting Othello—and shatters the occasion's fragile tranquility.

Will this production send students back to the text? I doubt it. I don't believe that the modern media encourage reading. How can they, when they do most of the imagining for us? Assuming students do return to the text, they are likely to believe that they already know Iago's motivation, a belief that will be almost immediately confirmed by Iago's conversation with Roderigo. As Ed Siegel says in his review, however, Shakespeare "is *not* specific about motivation."[22] What is likely to happen, then, is that TV will impose its invariably simplistic meanings on the inherited script. First times have nothing with which to compare themselves, and primacy theory suggests that the first experience is normative. Here, the mystery of human iniquity is answered by the current formulae of ambition and police brutality. Ambition is *not* a "virtue" in the world of Shakespeare's *Othello*, except, as Othello tells us, in the instance of "big wars." The thematics of racism, if developed in this production, might have provided some glimpse of the unquenchable fires burning within Jago. The story is not about love, though perhaps the world within the frame believes that. Jago should, then, be shown talking about it to the Prime Minister, as opposed to confiding in us. If students do visit the text, they are likely to conclude, as I have done, that the current effort would have benefited had it been called anything but *Othello*. A new title, though, does not necessarily enhance a derivative work, as demonstrated by Jane Smiley's dreary *A Thousand Acres*.

A return to the text will show a student that the world of the play learns that the murder occurs in the "close-shut, murderous room," not because Othello's cannot "handle" Desdemona, but because Iago has encouraged Othello's self-estrangement. Within the narcissistic syndrome, his own perfection depends upon Desdemona's. By not opening that room to public view, this production robs Othello of the final moment that validates what he has said about himself. At the end of the play, he assumes command one last time and executes an enemy of the state who happens to be himself. John Othello might also have been that fell sergeant. Instead, Jago rides in his limo to his investiture as commissioner. As at the end of the Polanski *Macbeth*, where Donalbain approaches the Weird Sorority in the service of his own ambition, evil is a recyclable commodity that serves only the powerful. At the end of Shakespeare's *Othello*, Iago promises silence. The meanings within that silence have resonated for almost 400 years and continue to, regardless of how productions fill in that terrifying blank. *Othello* does not fit cozily into our own *episteme*, for all of our depravity. Contemporary adaptations seem incapable of bringing forward a character emerging from a fabulous and exotic background, a woman at once as courageous and as virtuous as Desdemona, or a character as deeply evil as Iago. We can find modern analogues, perhaps, in Mohammed Ali or in modern pathology, but our analogies are shallow and merely contemporary. The play drives us into zones that are deeper and more mysterious than the "explanations" we try to provide for them.

To find modern analogues for the play, its characters, and its action, is to diminish the still-available potency of our confrontation with the original script, which can resemble the experience depicted in the play, as Venetian society encounters this extravagant stranger from places that have never been mapped, and as we meet Iago, a character from an even more frightening zone.‡

Notes

* Robert F. Willson, Jr. points out that one effort to trap Anthony John resembles "a *Hamlet*-like 'mousetrap' to catch the conscience of the killer" (91). An actress is made up to resemble Pat Kroll, the woman John has murdered. The actress even wears the earrings that Kroll had been wearing on the night that John did her in. As the actress comes to take his order in a bistro, John is startled and leaves abruptly, thus convincing the observers who have planned the trap of his guilt. The moment also resembles the Banquet Scene in *Macbeth*, as Banquo's dead body materializes in some state this side of ghosthood. Whether Claudius reveals his guilt is a matter of performance. Macbeth, when confronted with a murder about which only he of those present can know, certainly exhibits questionable behavior: "Thou canst not say I did it."

† On these animations, see also Thomas A. Pendleton, "Animated Shakespeare on HBO." *The Shakespeare Newsletter* XLII: 3/214 (Fall, 1992): 38, 40.

‡ For a discussion of *Othello* on film and TV as a resource for teaching, from which this chapter is excerpted, see my "Teaching *Othello* on Cassette," *Shakespeare and the Classroom* 11/2 (Fall 2003): 26–38.

Chapter 4
King Lear

King Lear is not a play for all seasons. For about 150 years—from the late 17th to the early 19th centuries—Shakespeare's play was not performed. A version written by Nahum Tate held the stage. Tate permits Cordelia to survive and marry Edgar—France having been conveniently eliminated—while Lear and Gloucester also survive into contented old age. Although Shakespeare's play was gradually restored to the performance canon, it was considered "too large for the stage" during most of the 19th century and for the first half of the 20th century. After World War II, however, the play began to be performed regularly. The stage of history had finally shown events huge enough to permit the world to accept the "image of that horror" that Shakespeare creates in *King Lear*.

The world of the play is "syncretic"; that is, a mixture of pagan usage and Christian insight. It can be said that the world of *King Lear* struggles toward the best of Christian meanings, mercy and forgiveness (as opposed to the strident hypocrisy that passes for "Christianity" on television and in politics these days). The death of Cordelia cancels the positive movement of the play. Lear's awakening represents a kind of resurrection. "You do me wrong to take me out of the grave," he says. The hanging of Cordelia, however, is a version of crucifixion, so that Shakespeare has taken the great archetypes of Christian mythology and *reversed* them. No wonder Tate wanted a happy ending! No wonder the 18th century preferred that happy ending! The play, though, does not incorporate the specifics of Christian usage that is, a sense of a single God or a knowledge of Christ and the Apostles. Instead, the pagan gods—Apollo and Jupiter—are on the tongues of the characters, and the gods are plural: "thou swear'st thy gods in vain"; "the clearest gods"; and "The gods themselves throw incense." Edmund can sneer at astrology—"Fut, I should have been that I am, had the maidenliest star in the firmament twinkled on my bastardizing"—but he makes "nature" his "goddess" and asks that the "gods ... stand up for bastards." Kent, meanwhile, says that it is "the stars ... that govern our conditions." Opposing this pagan structure, where an Epicurean like Edmund can sneer at prophecy and a Stoic like Kent can believe in a determinism riding the wheel of the Zodiac, is the "Cordelia ethic." It represents a lack of calculation, a lack of material desires, and a love that is not premised on the mere advantages that accrue to professions of love. If it is permitted to survive, the world swings into a new value system in which, as she says, "kind gods ... Cure." Apollo is not just a curse word in Lear's mouth. He is the god of medicine and of light. Nature, for Cordelia, is not a power whereby bastards may ascend the wheel of fortune, but of "blest secrets [and] unpublish'd virtues of the earth," energies that are "aidant and remediate," forces of "restoration" that "repair." Her nature—both her human nature and the nature in which she believes, which is a potentially benevolent *super*nature—opposes the *un*natural in this world, those who vie for political, material, and sexual advantage. The latter die, of course, victims of what Albany calls "This judgement of the heavens." At the end, Cordelia also lies "dead as earth." The earth that she hoped would spring with healing herbs lies dead with her.

While we can understand why a previous age would prefer a different ending, what we must do is to pursue the remorseless logic of Shakespeare's version of events. I suggest that Lear makes one huge error at the outset, survives that error to achieve a "comic" ending, but makes a further error deep in the play that dooms his daughter, and the vision she manifests. The play dramatizes the movement toward the terrible still-birth with which it ends.

Lear's division of the kingdom at the outset is obviously an error in judgment. To prevent "future strife" by dividing a polity is, as our history tells us, only a way to war, as Korea, Northern Ireland, Vietnam, and Yugoslavia suggest. Furthermore, Lear empowers the acquisitive and calculating element in his kingdom, particularly Goneril and Cornwall. It may go unnoticed, but the opening upheaval permits Edmund to hang around and work his mischief. The thesis he attributes to his legitimate brother, Edgar, is the same one that Lear has enunciated at the outset "sons at perfect age, and fathers declining, the father should be as a ward to the son, and the son to manage his revenue." Lear wants to be cared for, but he also wants the good things that go with kingship. This is not a renunciation of the world for the sake of achieving one's soul. It is as if

Richard Nixon had said, "I am willing to resign, but Pat and I have grown fond of the White House and Air Force One, so, I'll surrender the office of president if you let me keep the perks." Lear says, "while we unburdened crawl toward death." He should say "I," since it is the physical man who dies, not "kingship" as principle. He has been king for so long, however, that he fails to make the distinction between the person ("I") and the office ("We"). A large part of the play is taken up with his learning the difference the hard way: "The art of our necessities is strange, / That can make vile things precious"; "They told me I was everything; 'tis a lie, I am not ague-proof." Edmund may worship his mother—"nature"—and he may, for the moment, want the unsanctified "sport" of his "making" to become a law of the land that gives him a wide-ranging space in which to exercise his skills, but he wants the most conventional of rewards: to be Earl of Gloucester. He gets there, unofficially, but the chaos that Lear has unleashed and that Edmund represents does not yield tamely once certain people have attained their wishes. As Claudius and Macbeth discover that, having killed their former kings and become kings themselves, the world does not "return to normalcy," so Edmund finds that, having clambered aboard fortune's wheel, "The wheel is come full circle."

Lear's initial decision draws Cordelia's refusal to go along with his auction sale. She is banished. Kent is banished. Lear, however, has not killed Kent's or Cordelia's love for him. In disguise, Kent offers his service to Lear. Then Cordelia returns, but to a divided Britain. While she upholds her father's right, she represents an invader at the head of a foreign army. It is not "good vs. good," or "good vs. evil," but, as A. C. Bradley says of *Richard II*, "an inextricable tangle of right and unright."[1] Lear's initial division of Britain has badly confused the political and moral situation. Albany and Edmund find themselves in the same army, with Edmund assuming more command than Albany is willing to grant. At the outset, however, Lear had given the land to his daughters and the emblem of power (the coronet) to the sons-in-law. Who is in charge here?

The reconciliation of Lear and Cordelia, then, is not the final act of a "romance," in which long-separated parents and children are restored to each other amid the wash of happy tears. Lear and Cordelia come together again amid the sway of armies vying for whatever dubious prize they think they are fighting for. It is, however, a beautiful moment—almost wordless, virtually "out of time." Lear believes he has been taken "out of the grave." He thinks Cordelia is a "soul in bliss," someone viewed from across the gulf of eternity in a brilliant instant borrowed from the Dives-Lazarus story in Luke (16: 19–26). She reiterates her love. When Lear says that she has "some cause" to hate him, she murmurs, "No cause, no cause." This is the end of a comedy, wherein the foolish character has learned his lesson and been rewarded with a reentrance to a society that contains new insights and the ones he loves. But his scene is not the end of the play.

So delighted is Lear to be reunited with his "child, Cordelia" that he neglects to recognize the position they are in. They are prisoners—political prisoners (an ex-king and a foreign queen)—going off to the dungeons of the enemy. Cordelia wants confrontation—to "see these daughters and these sisters"—but Lear talks of "blessing" and "forgiveness," of singing "like birds in the cage." "Have I caught thee?" he asks. We recall that he had hoped "to set [his] rest on [Cordelia's] kind nursery," and now his goal has been achieved. He commits a "hubris of consciousness" by overstating the moment and finding in it more than it can contain within the process of time. What he does is similar to what Othello does on landing on the shores of Cyprus. To grasp the "mystery of things" is not to have achieved stasis in human life, or any arrival at perfection. Life is a process of individuation, not completion. And so the Lear who "might have sav'd" Cordelia, as he says, stares at her, knowing "she'll come no more." His final words—"Look there! Look there!"—were once taken as proof of "an unbearable paroxysm of joy," as A. C. Bradley says, as proof that Cordelia is alive.[2] He dies happy, then. Modern King Lears, like Morris Carnovsky at Stratford, Connecticut in 1964, do not reflect that delusion. Their "Look there! Look there!" is a final, unblinking look at death. For that death, Lear is responsible, in what is the "second tragedy" of the play, his failure to recognize the danger that Cordelia is in as they go off to Edmund's prison.

Dr. Samuel Johnson, the greatest literary critic of the 18th century, admits that he could not bear to read the final scene of *King Lear* until he came to edit the play.[3] He does not condemn the play for not conforming with a "virtue rewarded" ending. Instead, he says, "A play in which the wicked prosper and the virtuous miscarry may doubtless be good, because it is a just representation of the common events of human life." Our own times—via the bomb and the Holocaust, both sudden revelations that struck the world in 1945—have demonstrated to us that the play is a "just representation." It helps us understand our own moment in history. In Shakespearean tragedy, we notice, the terrible events are not accidental but are motivated, a chain of events linked to human decision. In *King Lear,* that motivation comes from the title character, who must at last look down at his dead daughter, whom he might have saved.

Two other questions remain. What is the Fool's function? What is the subplot doing in the play? The Fool is a truthsayer. He keeps pointing with songs and jests at Lear's folly. His role is to puncture the pretensions of power. Notice that he is silent in the opening scene. Regan's cruel line "What need one?" can be directed at the Fool. Lear learns the Fool's lesson, of course, and ultimately descends to madness—a variation on the epic journey to the underworld. No compensatory voice can reach Lear then, and so the Fool disappears. The subplot—the story of the loyalty and disloyalty of Gloucester's sons—obviously reinforces the narrative of Lear and his daughters. I would suggest that it is more of a contrast than a comparison. It seems almost as if the rigorous allegory through which Edgar forces Gloucester is a revenge for Gloucester's having cast Edgar off so readily early in the play. Through Edmund, the subplot explores evil, but it does not come close to transmitting a sense of what Cordelia represents in the main plot.

Several good productions of the play are available on cassette. A silent Italian film of 1910 features the beautiful Francesca Bertini as Cordelia, superbly tinted shots, and some splendid location scenes. Two films made simultaneously in the early 1970s—the Peter Brook and the Grigori Kozintsev—provide a different take on the script. Brook's film, featuring Paul Scofield as Lear and Irene Worth as Goneril, is shot in black and white, like a documentary, and provides the bleakest vision possible of the inherited play, cutting all positive elements. The film was conditioned by Brook's despair over the inexcusable United States war in Vietnam. Kozintsev's is a wide-screen epic in 70 mm Sovscope which also has a documentary quality, at times resembling the Nazi films of the invasion of Poland in 1939 and of the Soviet Union in 1941. It is set in a Christian world, and full of brilliant insights. Edmund, for example, cannot understand the happiness of Lear and Cordelia going off to prison. Don't they know they've lost? He goes into his combat with Edgar still puzzled and thus gets nailed. Three worthwhile television productions exist. The BBC production of 1982, with Michael Hordern, has an excellent Edmund in Michael Kitchen, who plays the role as a calm, ironic outsider, an observer of events he only partly motivates. The Michael Elliot production of 1983 features a frail Lawrence Olivier in a production that is largely homage to the great actor. The Richard Eyre version of 1999 is a translation from a stage production, with Ian Holm as a superb King Lear. Of the television productions, I find it easily the best, though it does suffer from a televisual scale too limited to capture the larger dimensions of its play. One of Eyre's brilliant touches was to have Lear wear the Fool's cap after the Fool had physically disappeared.

Since *King Lear* does not announce its worldview, productions can create zones of good and zones of evil within whatever overriding concept of production prevails. That means that placing the *praxis* in a criminal or a Wild West context can work effectively, as opposed to a profoundly Christian play like *Macbeth*. *King Lear* will forever remain open to a range of interpretations denied to *Macbeth*.

Recontextualizations include *Harry and Tonto* (1974), in which Harry (Art Carney in a role turned down by the retired James Cagney) has Lear-like experiences in a cross-country journey. That includes his identification of the body of an old friend at the morgue (an analogue to "I know you well enough. Your name's Gloucester.").

Most reworkings place the Lear *praxis* either in a criminal setting or in a Western film. The former permits the dividing of an opulent kingdom and the release of murderous competition already more than latent. The latter allows the divvying up of vast pieces of land, though the impulse toward greater acquisition is more typical of the 19th century West. Division, however, encourages deadly rivalries. Each context can work, as one example from each category proves. Since the script is imprecise as to when events occur, and since it does not incorporate a medieval worldview, it is flexible. *King Lear* challenges all received assumptions, except that the weather is bound to get worse.

House of Strangers (1949), the film of which *Broken Lance* (1954) is a remake, is a *King Lear* derivative. Yet it has received scant attention. Its basic "*Lear* moment" occurs when Gino Monetti (Edward G. Robinson), having been indicted for bank fraud asks his four sons, "How much you want to be my son?" Max (John Conti), a lawyer, has suggested that they split the responsibility for the fraud four ways and thus make the charges impossible to prove. No one will know who did what, he argues. Joe (Luther Adler) claims that he "never had enough responsibility to divide." Joe has complained previously about his salary of $65 a week and has been told "Go back to your cage." "For a few more dollars a week I coulda had a good son," Gino grouses, reconfiguring the love-for-material-reward thesis of Lear. Tony (Efrem Zimbalist, Jr.) doesn't "want to stick [his] neck out." Pietro (Paul Valentine), a six-round preliminary pug with a glass jaw, clearly cannot take the fall for a sophisticated swindle. "You have brought up a house of strangers," Max tells Gino.

Max attempts to bribe a juror, but Joe sets him up. Max is arrested and goes to jail. Gino is shut out of the new bank that develops. He complains to Max that the other brothers have told him to sit on a bench in the park and feed the pigeons. "You gotta make them pay," Gino tells Max.

That narrative occurs in a long flashback. The film begins with Max's return from jail after seven years. It is now 1939. Gino has died. A bust of Mussolini adorns the sleek offices of the bank. The brothers offer Max $1,000 to get lost—a sum that seems tiny. Even in 1939 that would not have bought a new LaSalle. Joe recognizes that "a man who turns away money is a big worry, a big problem."

Max heads off to Park Avenue where Irene (Susan Hayward) has been waiting for him for all these years. She has asked, "Do you think women live in vacuum-sealed containers, like tennis balls?" She has tried to rid herself of Max, but it hasn't worked. Now, she recognizes that for Max revenge is "like a rare wine, a joy divine." She tells him that his father still controls him. Gino, she says, is "a dead man, an evil man." Max "is filled with his poison. It breathes in" him.

Max returns to Gino's mansion. Irene has convinced him. He says to Gino's eerily alive portrait above the fireplace, "Rest easy. You are dead. You've had all you are going to get." The brothers trap him, however, and are about to throw him from an upper window, when Joe calls Pietro "Dumbhead"—his father's consistent epithet. Tony recognizes that "if you kill him, Joe, you'll kill him for Pa." They have all been controlled by the dead man. Max and Irene ride westward toward San Francisco in her '39 Buick convertible.

This is an excellent *noir*. The bust of Mussolini echoes the "foreign authority" the father exercises, even in death, over all the brothers. The inevitable tavern scene is highlighted by Dolores Parker, who had sung with Ellington, singing "Can't We Talk It Over." The song becomes the film's theme, or at least, Max's theme. Gino's had been the tenor solo, *Ach so fromm*, from Flotow's *Martha*, a somewhat esoteric choice for an Italian immigrant.

In discussing the western, André Bazin tends to conflate tragedy and epic.[4] I would suggest, however, that the nature of "heroism" in each genre is remarkably different and that the tragic hero does not fit in with the *praxis* of the western, which almost invariably finds virtue rewarded and evil punished. The western tends to be a Manichean universe where "outlaws" or "Injuns" threaten the establishment of "civilization" in desert places. Its world is reduced to simplistic notions like "You're either with us or against us." The tragic hero tends to become more human as a result of his experience. He or she tends to move from "Alone I did it! Boy!" to "Holds her by the hand, silent." Euripides's Medea is an exception as she rides off in a dragon-drawn chariot at the end, casting off humanity and becoming a demon-goddess. Shakespeare's Cleopatra combines the elements of the human and the divine as she feels "a lover's pinch" and creates a romantic poem in which she returns to Cydnus and begins again with Antony, free of the inhibiting power of Caesar. The norm for tragedy, though, is Oedipus's acknowledgment of Apollo. His defiance of the god and his insistence on his human will have empowered Apollo. The epic hero tends to be superhuman and stands for what is great about his country or race—as opposed to what is great about human beings—like Macbeth in the bleeding captain's description at the outset. Macbeth descends from "Bellona's bridegroom" to a claim of human numbness, in a world where the order of sparrows and eagles, hares and lions is turned upside down, so that mousing owls are superior to falcons. Yet Macbeth will still claim his "better part of man" when he confronts Macduff. Lady Macbeth descends from a superhuman hubris to the depths of human madness and a perception of her own damnation. But in "hell" she is most human.

Bazin points out that the western coincides with the invention of film. Indeed the first narrative film is "The Great Train Robbery," which was filmed in the wilds of New Jersey but "occurs" out west.

"The western was born of an encounter between a mythology and a means of expression."[5] The western, Bazin says, is "faithful... to history"[6] and represents an "epiclike idealization based on comparatively recent history."[7] As with the knight of the Grail Legend, the hero must "pass through a series of fabulous trials" until he can save "his elected bride."[8] The western particularizes "an already specific dramatic plot, the great epic Manicheism that sets the forces of evil over against the knights of the true cause."[9] "The Indian, who lived in this world, was incapable of imposing on it man's order. He mastered it only by identifying himself with its pagan savagery. The white Christian ... is truly the conqueror of a new world."[10] Although Bazin does not adduce *Birth of a Nation*, his formula defines Griffith's exploitation of this mythology. The film anticipates a hundred more, in which the United States Cavalry (not the Ku Klux Klan) rides, in a sequence of crosscuts, to the rescue of the wagon train surrounded by a whoop of hostile Indians.

Bazin is right to find "at the source of the western the ethics of the epic and even of tragedy."[11]

Matt Devereaux's conflict in *Broken Lance* (1954) is between his pride in accomplishment in domesticating a hostile environment and the competing commercial interests and their paid-for legality that arrive after the world is tamed. In other words, it is a conflict between individuality and legality. Devereaux's *hubris* lies in his insisting on the former as a valid manifestation of a previous generation in defiance of the latter—the inevitable process that comes with the railroad and "civilization," as depicted in Stephen Crane's story *The Bride Comes to Yellow Sky*. "The epic and tragic hero is a universal character," says Bazin. "The migration to the west is our Odyssey."[12] I would suggest, though, that epic (Odysseus) and tragic (Achilles) are not the same, or, that they do not manifest their epic and tragic characteristics at the same time. Devereaux (Spencer Tracy), for example, moves from epic to tragic hero. Matt's past is epic. He has conquered the wilderness. His triumph, however, results in the tragedy of a man with virtues that are at once "old-fashioned," in that he refuses to compromise with "progress" (he will not open an office in town) and "modern," in that he is tolerant of other races and of those less fortunate than himself. The climax comes when he defies the court system that has replaced his less formal, less complicated version of justice.

Robert F. Willson, Jr., suggests that the film "subsumes in its main action characters and themes from both plots of *King Lear*."[13] Devereaux would banish two of his sons for cattle rustling were it not for the intercession of his youngest son, Joe (Robert Wagner). It is Devereaux's lawyer (Carl Benton Reid) who suggests that Matt divide his vast holdings to avoid legal problems. The elements of hubris, banishment, and division of the kingdom are strongly present. The story of Joe and Barbara (Jean Peters), however, is a version of *Romeo and Juliet*, in that her father, the Governor (E. G. Marshall), objects to their relationship. It is the "modern" *Romeo and Juliet:* he is half-Indian and she an eastern-educated lady. The relationship reflects Director Edward Dmytryk's social agenda, as do so many 20th century reconfigurations of *Romeo and Juliet*. That is, the impulse of an egalitarian worldview to produce harmony from ethnic and social diversity.

The film's flashback technique insists that we concentrate on time and on the changes that time has brought to what had been until very recently a wilderness. The flashback allows the tragic to be folded into the epic. It is something like the *King Lear* design, where the comedy—the reconciliation of Lear and Cordelia—is surrounded by the tragedy—Lear's initial errors in judgment and their ramifications. As in *House of Strangers* (also written by Philip Yordan), a brother goes to prison for his father (Joe Devereaux serves only three years), returns to find his father dead and to his brothers' attempt to buy him off, and talks to an overpowering portrait of the old man toward the end of the film. In *Broken Lance*, the name Joe seems also to allude to the story of Joseph and his brothers in the Bible and the Koran. Joe Devereaux breaks the lance he had thrown defiantly into the ground at his father's funeral. The breaking of the lance signals his renunciation of revenge. But he still must fight his brother Ben (Richard Widmark), who had sneeringly called Joe "father's pet" earlier. Just as Joe is about to get shot, Ben is picked off by the faithful Two Moons (Eduard Franz).

Bazin calls it "a good script, at once classic and novelistic, but treated without great inventiveness: "classic," one assumes, in the sense of "western," and "novelistic" apparently because of its use of a long flashback to cover the three years between Joe's incarceration and his release from prison. The film uses tracking and panning shots of Arizona, "restor[ing] to space its fullness," says Bazin.[14] Regardless of its indebtedness to *King Lear*—and Willson makes a good case against Bernice Kliman's objections[15] —this is a fine western. Even as Joe and Jean ride off in the surrey with the fringe on top, a sad look from Joe's mother (Katy Jurado) suggests that all problems have not been solved. Will California be any more tolerant of half-breeds like Joe, and of mixed marriages, than Arizona has been?

Godfather III (1990) may have had its genesis in the middle of *Godfather II* (1974). Hyman Roth (Lee Strasberg) decides to cede his empire in Havana to Michael Corleone (Al Pacino) and others. Roth is very specific about which hotels (or gambling rights) he is giving to whom. The problem is that this division of a kingdom occurs on the eve of the Cuban Revolution. Nothing, then, is divvied up, until years have passed and it is time for Michael to take on the role of King Lear.

At the end of *Godfather II*, Michael closes the door in his wife's face. This is Diane Keaton, hopelessly lost, as character and actress, in the criminal morass. Michael ponders the murders he has ordered, including that of Fredo, his brother (John Cazale), shot in the back of the head as he recited the "Hail Mary" (the better to catch fish with in Lake Tahoe). That is a good ending to a film that never knows what story it wants to tell and so tells the same story in two different times: the rise of the immigrant (Robert De Niro) at the beginning of a new century by means of murder and assassination, and the spread of power by the immigrant's son in the middle of the century by the same means. The stories neither reinforce nor conflict with each other. They merely repeat themselves, and we know where we are by the automobiles driving past. The ending, though, casts a shadow of doubt retrospectively over the success of the Mafia don, and thus serves one of the purposes that art used to serve: "to instruct."

But now the man repents. In the video cassette for *Godfather III*, the director, Frances Ford Coppola, says, "He hasn't set things right." He is, after all, "a metaphor for the American way," says Pacino. And one is forced to agree, given the criminality rife in the upper reaches of our politics and government and given a criminal foreign policy. So now we have a story of "redemption," Coppola says.

Corleone gives $100 million to Sicily by means of the Catholic Church and becomes a member of the Order of San Sebastian. He has purchased legitimacy. It is another of the ceremonial moments in these films, as so often in *Hamlet*, that are somehow corrupted. The best was in *Godfather I* (1972), where a series of murders are conducted during the christening ceremony at St. Patrick's. This time, Kay (Keaton) says, "I preferred you when you were a common mafia hood." But Michael, as Vito's son, never had been a common hood. Rather than point that out, Michael tells her that he "did what I could to protect all of you from the horrors of this world." It was all for family—including the murder of family members. It became necessary to destroy the family in order to save it. Michael gives his associates their share of the Atlantic City operations, but the ceremony is slightly marred by an attack from helicopter gunships, from which Michael escapes. So much for that effort at being the gracious figure resigning his throne. He finally accomplishes this resignation when he names the bastard, Vinny Mancini (Andy Garcia), the new don. Vinny is the Edmund figure here, and in case we miss that we are told that "All bastards are liars. Shakespeare wrote poems about that." Vinny must surrender Michael's daughter, Mary (Sophia Coppola, the Cordelia figure) to secure the position. But she is shot down on the steps of Palermo's opera house by a bullet intended for Michael. The assassin (Salvatore Billa) is, of course, disguised as a priest.

That death is but one of the many that punctuate the end of the film. The crooked Archbishop Gilday (Donal Donnelly) is assassinated as he walks up a set of steps wearing his ceremonial garb. He is tossed down from those heights—a result of hubris, and a shameless theft from Hitchcock. Gilday, I assume, is modeled on Archbishop Paul Marcinkus of Chicago, a Vatican banker of that era (as opposed to the bigot, Francis Cardinal Spellman, Archbishop of New York until his death in 1967). The Pope, John Paul I (Raf Vallone), is murdered. John Paul I did die mysteriously after a reign of 33 days on 29 September 1978 and his body was speedily embalmed. A hanged figure (Helmut Berger) is, I assume, an allusion to Roberto Calvi, whose Banco Ambrosiano failed to the tune of $1.25 billion. His body was weighted down with bricks in 1982 when it was found under Blackfriars Bridge—to point at the Masons as the culprits—but British police have recently decided that it was a murder ordered by the Mafia. Calvi, it seems, had caused some $400 million to simply disappear, a lot of it mafia drug money being laundered. I am not sure how we are to grasp this allusion, since the Calvi figure is scarcely sketched in the film.*

For all of Michael's disclaimers "The higher I go, the crookeder it becomes," and "All my life, I wanted out," we are convinced by the corruption here, not by the impulse toward contrition and forgiveness. The film's final shot shows Michael sitting all alone in the sunlight. He falls off his chair, to be sniffed at by his faithful dog. The original ending had him dying on the opera house steps. Kay asks, "Are you dying?" He says, "No," and dies. That would have been a final and appropriate instance of the denial that has been his mode almost throughout the film. At one point, he says "I am beyond redemption." And that is perhaps the one true thing his character is given to say.

The scene in which Zasa (Joe Mantegna) is assassinated during a Catholic festival is stolen directly from *China Girl* (1987). In that film a religious procession wends its way through Little Italy as Alby (James Russo) is murdered by Chinese hoods. As they escape through the throng of celebrants, the plaster statue of the Virgin tumbles from its pedestal and shatters, leaving only Mary's severed head in the gutter. In *Godfather III*, some of the men carrying the icon during a similar festival set down their honorable load to become gunmen. Mary's golden image crashes to the pavement. Some will say that Coppola "alludes" to the earlier film. A theft should be acknowledged as such.

King of Texas (2002), another *Lear* in the Wild West, begins promisingly. The silhouettes of two men lean from a ruined cottonwood, the only vestige of tree within a hundred miles. Are we watching *Lonesome Dove*? A Mexican rides furiously into a heavily guarded stockade and accuses John Lear (Patrick Stewart) of killing the men. Lear admits as much. They were eating one of his steers. "They were starving," the Mexican retorts. The rich vs. poor conflict, prominent in both the main and subplots of the Shakespeare script, never surfaces again. Indeed, the Mexican to the south of Lear's 200,000-acre spread lives very well, with more servants and amenities than his neighbor to the north. No wonder Claudia (Julie Cox) flees to Mencacha's (Steven Bauer) ranch after she is booted out by Lear.

When Lear asks his "gals" to tell him how much they love him, our suspension of disbelief, slender at best on television, evaporates. On stage, we can accept the lovetest, and we might do so in a more realistic medium were the setting ancient ("once upon a time") or otherworldly ("on a remote planet in a faraway galaxy"). But this is Texas, right after the Alamo, where Lear's son-and-heir has been killed.

The dust devils, tumbleweeds, the sweat on the flanks of the horses, along with Lear's up-from-drygulch background, make his sudden demand for words of love noncredible. His reason is that "you three gals won't be fightin' amongst you when I'm gone." Claudia loses her "husband/father" comparison, which can be telling on stage, since it comes when Cordelia has said almost enough to placate Lear. Here it would have been, "Pappy, these gals got men a their own now. How come they say they love you completely?"

The oldest, Susannah (Marcia Gay Harden), praises Lear's manhood: "I love you for your strength." Rebecca says, "Daddy, I don't know what to say," but she struggles through. "It's not a speakin' thing. It's a feelin' thing." With "some prime land left," Claudia has "nothin' to say." "You best heed your words, lest you throw away your fortune," Lear warns. Free of the constricting underwear of Captain Picard, Stewart lets the rhetoric rip. "She has no more feelin' in her than a lowdown rattlesnake. Poison! I can't keep no rattler in this house. Go, git!"

Lear's rage is out of proportion to Claudia's reticence. She has been taking care of him for some time now. Lear is *already* a beneficiary of "her kind nursery." Lear has not, it seems, permitted any suitors to get close to Claudia. Part of the problem of this opening is that we have had no preparation for the division of Lear's vast holding. The irrelevant episode of the starving Mexicans substitutes for the discussion between Kent and Gloucester that opens the play. The opening auction sale in the play does not startle us as it does here. But the division of Lear's spread in Texas is just as irrational as the carving up of Lear's Britain. King James, after all, hoped for a unification of England, Scotland, and Ireland. A Texas cattle baron would always need more land, and would never risk its descent into farmland. (The issue arises in *Oklahoma*—"The Farmer and the Cowman Should Be Friends," perhaps, but their concepts on the use of land are radically different.) In other words, the opening of *King of Texas* defies the history of a time much more recent, and much more specific than that of *King Lear*.

Stewart grew a white wig for the role of possessive father, but never for a moment does this version suggest that the character is worthy of loyalty or love. Without that quality, hidden even from Lear himself—the "Authority" of authenticity—the production has no emotional center.

Anita Gates claims that *King of Texas* "makes a solid connection with time and place."[16] If she is correct, the trade-off is considerable. The "solid connection" collides with what we know of history. Furthermore, Shakespeare's language insists upon a world in which it can occur. In a *Richard III* set in London in 1937, or a *Hamlet* set in New York in 2000, Shakespeare's words collide anachronistically against the *mise en scene*. In *King of Texas*, the language is translated into a patois that the writers believe characterizes Texas talk in the mid-19th century. Exceptions include "If this feather stirs she lives," and "Look there! Look there!" The exceptions prove that some of the almost wordless simplicity of the ending does not need rephrasing, and perhaps that Shakespeare's language might have worked here, had the actors been up to it. At other times, while the substitutions are not as bad as in *Joe Macbeth* (1955) or NBC's *The Tempest* (1998), they have been stolen from ancient cowboy flicks. "Musta gotten wind we was comin' and skedaddled." I don't think that Lear got his vicious curse of Goneril—"into her womb convey sterility"—but it would have come out like this: "If she do have chillen, let 'em trouble her sorely, like she done her pappy."

Some of the location shots—the distant gallows-tree, horses clopping through a river, riders dwarfed by vast or overarching landscapes—are on loan from a thousand cowboy flicks. The filmmakers seem not to recognize that, while such footage can be powerful on a movie screen (particularly in black and white), it is inevitably miniaturized on most TV screens. Another film technique, music designed to reinforce emotional content, merely underscores the emptiness of what is happening in this production. When the music becomes most of what we notice, nothing much is happening within the frame.

Gates claims accurately that the *King of Texas* "script has thrown away all of the play's insight."[17] The production provides data where the play shows process. And here, the shallow depth of TV is at fault. Without a visual field of depth, emotional or imaginative depth is inhibited. Lear, riding off to visit daughter number two, suddenly loses his way. Heatstroke? Rapture of the plains? No. We are told that he is going mad. The problem is not that this descent has not been prepared for, but that John Lear has been bonkers from the beginning. Lear tries to pull Rebecca (Lauren Holly) away from her nasty husband (Patrick Bergin): "It's you and me from now on." This odd assertion might have had some impact had Claudia gotten her line earlier about her sisters "loving their father all." When Rebecca resists, Lear launches into nonsense about the linkage between her and disease. As he rides angrily off, she cries "Daddy!" heartbrokenly across the mesquite, having not internalized Sylvia Plath's insight about all fathers.

A thunderstorm enters above, so that Lear can shout "Come and git me!" and "You missed me!" to the lightning. (He does avoid the Texas bravado of "Bring 'em on!") We next see Lear watching an eagle, saying that he himself is on the way "to the place where he's goin'." That turns out to be around a butte, and Lear cannot follow. A bird flaps after Claudia dies. The production attempts to compensate with clumsy symbolism for all that is not happening within it.

Claudia is killed during the final battle, after Lear wanders off and tells the soldiers to stop shooting. We are not told that he suddenly—or gradually—recognizes that this is all his fault. When Lear carries Claudia in his arms out through the gate of the besieged fortress, the shooting stops. Why didn't the defenders of the Alamo think of this one?

The blinding of Westover (Roy Scheider), after he finds Lear lost in a gully, is similarly unmotivated here. It is gratuitous violence, until

Susannah gets that other eye in revenge for her husband (Colin Meaney) who has been plugged by one of Westover's servants. Just as Rebecca and Susannah are poised to scratch each other over the Edmund figure (Matt Letscher), Susannah pauses to ask, "What are we doin', Rebecca? What's become of us?" Sudden insight is not a quality that, so far, has been part of her characterization. This may be our question, but it is certainly not hers. The script is driven by the necessity of including elements apparently supposed to be there, but is seldom motivated by character or by the inevitable consequences of word and action. Furthermore, I don't find any reflection or doubt in Shakespeare's Goneril.

The contrasting and reinforcing plots of the play are confusingly intermingled here. A well-made TV drama—as *The Waltons* used to be—can develop metaphors between plot and subplot. A subplot could represent in material terms a more intangible quality of the main plot, for example. *King of Texas* makes a clumsy attempt to do so here. "I was blind before," says the blinded Westover. "I couldn't see the hate in Emmett's heart." "All I've ever felt for you is hate," says Susannah to Lear. In spite of her lapse in asking "What's become of us?" she re-achieves her chilly blood as she views the bodies of Lear and Claudia. "It needed doin'," she says. So hatred inhabits each plot? So what?

On Shakespeare's stage we know the villain's intention and overall strategy. Richard III, Iago, Edmund, Iachimo, and *The Tempest*'s Antonio, tell us what they are going to do or describe what they are doing as they go along. We participate vicariously in their virtuosity. Here, we don't learn until later that the man who beats Rip, Lear's trusty cook (David Alan Grier), is Susannah's servant. This fact foments her fight with Lear. We don't learn until after Thomas (Liam Waite) has been thrown out by Westover that Emmett had convinced Westover that Thomas stole and sold the horses in the Westover corral. The writers do not recognize that TV's constant present and strictly chronological movement of time do not permit expostfacto insights. Thus events are often confusing here, and are not clarified when later explained. We have to know things "at the time" on TV. Flashbacks, for example, seldom work in "straight" TV drama, as opposed to soap operas, which subsist on digressions. Film, obviously, is a more flexible medium and can work on TV because we understand the conventions even if we are watching a film on a cathode ray tube. Films made for TV, however, are as limited in their treatment of time as they are in their field of depth. Shakespeare's stage permits characters to remember the past—the dying Mortimer, the Duke of York in *Richard II*, Henry IV, the newly crowned Henry V, and Prospero, for example—to tinge the past with retrospective irony or to set up expectations for the immediate future. And the Shakespeare script can work on TV, particularly when the production is reconfigured from a theatrical version (as in the several successful productions by Trevor Nunn). In those instances, the productions can pick up a modicum of "suspension of disbelief" that helps them to work on our imaginations.

Whether Stewart could have delivered King Lear to us—in the mode of the pint-sized Lear that can be powerful (Yuri Jarvet and Ian Holm, for example)—is questionable. It may have been a bad script that limited him to the alternating modes of forced joviality or tantrum and a blessedly brief over-the-top shouting match with the lightning. "Stewart often sounds like Jeb (Buddy Epson) in *The Beverly Hillbillies*," says Richard Burt.[18] After his superb Prospero in a flawed 1995 *The Tempest* in New York, he was reported to be considering *Antony and Cleopatra* with Lisa Harrow, a logical progression from his great Enobarbus in the Nunn production of the early 1970s. Instead, he did the pale-face Othello in D.C., surrounded by about a dozen black actors who had essayed the title role previously. It is a shame that an actor as well-known as Stewart did not lend his prestige and talent to Shakespeare's *King Lear*. The effort would have called attention to a great work of art and, most likely, extended our understanding of it. This travesty does nothing of the sort. It is like watching a production of one of Shakespeare's sources and wondering how Shakespeare took such unpromising material and crafted it into such magnificence.

Notes

* On this tangled story of high and low finance, see Giancarlo Galli, *Finanza Bianca: La Chies, I soldi, Il Potere*. Rome: Mondadori, 2004.

Alexis Bledel of "The Gilmore Girls." Photo reprinted with permission from *New York Times*.

Conclusion

"Bless thee, Bottom! Bless thee! Thou art translated," says a frightened Peter Quince. In the 1935 film, the donkey that had pulled the prop-cart out to the woods bolted in terror at the sight of James Cagney's ass-headed Bottom. To the donkey, this strange relative was a version of Banquo's ghost. The film captures at that moment the inversion in the natural order that *A Midsummer Night's Dream* explores.

Nowadays, Shakespearean translations on TV are likely to represent an inversion of what we might consider the Shakespearean "script." They are unlikely to suggest something about that energy or quality we call "Shakespeare" but will probably remind us of Bottom's rejoinder to Snout: "You see an ass-head of your own, do you?" The productions will either distort a given script into a context it will not support—like the Mafia for *Macbeth*—reflect their commercial premises blatantly, or reduce Shakespearean dimensions to narrower modern modes, like a high school, or a ranch in Texas, or a police force in London. The modernization tends to reflect us back at ourselves. Shakespeare, of course, has always been subject to commercial pressures. When the hat was passed after carts had delivered medieval miracle or morality plays, the throng tended to dissipate, its coinage intact. The enclosure of the playing space permitted Shakespeare to purchase New Place. Only recently, however, has Shakespeare been *submerged* by commerce.

Two of the final Shakespeare films of the 1990s seemed to promise a very positive new millennium. *Shakespeare in Love* followed up on Trevor Nunn's witty exploration of gender in his 1996 *Twelfth Night*. In that film, Nunn had gone after the issue directly by showing how difficult it is for his Viola (Imogen Stubbs) to master the variety of activities in which aristocratic males of the late 19th century engage. Stubbs's brilliant performance demonstrated, by implication, the problems inherent in a life of external accomplishment and inner emptiness at any moment in time. One of the lessons of Nunn's comedy is that her assumption of the role helps to destroy its necessity.

Julie Taymor's *Titus Andronicus* portrays a politics gone mad and offers a salutary warning about any politics in any moment of history. The film's sentimental ending does not vitiate its vivid exposé of the self-destructive impulse at the core of "official" actions and decrees. While the film pressed an oppositional energy into the morass of clichés that Hollywood was promoting, it did not make money, and thus helped doom efforts at producing further Shakespeare films, as *A Midsummer Night's Dream* and *Romeo and Juliet* had done in the 1930s.

Shakespeare in Love survives some of its earlier lapses into anachronism, such as the silly 1970's trip to the shrink, which trades on self-congratulatory recognitions on the part of members of the audience, to move into a late-1990's vision of Elizabethan London, as if Sam Wanamaker's Globe Theatre had spread down Bankside and slid its tentacles across several bridges to the City, there to erase the steel and glass towers and replace them with squatter structures of timber, mortar, and brick, and avenues gridlocked not with Jaguars but with wagons on muddy lanes. The film visualizes what Shakespeare's plays can suggest—the great network of a city surrounding the theaters, with its Chertsey, Crosby House, Whitefriars, and Holborn, where the Bishop's strawberries grow. The architecture, streets, and costumes of *Shakespeare in Love* convey "authenticity" and are not really much different than the black-and-white mise-en-scéne of the opening of the 1929 *The Taming of the Shrew,* though the latter features more live dogs. Most important, the settings for *Shakespeare in Love* place the love story and its conflict in its time: an arranged marriage struggles against romantic love, which, in turn is the conflict central to the play-within-the-film, *Romeo and Juliet*. Conceptual space and the story told within that space coincide perfectly and help make my point that Shakespeare can succeed in *his* time (that is, within our conception of "early modern history"). Furthermore, the film emerges from a tradition of films about the production of plays or musicals or films in which backstage and onstage worlds tug at each other, perhaps opposing, perhaps reinforcing what is happening "on stage." In this genre, the onstage world sometimes resolves the offstage dilemmas. Marion Davies's wonderful silent film *Show People, Singin' in the Rain*, Mickey-and-Judy flicks like *Babes in Arms,* and Cole Porter's masterpiece, *Kiss Me, Kate!,* are examples of a genre that seldom fails, though it can do so, as in *Goldiggers of 1937,* which consistently trespasses beyond the boundaries of credulity, and, recently, in Branagh's *Love's Labour's Lost*, which founders at precisely the point where Nathan Lane usurps the play's agenda for "There's No Business Like Show Business." Branagh's film never recovers from its foray into *Annie, Get Your Gun*. *Shakespeare in Love* benefits from its *not* having a happy ending. Unlike the examples I give or almost any other instance in the genre (with the possible exception, of course, of *Love's Labour's Lost*) the two young lovers don't end up together. That separation lifts the *Shakespeare in Love* above its generic counterparts. It is, as the comparison with old-fashioned films suggests, an old-fashioned film, telling a story that film usually tells well. Above all, it is thematically unified from its depths to its surfaces.

"Those whom God has joined together not even I can put asunder," says the Queen. Based on one divorce, her church cannot condone another. Until the end, however, it is a great love story intercut with scenes from other love stories, particularly *Romeo and Juliet* and *Twelfth Night*.

After many actors have auditioned for Will's new play with Faustus's speech to Helen, Master Kent, the disguised Viola, shows up reciting Valentine's soliloquy on Sylvia (3.1), which looks ahead in its "banished" and "banishment' to *Romeo and Juliet*. She takes on a male role here, even the role of stereotypical lover. Her brief recitation, though, pulls Will's soul toward her. In love with his own verse, he begins the movement from a paralyzing narcissism through other layers of clothes and of awarenesses. Will's writer's block dissolves in a flash of lust.

In Ian Judge's 1994 *Twelfth Night* for the RSC, Orsino (Clive Wood) kissed Cesario (Emma Fielding) before "his" embassy to Olivia, then backed away, touching his lips in puzzlement. Who am I? What am I becoming? The homoerotic experience was a prelude to a heterosexual relationship, of course. We knew that. Orsino did not. He had begun a necessary questioning of his own arrogant assumptions about himself. In a film of many borrowings, *Shakespeare in Love* steals this moment. As Will rows Master Kent, his boyactor, across the Thames within a superbly visualized nightscape and rhapsodizes about his love for the "absent" Viola, he falls in love with the stand-in, Master Kent, and kisses "him" just below the moustache. It may be homoerotic to a confused Will-Orsino, but we know what lies beneath the strapped-down breasts, so that the instant is a bit of foreplay in what becomes a fiery romance, conducted in moments stolen from the prying eyes of a rival. Viola has been Virginia Woolf's Judith Shakespeare, but instead of waiting futilely at the stage door, she borrows a page from Will's *Two Gentlemen of Verona*, dons doublet and hose and steps inside the male-dominated Globe.

The issue of gender is neatly carried forward into what is probably the film's finest sequence, a series of cuts between the actual romance and Will's new play, with boy actor playing Juliet and girl, disguised as male actor, playing Romeo. The lines of the balcony scene flash back and forth across the river, from Viola's bed to the rehearsal at the Rose, which entrances the assembled company. The sequence may show, as Janet Maslin suggests, "the bond between tempestuous love and artistic creation."[1] It *does* show how montage can suggest much more than its parts; in this case the instability of gender, perhaps the fusion of gender at some level deeper than the physical. The words refuse to stay within their gender designation. "Wilt thou leave me so unsatisfied?" says Will, in bed with Viola. "That's my line!" she protests, as actor and as woman. Will's appropriation of "I will come again"—Juliet's line in the play—has a different meaning here. The sequence culminates in Will's unwrapping of Master Kent backstage. All of this demonstrates passion most convincingly. Whether it convinces anyone of the equation between sex and artistic creativity is another matter. The backstage bout of concupiscence is spied upon by a young vagabond named John Webster, who is thinking that "The gates of heaven are not so highly arched / As prince's palaces. They that enter / There must go upon their backs." Elizabeth has the last word on the issue of gender: "I know something of a woman in a man's profession."

Stoppard moves the scenario in and out of planes of reality, as the camera does in his film of *Rosencrantz and Guildenstern Are Dead*. As the Montagues and Capulets square off in rehearsal, a rival party of actors, Burbage and the Chamberlain's Men—enraged that Will is letting Henslowe do a play promised to them—storms the theater. The groups engage, Capulets and Montagues suddenly united against an invader, to the delight of Mr. Fennyman, the backer (Tom Wilkinson), who thinks it's part of the show. He begins to unsuspend his disbelief, though, when valuable props shatter.

At the end of the film, Will takes on the role of Romeo because Master Kent has been found out. The boy actor assigned to the role of Juliet discovers that, overnight, his voice has become that of a bullfrog. Viola, having absconded from her marriage to Wessex, rushes down to play Juliet. She knows the part, of course, because it is a product of her love affair with Will and it has been recited to her even as the ink on the parchment dries. The words have been waiting for *her*, as woman and as actor. The film anticipates the Restoration, when women were at last permitted on the public stage. Will's love has permitted him to write both parts for the stage because he's been inspired by his backstage romance, which has been more than mere infatuation. (Will's previous play, *Two Gentlemen of Verona*, has been a hit only because of Crab, the dog.) Master Kent has been playing Romeo. The transition and their own impending separation allow them to play the scene in the Capulet tomb with remarkable conviction. It is their last scene together, on stage or off, and they know it, so subtext and script coincide powerfully.

The ending is more satisfying than the conventional "ever after," because Will and Viola's passion is at its height, like that of Romeo and Juliet. Will and Viola part sorrowfully, but they will never know disillusionment at the decline of the first splendid flood of love and lust. It is, as Will writes it, "too rash, too unadvis'd, too like the lightning," but not (to borrow from Keats) like "All human passion ... / That leaves a heart high-sorrowful and cloy'd / A burning forehead, and a parching tongue." Theirs will always be first love, with the ache at its loss turning gradually to the memory of yearning that every spring will bring. The film has the grace to grant us our own sense of what passion is all about.

The innermost fictions of the film become "the truth" the film delivers. Viola, now Lady Wessex, bound for Virginia with her colonist husband, will remain forever young for Will. She will be the inspiration for a host of young women playing boys and played by boys in plays to come. It would be better, admittedly, for the film's thesis, had Shakespeare not already exploited this device through Julia in *Two Gentlemen of Verona*, but not too many filmgoers will launch this quibble. While the next play that Shakespeare will write is not *The Tempest*, as the *New York Times* reviewer says[2] —that cuts out a few good scripts between *Romeo* and 1610—we can sense an older Will, whose every third thought may be the Avon, ceding a young Miranda (a still young Viola) to Ferdinand, the two to live out the life denied to Viola de Lesseps and Will Shakespeare. The brief romance has been the seedbed of Shakespeare's genius, the one love affair that remains the one. First times have nothing to compare themselves with and so invite their constant reinvention, at least until *Macbeth* and *Antony and Cleopatra* explore the far side of marriage. Kenneth Rothwell calls the film a "farce"[3]—that is, a complicated series of situations in which "the truth" is concealed from at least one of the characters in the frame. John Lardner labels the film a "fantasia."[4] I see it as a "romance," full of improbable but pleasing coincidence that becomes synchronicity. The ending involves a physical separation but also a merging of Shakespeare and the creativity that would carry him for the next decade and a half—and a lot of us since then. Shakespeare was more a product of a craftsmanship deployed within the very specific architecture of Elizabethan theaters than of a sudden crystallization around a girl of his dreams untimely snatched from his embrace, but the latter scenario makes a better story and a much more sensuous film than could be made from dust, goosequills, and the slow, secret process of mastery.

At the end, Will is working on *Twelfth Night,* in which he makes Viola a boy coming to an infatuated Duke, seeking in language and music what he cannot attain in life. At the end, of course, Viola is to return in her woman's weeds to wed. It is the ending that Will can write but cannot attain. *Shakespeare in Love* borrows a storm scene from Trevor Nunn's wonderful *Twelfth Night,* so among the fringe benefits of Stoppard's film may be a renewed interest in Nunn's film, which deserves more attention than it has received. Both films demonstrate that Shakespeare can interrogate gender issues in ways more illuminating than, for example, *Sex in the City* or a static remake-for-TV of *The Goodbye Girl.*

Taymor's *Titus Andronicus* begins when Titus inspects the ranks. We have a leader established, as opposed to the puzzling lad who has been kidnapped to this underground space. Titus finally addresses the Romans. "Hail Rome, victorious in thy mourning weeds!" Soon, though, Titus encounters problems. In Shakespeare's late 4th-century Rome, rituals are empty of their meanings. The film shows Titus filling the empty combat boots of his dead soldiers with dirt sifted from his hand. Titus shows no conviction in condemning Alarbus. It is a formula. Titus consumes some wine as the disembowelment is conducted, but the wine is not linked to the pagan ceremony of redress. "The signs of decadence, corruption, and loss of cultural confidence are everywhere," as Katharine E. Maus says of the play. "The distinction between legitimate and illegitimate behavior seems ... remarkably indistinct."[5] Titus acquiesces in the burial of Mutius simply because it makes no difference what happens. He is not torn between ancient family-based values and an emerging civic order, as are Sophocles's Antigone and Aeschylus's Orestes, though Titus is in a position to negotiate this transition, and evades the responsibility. This play comes the closest in the Shakespeare canon to exploring the issues that the great Greek tragedians were probing within their evolving city-state. In *Titus*, though, the interrogation occurs during the period of decline and fall. Titus is a transitional figure, a fact particularly underlined in Taymor's film, since she first shows Titus in absolute command as he returns to Rome, then swings to the brawling factions of Saturninus and Basianus, then to Titus's weighting of the election to Saturninus. The problem with this transposition, of course, is that the play shows Titus returning in the middle of the ongoing election contest. Taymor creates so powerful and iconic a figure that Titus's preference for Saturninus seems like an incomprehensible surrender and a refutation of what the film has already established. Titus comes close to "tragic" status in that he can be seen as refusing to make the decisions that would smooth Rome's movement into a positive future. The problem, however, within the Aristotelian formula is that we do not witness Titus's awareness of his culpability.

In *Titus*, old codes are a memory of the past, not a living guide to present behavior. Their observation, then, tends to violate a sense of "right" that may be evolving, but has yet to be articulated. Tamora can only appeal for Alarbus on the basis of family, but that is also Titus's point: "These are their brethren [who] Religiously ... ask a sacrifice." Tamora must express what Titus is doing through oxymoron: "O cruel, irreligious piety!" By the time the play arrives at the "Antigone-Creon" conflict between Titus and the brothers of Mutius, the distinction between family and state is irrelevant. Rome, having taken in the Goths through Tamora's marriage to Saturninus, is shrouded in a moral murkiness similar to that that Dreiser explores in *An American Tragedy*, where a young man who may or may not be a murderer, but who certainly is a product of the tantalizing promises held out to him, goes to his death primarily because he had found himself on the borders of that promised land. The only decision that we can applaud in *Titus* is Titus's to revenge. The play, then, is mostly a prologue to his freedom to make that decision. Once the film really begins—after its irrelevant prologue—it provides images and performances as good as anything we are likely to find in Shakespeare on film, as well as "a parable for our own potential decline and fall," as Samuel Crowl accurately claims.[6] As the film recedes into its financial failure, this country trembles on the brink of a right-wing coup d'etat.

These two films promised a further exploration and understanding of gender issues and a further exposure of destructive politics. But each promise remained within its film. Too soon, it was 2000. It seems now that we are asked, not so much what to make of the diminished thing (to paraphrase Frost) that Shakespeare becomes on TV, but also what to make of the world that Orwell predicted would arrive 20 years before it did. It is no accident that two of the best and most politically profound Shakespeare derivations—*The Bad Sleep Well* and *Shakespeare Wallah*—appeared some four decades ago. Nor, it would seem, is it unremarkable that Taymor's vivid interrogation of politics in *Titus* has been forgotten, or replaced by a shallow and merely contemporary *Fahrenheit 9/11*. As Memorial Day 2004 rolls around, the flag-covered coffins produced by war are hidden from public view. It would seem that the makeover show, "The Swan," wherein reality is transformed into what the western world considers "a pleasing shape," is emblematic of where we are, and where we wish to be. Joe Margolis argues that "popular culture is just a post modern term for entertainment." A film full of car crashes and karate chops, he says, "allows its viewers to escape the world for a short while."[7] Even films like *The Passion of the Christ* on one hand and *Fahrenheit 9/11* on the other merely reinforce the biases of their auditors. Films aimed at the teenage market—and that seems to be most of them these days—merely create a world that flatters its audience. In other words, entertainment has flattened out to a way of paying money to kill time. Even films that claim to emerge from the generic premises of earlier films deny any sense of their heritage. A truly awful film of 2003, *Intolerable Cruelty*, claimed to be a "screwball comedy" in the tradition of Claudette Colbert, Carole Lombard, and Miriam Hopkins. It had neither pace nor humor nor a shred of believability, and dropped its single good idea early, which was the ways in which narratives can be reinterpreted by clever lawyers. Yet it was so well reviewed that people like me were encouraged to see it.

In *Shakespeare Wallah*, Shakespeare represents a dying voice in an emerging nation that celebrates meretricious "native" work. And it takes no ghost to come from the grave to tell us that we have translated Shakespeare into the meretricious. The issue, however, goes beyond the mere trivialization of a *Strange Brew*, or the expropriation of *Romeo and Juliet* as a validation of teenage "values." *A Double Life* convinces us of the somewhat improbable fiction that a professional actor can be inhabited by the roles he plays. The imaginary construct called *Othello* becomes reality for Anthony John. A fictional murder promotes a real murder. Once we accept the premise, the film develops inexorably and powerfully. Crucially, the parallel between Shakespeare's play and modern world is merely individual and, for Anthony John, psychological. A production must close, or go on with an understudy, a restaurant must find a new waitress, but the results of Anthony John's madness are not widespread. Nor are the results of Othello's aberration. *O* attempts to parallel "the world" of *Othello*, which is circumscribed and island-bound, but does deal with important people and important issues. Palmetto Prep and its miniature basketball team fail as a model. So does Texas on television. For better or worse, Texas demands a film. And, I would argue, *O* and *King of Texas* force their parallels. They do not emerge easily from context, as they do in an admittedly minor film like *Strange Illusion.*

The issue of TV is not merely one of scale. Trevor Nunn and Jane Howell show how the medium can work for "straight" Shakespeare. For 19th century Texas or modern London, the necessary details must be *explicit*, not suggestive, and thus the *mise-en-scène* simply takes over from whatever archetypes may be lurking down there under the translation. Television drama is remarkably ahistorical, even if it inevitably reflects zeitgeist. That is not to say, however, that history plays cannot work on TV. Deborah Warner's *Richard II* with Fiona Shaw is a spare production. No flowers grow in its garden. That paucity permits language and characterization to emerge powerfully. Shakespeare on television demands a metonymic approach: billowing curtains and huge pillows vs. columns and armor for Nunn's brilliant *Antony and Cleopatra*, a flexible playground that lighting can change to a throne room or a battlefield for Howell's vibrant *Henry VI* sequence, bugle calls to mark off the dimensions of a given day in the military environment of Nunn's powerful *Othello*. Occasional successful exceptions to the rule—David Thacker's police-state *Measure for Measure* (1994), and Jonathan Miller's cluttered, Victorian *Merchant of Venice* (1970)—do exist. They are rare, however. TV is a close-up medium. For all of the recent changes in definition, TV will always lack the field of depth that film can enjoy. And here, as with Shakespeare in any medium, observant and detailed performance criticism is more useful than a thousand theories.

Directors of the plays on stage are still seeking the parallels in the script that reinforce and/or contrast with each other. They still look for themes that will render their productions coherent. When the plays are subversive as contemporary politics suddenly reflects its lurid light on them, good directors avoid coercing the scripts into contemporary "relevance." America today is probably less tolerant of the "mirroring" effect of the script in the right-wing state engendered by the terrorist attacks of September 2001. If not it is too susceptible to the easy analogy: O.J. and Othello, or Richard II and Watergate, for example. Again, the rare exception—Welles's fascist *Julius Caesar* of the late 1930s— proves the point. Stage directors may be old-fashioned. I don't find their notes full of the current jargon. Since production is where Shakespeare *is,* that is to the good. Directors may be running scared in the frightening environment created by terrorists and by official response to terrorism, and may therefore be presenting tame and unoffending productions. But that is preferable to productions that all too easily evoke the postmodernist standards of disunity and dissonance. They inevitably result in an incoherent production where scenes seem to be competing against each other, rather that than co-operating to evoke a satisfying final cause.

Current "theorizing" does not account for the thinness of Shakespeare on TV. Here, theory becomes irrelevant. It takes no discussion of the work of art in an age of mechanical reproduction or of the cultural logic of late capitalism to tell us what TV is, and what it is likely to make of Shakespeare. Commercial TV is by definition commercial, within, and around, its ostensible drama. TV subordinates its content to its agenda. We can study *how* this happens, but we know why.

Jorg Helbig shows convincingly how recent filmed Shakespeare attempts to appeal to what Kenneth Branagh calls the "batman audience."[8] "Clearly," says Helbig, "contemporary Shakespeare films are no longer restricted to art-house audiences, but have become a mass-cultural phenomenon."[9]

Helbig responds to Roger Ebert's question, apparently posed with tongue-out-of-cheek: "Why is Shakespeare so popular with filmmakers when he contains so few car chases and explosions?"[10] Helbig suggests that the recent films explore topical issues like war, gender, and homosexuality; that they allude to other cinematic icons that a film-savvy audience will recognize; and that they often include stars in their casts. The problem is that, assuming that the audience for

Luhrmann's *Romeo + Juliet* has grown up by now, it did not grow up as an audience for more Shakespeare. The teenage years apparently were also their Shakespearean moment. That is another way of saying that the more challenging *Titus Andronicus* failed at the box office. That means that for the time being, and into the foreseeable future, Shakespeare on screen is likely to be reduced to translations into settings and zeitgeists that insist on dysfunctional marriages between the inherited script and the production, or to the efforts of young people to produce *Romeo and Juliet* in a sometimes well-meaning but clumsy and sometimes hostile "adult" world.

Mary Pickford, in the 1919 version of *Daddy Longlegs* in which she forgets her lines as Juliet.

Citations

Introduction

1. According to Michael Goldman, *Praxis* corresponds to the action the characters perform and equates to Aristotle's "imitation of an action." *Poesis* is the actors' creation and projection of their roles. *Theoria* is the audience's action in possessing the dramatic experience. *Acting and Action in Shakespearean Tragedy* (Princeton: Princeton University Press, 1985).
2. D. Traister, "Review." *Choice* (September 1999).
3. Ruby Cohn, *Modern Shakespearean Offshoots* (Princeton: Princeton University Press, 1976).
4. Daniel J. Vitkus, "Turning Turk in *Othello*: The Conversion and Damnation of the Moor." *Shakespeare Quarterly* 48/2 (Summer 1997): 176.
5. Peter S. Donaldson, "Cinema and the Kingdom of Death: Loncraine's *Richard III*," *Shakespeare Quarterly* 53/2 (Summer 2002): 244.
6. Peter S. Donaldson, 2002: 244.
7. H. R. Coursen, "Filming *Richard III*," *Shakespeare: The Two Traditions* (Madison, N.J.: Fairleigh Dickinson University Press, 1999), pp. 137–161.
8. Christopher Lasch, *The Culture of Narcissism: American Life in an Age of Diminishing Expectations* (New York: W.W. Norton, 1991).
9. Coppelia Kahn, "They'll All Kow-Tow." *Shakespeare and the Classroom* 1/2 (Autumn 1993): 4.
10. Stuart Klawans, "Blind Faith." *The Nation* (15 March 2004): 26.
11. Klawans, 2004: 26.
12. Klawans, 26.
13. Klawans, 26.
14. Frank Rich, "Review." *New York Times* (14 March 2004): Arts, 2.
15. David Denby, "The Current Cinema." *The New Yorker* (23 March 2004): 85.
16. Denby, 2004: 84.
17. Denby, 84.
18. Denby, 86.
19. Kenneth L. Woodward, "Do You Recognize this Jesus?" *New York Times* (25 February 2004): A 27.

20 H. Richard Niebuhr, qtd. in Woodward, 2004:A27.
21 David Brooks, "You'll Never Walk Alone." *New York Times* (21 February 2004): A29.
22 Barbara Hodgdon, "From the Editor," *Shakespeare Quarterly* 53/2 (Summer 2002): vii.
23 Peter Singer, *The President of Good and Evil: The Ethics of George W. Bush* (New York: Dutton, 2004).
24 Bob Woodward, *Plan of Attack* (New York: Simon & Schuster, 2004). For other carefully researched examinations of the Bush presidency, see Richard Clarke, *Against All Enemies: Inside America's War on Terror* (New York: Free Press, 2004); David W. Corn, *The Lies of George W. Bush: Mastering the Politics of Deception* (New York: Crown, 2003); John W. Dean, *Worse than Watergate: The Secret Presidency of George W. Bush*; (Boston: Little, Brown & Company, 2004), Geoffrey Hodgson, *More Equal than Others: America from Nixon to the New Century*, (Princeton: Princeton University Press, 2004); Molly Ivins and Lou Du Bose, *Bushwacked: Life in George W. Bush's America* (New York: Random House, 2003); Paul Krugman, *The Great Unraveling: Losing Our Way in the New Century*, (New York: W. W. Norton, 2003); Ron Suskind, *The Price of Loyalty: George W. Bush, the White House, and Paul O'Neill* (New York: Simon & Schuster, 2004). Some recent books that illuminate the current national debate include Niall Ferguson, *Colossus: The Price of America's Empire* (New York: Penguin, 2004). (The United States is an empire, not a modern state, whether we like it or not, and we had better learn to behave like one. When Rome, do as Rome did.) Michael Ignatieff, *The Lesser Evil: Political Ethics in an Age of Terror.* (Princeton: Princeton University Press, 2004). (In the face of terrorism, torture becomes relative. It is justified by greater evil. If we don't use torture, the terrorists have won?) Michael Hardt and Antonio Negri, *Multitude: War and Democracy in the Age of Empire* (New York: Penguin, 2004). (This is a woolly-headed indictment of globalization. I would suggest that not some vague "democracy," but the developed institutions of the modern nation-state, regardless of political system, are required to take advantage of globalization.)
25 Courtney Lehmann, *Shakespeare Remains: Theater to Film: Early Modern to Postmodern* (Ithaca and London: Cornell University Press, 2002). Lehmann treats *A Midsummer Night's Dream*, *Hamlet*, *Romeo and Juliet*, and *Shakespeare in Love*. For other recent approaches to the filmic canon, see Courtney Lehmann and Lisa Starks, eds. *The Reel Shakespeare: Alternative Cinema and Theory* (Madison, N.J.: Fairleigh Dickinson University Press, 2002). The book includes essays by Lia M. Hotchkiss on *Prospero's Books*, Kenneth Rothwell on silent *Hamlet*s, Alan Walworth on Godard's *King Lear*, Kathy M. Howlett on *My Own Private Idaho*, Peter Donaldson on Peter Hall's *A Midsummer Night's Dream*, Bryan Reynolds on the Polanski *Macbeth*, Starks on Taymor's *Titus*, essays on pedagogy by Douglas Green and John Brett Mischo and José Ramon Diaz-Fernandez's invaluable filmography, James R. Keller and Leslie Stratyner,

eds. *Almost Shakespeare: Reinventing His Work for Cinema and Television* (McFarland, N.C.: Jefferson, 2004). Its essays deal with *My Own Private Idaho, CSI-Miami, One Thousand Acres, O, 10 Things I Hate About You, Get Over It,* and *The West Wing, Cineaste* 14/1 (1998), with essays by Gary Crowdus, Samuel Crowl, Russell Jackson, Kenneth Rothwell, Thomas Pendleton, and a "Director's Symposium" with Peter Brook, Peter Hall, Richard Loncraine, Trevor Nunn, Oliver Parker, Roman Polanski, and Franco Zeffirelli, and Stephen M. Buhler, *Shakespeare in the Cinema: Ocular Proof* (Albany: State University of New York Press, 2002), along with Kenneth S. Rothwell's discussion of Buhler's taxonomy in *Shakespeare Bulletin* 20/1 (Winter 2002): 40, and *Shakespeare, The Movie, II.* Lynda E. Boose and Richard Burt, eds. (London: Routledge, 2002), which contains essays by Burt on "race, and the small screens of popular culture," Katherine Rowe on Almereyda's *Hamlet*, Michael Anderegg on *Romeo + Juliet* and *Shakespeare in Love*, Katherine Eggert on Branagh's *Love's Labour's Lost*, and Nunn's *Twelfth Night*, Barbara Hodgdon on *Othello*, Peter S. Donaldson on *Prospero's Books*, Diane E. Henderson on *Shrew*, Laurie Osborne on The Animated Shakespeares, Douglas Lanier on the *Midsummer Night Dream*s of Hoffman, Noble, and Edzard, James N. Loehlin on the Loncraine *Richard III*, Thomas Cartelli on Pacino's *Looking for Richard* and Bedford's *Street King*, Donald K. Hedrick on Branagh's *Henry V*, Courtney Lehmann on *Macbeth* (including a discussion of *Scotland, PA*.: 245–246), Amy Scott-Douglas on European cinema and Richard Burt on "Shakespeare and Asia." The latter essay includes a discussion of the generic problems of *China Girl* (283–286).

26 Richard Burt, "Introduction." *Shakespeare: The Movie, II* (London: Routledge, 2002), p. 18.
27 Mark Thornton Burnett, "Review." *Shakespeare Quarterly* 54/4 (Winter 2003): 470.
28 Charles Forker, "Review." *Shakespeare Bulletin* 53/3 (Fall 2003): 71 and 82.
29 Thomas B. Hughes, *Human-Built World: How to Think about Technology and Culture* (Chicago: University of Chicago Press, 2004).
30 Zbigniew Brzezinski, *The Choice: Global Dominance or Global Leadership* (New York: Basic Books, 2004).
31 James Mann, *Rise of the Vulcans: The History of Bush's War Cabinet* (New York: Viking, 2004), p. 17.
32 Elaine Pagels, *Beyond Belief* (New York: Random House, 2004), p. 137. See also her *The Gnostic Gospels* (New York: Vintage, 1979), and *Adam, Eve, and the Serpent* (New York: Vintage, 1988).
33 Louis Menand, "Nanook and Me." *The New Yorker* (August 9 & 16, 2004): 96.
34 Frank Rich, "Saving Private England." *New York Times* (18 May 2004): 2: 1 and 8.
35 Robert F. Willson, Jr., *Shakespeare in Hollywood: 1929–1956* (Madison, N.J.: Fairleigh Dickinson University Press, 2000), pp. 94–101.

36 On *Scotland, PA.*, see Robert F. Willson, Jr., "*Scotland, PA.*" *Shakespeare Bulletin* 20/3 (Summer 2003): 41–42
37 See Barbara Hodgdon, "Katherina Bound: or Play(K)ating the Strictures of Everyday Life." *PMLA* 107/3 (1992): 538–553.
38 Jack Oruch, "Shakespeare for the Millions." *Shakespeare on Film Newsletter* 11/2 (April 1987): 7. See also Diana Henderson, "A Shrew for the Times," *Shakespeare the Movie: Popularizing the Plays on Film, TV, and Video*. Lynda Boose and Richard Burt, eds. (London: Routledge, 2000), pp. 164–165.
39 Robert F. Willson, Jr., "Shakespeare in *The Goodbye Girl*," *Shakespeare On Film Newsletter* II. 2 (April 1978): 1, 3 and 4. *Shakespeare in Hollywood: 1929–1956*. (Madison, N.J.: Fairleigh Dickinson University Press, 2000), pp. 162–163.
40 Ned Martel, "Goodbye girl grows up and loses her gags," *Financial Times* (10/11 January 2004): W7.
41 See Willson, *Shakespeare in Hollywood*, pp. 101–109.
42 Jay Bobbin, "Shakespeare's *Tempest* Brews Anew on NBC." *TV Week* (13–19 December 1998): 2
43 Quoted in Wendy Williams, "Fonda Takes On *The Tempest*," *Satellite TV Week* (22–28 November 1998): 2.
44 Bonamy Dobree, "The Last Plays," *The Living Shakespeare*. Robert Gittings, ed. (New York: Fawcett, 1961), p. 158.
45 Qtd. in Wendy Williams, 1998: 2.
46 Kenneth S. Rothwell, *A History of Shakespeare on Screen: A Century of Film and Television* (Cambridge: Cambridge University Press, 1999), pp. 225–227.
47 Rothwell, 1999, p. 219.
48 Rothwell, p. 219.
49 Kathy M. Howlett, in Lehmann and Startks, 2002, p.168.
50 Qtd. on "Frontline: The Jesus Factor." Public Broadcasting Service, 29 April 2004.
51 Frank Rich, "3 Hours, 4 Nights, 1 Fear." *New York Times*. Section 2 (25 July 2004): 1.

Chapter 1 – Romeo and Juliet

1 Douglas Lanier, "Shakescorp *Noir*," *Shakespeare Quarterly* 53/2 (Summer, 2002): 162. For the "oppositional" argument, see Lawrence W. Levine, *Highbrow/Lowbrow: The Emergence of Cultural Hierarchy in America* (Cambridge, Mass.: Harvard University Press, 1988).
2 See for example: Theodor Adorno and Max Horkheimer, "The Culture Industry: Enlightenment as Mass Deception," *Dialectic of Enlightenment*, trans. John Cumming (New York: Continuum, 1972): 120–167. Walter Benjamin, "The Work of Art in the Age of Mechanical Reproduction." *Illuminations*, ed. Hannah Arendt, trans. Harry Zohn (New York: Harcourt, Brace and World, 1968): 219–253. Frederic Jameson, "Postmodernism and Consumer Society."

The Cultural Turn: Writings on the Postmodern: 1983–1996 (London: Verso, 1998): 1–20, and *Postmodernism: The Cultural Logic of Late Capitalism* (Durham, N.C.: Duke University Press, 1991).
3   Lanier, 2002: 179.
4   Peter Blos, *On Adolescence* (New York: Free Press, 1952).
5   Frederic Jameson, *The Political Unconscious: Narrative as a Socially Symbolic Act* (Ithaca: Cornell University Press, 1981), pp. 103–150.
6   Valerie Wayne, "*Shakespeare Wallah* and Colonial Specularity." *Shakespeare: The Film*, Lynda Boose and Richard Burt, eds. (London: Routledge, 1997): 97.
7   Tony Howard, "Shakespeare's Cinematic Offshoots." *The Cambridge Companion to Shakespeare on Film*, edited by Russell Jackson (Cambridge: Cambridge University Press, 2000): 309.
8   Doug Stenberg, "The Circle of Life and the Chain of Being: Shakespearean Motifs in *The Lion King.*" *Shakespeare Bulletin* 14/2 (Spring 1996): 37.
9   On *Titanic*'s relationship to *Romeo and Juliet*, see Richard Burt, "No Holes Barred: Homonormativity and the Gay and Lesbian Romance with *Romeo and Juliet.*" *Shakespeare Without Class: Misappropriations of Cultural Capital*, edited by Donald Hedrick and Bryan Reynolds (New York: Palgrave, 2000): 153–186.
10 Richard Burt, "Slammin' Shakespeare." *Shakespeare Quarterly* 53/2 (Summer 2002): 214.
11 Barbara Hodgdon, "From the Editor." *Shakespeare Quarterly* 53/2 (Summer 2002): vii.

Chapter 2 – Hamlet

1   On the patterns of the Elizabethan revenge play, see my chapter on Taymor's *Titus Andronicus* in *Shakespeare in Space: Recent Shakespeare Productions on Screen* (New York: Peter Lang, 2002): pp. 129–141.
2   On the Townswoman of Lynn, see O. B. Hardison, "Three Types of Renaissance Catharsis." *Renaissance Drama*. New Series II (1969): 4, and Thomas Heywood, *An Apology for Actors*, Richard A. Perkinson, ed. (New York: Scholars' Facsimiles & Reprints, 1941), #27.
3   W. H. Auden, "The Christian Tragic Hero." *New York Times Book Review* (16 December 1945): 1.
4   Cf. Michael Pennington, *Hamlet: A User's Guide* (New York: Limelight, 1996): 88–91.
5   Stephen Greenblatt, quoted in Adam Begley, "The Tempest Around Stephen Greenblatt." *New York Times Magazine* (28 March 1993): 33.
6   See, for example, Michael Billington, "A Hamlet perfect for the age of irony." *The Guardian;* (6 September 2000), Nicholas de Johgh, "This rare remarkable Prince gives the Hamlet of a lifetime." *Evening Standard* (9 June 2000); Lloyd Rose, "In London, a Truly Great Dane: John Caird's Haunting 'Hamlet.'" *Washington Post* (6 September 2000), and Charles Spencer, "Beale's great Dane rescues his master." *Daily Telegraph* (9 June 2000).

7   See my response in *Shakespeare in Space*, 2002, pp. 143–146 and 151–56.
8   Douglas Lanier, "Shakecorp Noir." *Shakespeare Quarterly* 53 / 2 (Summer, 2002): 171, 172.
9   Douglas Lanier, 2002: 171.
10 See Linda Charnes's brilliant reading of *L.A. Story*: "Dismember Me: Shakespeare, Paranoia, and Mass Culture." *Shakespeare Quarterly* 48 (1997): 1–16.
11 Robert F. Willson, Jr. 2000, p. 114.
12 Robert F. Willson, Jr. *Shakespeare in Hollywood: 1929–1956* (Madison, N.J.: Fairleigh Dickinson University Press, 2000), pp. 109–115.
13 See Eleanor Ruggles, *Prince of Players* (New York: Norton, 1953). The title comes from Thomas Bailey Aldrich's poem about Sargeant's painting of Edwin Booth. The film itself has received scant mention by Shakespeare-on-film critics. Kenneth S. Rothwell praises Burton's performance, arguing that Shakespeare will work on film if rendered by good actors. Kenneth Rothwell and Annabelle Melzer, *Shakespeare on Screen: An International Filmography and Videography* (Boston: Neal-Schuman, 1990), p. 63, and Kenneth Rothwell, *A History of Shakespeare on Screen* (Cambridge: Cambridge University Press, 1999), p. 226. On Edwin Booth, see Charles Shattuck, *The Hamlet of Edwin Booth* (Urbana: University of Illinois Press, 1969), and *Shakespeare on the American Stage* (Washington, D.C.: Folger Library, 1976), pp. 131–146, and Arthur Colby Sprague, *Shakespeare and the Actors* (Cambridge, Mass.: Harvard University Press, 1946) particularly pp. 214–116. On Shakespeare's influence on the Lincoln assassination, see Albert Frutwangler, *Assassin on Stage: Brutus, Hamlet, and the Death of Lincoln* (Urbana: University of Illinois Press, 1991), Gene Smith, *American Gothic* (New York: Simon and Schuster, 1992), and Michael W. Kauffman, *American Brutus: John Wilkes Booth and The Lincoln Conspiracies* (New York: Random House, 2004).
14 See, for example, Anthony Davies, *Filming Shakespeare's Plays* (Cambridge: Cambridge University Press, 1988), pp. 143–166, Robert Hapgood, "Kurosawa's Shakespeare Films." *Shakespeare and the Moving Image*. Anthony Davies and Stanley Wells, eds. (Cambridge: Cambridge University Press, 1999), pp. 234–249, Donald Richie and Joan Mellen. *The Films of Akira Kurosawa* (Berkeley: University of California Press, 1973), and Kenneth S. Rothwell, *A History of Shakespeare on Screen* (Cambridge: Cambridge University Press, 1999), pp. 191–200.
15 Robert Hapgood, 1999, p. 235.
16 Hapgood, 1999, p. 242.
17 Kenneth S. Rothwell, *A History of Shakespeare on Screen: A Century of Film and Television* (Cambridge: Cambridge University Press, 1999), p. 194.
18 Kenneth S. Rothwell, 1999, p. 194.
19 Tony Howard, "Shakespeare's Cinematic Offshoots." *The Cambridge Companion to Shakespeare on Film*, Russell Jackson, ed. (Cambridge: Cambridge University Press, 2000), p. 301

20 Kenneth S. Rothwell, 1999, p. 192.
21 Tony Howard, 2002, p. 301.
22 Howard, p. 302.
23 George Steiner, *The Death of Tragedy* (New York: Knopf, 1961), p. 15.
24 Elizabeth Wheeler, "Light It Up and Move It Around." *Shakespeare on Film Newsletter* 16/1 (December, 1991): 5.
25 Stephen Hawking, *A Brief History of Time* (New York: Bantam, 1988).
26 J. Dover Wilson, *What Happens in 'Hamlet'* (Cambridge: Cambridge University Press, 1935).
27 Qtd. in Maureen McKernan, *The Amazing Crime and Trial of Loeb and Leopold* (NewYork: Basic Books, 1957), p. 163.
28 Wendy Kaminer, *Review of The Strange Case of Dr. Kappler* (New York: Free Press, 1994) *New York Times Book Review* (27 November 1994): 27. See also the works of Henry Weihofen (*Psychiatry and the Law*, with Manfred S. Guttmacher, and *Mental Disorder as a Criminal Defense*), as well as *The University of Chicago Law Review* 22 (1955): 317ff, and Daniel J. Konstein, *Kill All the Lawyers?: Shakespeare's Legal Appeal* (Princeton: Princeton University Press, 1994).
29 Daniel Rosenthal, *Shakespeare on Film*. (London: Hamlyn, 2000) p. 20.
30 Doug Stenberg, "The Circle of Life and the Chain of Being: Shakespearean Motifs in *The Lion King*." *Shakespeare Bulletin*, 14 / 2 (Spring 1996): 36–37.
31 Qtd. in David Foster, "*Lion King*: Critics Say It's Full of Stereotypes." *Reading Eagle* (27 July 1994): A12.

Chapter 3 – Othello

1 A. C. Bradley, *Shakespearean Tragedy* (London: MacMillan: 1905), p. 145.
2 See Michael Long's excellent discussion of Venice's "courtesy culture" in *The Unnatural Scene* (London: Metheun, 1976), pp. 37–58.
3 See my discussion of the racial aspect of the script in *Watching Shakespeare on Television* (Madison, N.J.: Fairleigh Dickinson University Press 1993): pp. 126–162.
4 Robert F. Willson, Jr., *Shakespeare in Hollywood: 1929–1956* (Madison, N.J.: Fairleigh Dickinson University Press, 2000), p. 93.
5 Willson, 2000, pp. 122–129.
6 Willson, 2000, p. 92.
7 Laurie E. Osborne, "Poetry in Motion: Animating Shakespeare," *Shakespeare: The Movie*. Lynda Boose and Richard Burt, eds. (London: Routledge, 1997), p. 103.
8 H. R. Coursen, *Shakespeare in Space: Recent Shakespeare Productions on Screen* (New York: Peter Lang, 2002), pp. 113–128.
9 Laurie E. Osborne, "Mixing Media in Shakespeare: Animating Tales and Colliding Modes of Production." *Post Script* (Winter/Spring 1998): 77.
10 Glenn Kenny, "*O.*" *Premiere* (September 2001): 88.

11 Owen Gleiberman, "O." *Entertainment Weekly* (29 August 2001): 2 and 8.
12 Peter Rainer, "The Moor's Last Sigh." *New York* (10 September 2001): 166.
13 Glenn Kenny, 2001: 88.
14 Tim Blake Nelson, "There's a Price You Pay for Getting Too Real: Delay." *New York Times* (26 August 2001): 2, 8, 15.
15 Elvis Mitchell, "The Moor Shoots Hoops." *New York Times* (31 August, 2001): B1 & B12.
16 Mitchell, 2001: B12.
17 Peter Rainer, 2001: 166.
18 Owen Gleiberman, 2001: 8.
19 Tim Blake Nelson, 2001: 2.
20 Daniel Rosenthal, "Inspector Moor." *The Observer*. Screen (25 November 2001): 1.
21 Steven Oxman, "PBS 'Othello': Update of a Creepy Masterpiece." Reuters. Etonline.com. 28 January 2002.
22 Ed Siegel, "Modern *Othello* shows that Shakespeare still endures." *Boston Globe*. Living Arts (28 January 2002): 1.

Chapter 4 – King Lear

1 A. C. Bradley, *Oxford Lectures on Poetry* (Oxford: Oxford University Press, 1909), p. 255.
2 A. C. Bradley, *Shakespearean Tragedy* (London: Macmillan, 1904), p. 234.
3 Samuel Johnson, *Samuel Johnson on Shakespeare*, W. K. Wimsatt, Jr., ed., (New York: Dramabooks 1960), p. 97,
4 André Bazin, *What is Cinema?* Hugh Gray, trans. and ed. (Berkeley: University of California Press, 1971), pp. 140–157.
5 André Bazin, 1971, p. 142.
6 Bazin, p. 143.
7 Bazin, p. 143.
8 Bazin, p. 144.
9 Bazin, p. 145.
10 Bazin, p. 145.
11 Bazin, p. 147.
12 Bazin, p. 148.
13 Robert F. Willson, Jr., *Shakespeare in Hollywood: 1929–1956* (Madison, N.J.: Fairleigh Dickinson University Press, 2000), p. 117.
14 Bazin 1971, p. 157.
15 Willson, 2000, pp. 115–121.
16 Anita Gates, "Review." *New York Times* (1 June 2002): A20.
17 Anita Gates, 2002: A20.
18 Richard Burt, "Introduction." *Shakespeare, The Movie, II* (London: Routledge, 2003), p. 23.

Conclusion

1. Janet Maslin, "Shakespeare Saw a Therapist?" *New York Times* (13 December 1998): B16.
2. Sarah Lyall, "The Muse of Shakespeare Imagined as a Blonde." *New York Times* (13 December 1998): B22.
3. Kenneth S. Rothwell, "Orson Welles: Shakespeare for the Art Houses." *Cineaste* 14/1 (1998): 28.
4. John Lardner, "Close Up on Will." *Newsweek* (15 February 1999): 62.
5. Katharine E. Maus, "Introduction to *Titus Andronicus*." *The Norton Shakespeare* (New York: W. W. Norton, 1997), p. 375.
6. Samuel Crowl, *Shakespeare at the Cineplex: The Kenneth Branagh Era* (Athens, Ohio: Ohio University Press, 2003), p. 217. I highly recommend this book, which is at once cleanly spoken and deeply aware of current critical currents, along with Kenneth S. Rothwell's *History*, as previously cited, as sound guides to the films they treat, and the indispensable *Shakespeare on Screen*, Kenneth S. Rothwell and Anabelle Melzer, eds. (Boston: Neal-Shuman, 1990).
7. Joe Margolis, "Box Office Campaigns." *New York Times* (17 August 2004): 27.
8. Qtd. in Graham Fuller, "Two Kings." *Film Comments* 25 (1989): 6.
9. Jorg Helbig, "Cinematic Intertextuality." *Shakespeare in the Media*. edited by Stefani Brusberg-Kiermeir and Jorg Helbig. (Frankfort: Peter Lang, 2004). p. 171.
10. Roger Ebert, "William Shakespeare's 'A Midsummer Night's Dream.'" http://www.suntimes.com/ebert/ebert_reviews/1999/05/051404.html

Bibliography

Adorno, Theodor, and Max Horkheimer, 1972. "The Culture Industry: Enlightenment as Mass Deception." *Dialectic of Enlightenment*. John Cumming, trans. New York: Continuum: 120–167.
Auden, W. H., 1945. "The Christian Tragic Hero." *New York Times Book Review*, 16 December: 1.
Bazin, André, 1971. *What is Cinema?* Hugh Gray, trans. and ed. Berkeley: University of California Press.
Begley, Adam, 1993. "The Tempest Around Stephen Greenblatt." *New York Times Magazine* (28 March): 32–38.
Benjamin, Walter, 1968. "The Work of Art in the Age of Mechanical Reproduction." *Illuminations*. Hannah Arendt, ed., Harry Zohn, trans. New York: Harcourt, Brace and World: 219–253.
Biel, Steven, 1996. *Down with the Old Canoe*. New York: Norton.
Billington, Michael, 2000. "A Hamlet perfect for age of irony." *The Guardian*. 6 September.
Bloom, Harold, "Macbush," *Vanity Fair* (April 2004): 286–287.
Blos, Peter, 1952. *On Adolescence*. New York: Free Press.
Bobbin, Jay, 1998. "Shakespeare's *Tempest* Brews Anew on NBC." *TV Week* (13–19 December): 2.
Boose, Lynda, and Richard Burt, 2002. eds. *Shakespeare, the Movie II: Popularizing the Plays on Film, Tv, Video, and Dvd*. London London: Routledge.
——— and Richard Burr, 1997. eds. *Shakespeare, the Movie: Popularizing the Plays on Film, TV, and Video*. London and New York: Routledge.
Bradley, A. C,. 1909. *Oxford Lectures on Poetry*. Oxford: Oxford University Press.
———. 1905. *Shakespearean Tragedy*. London: Macmillan.
Brooks, David, 2004. "You'll Never Walk Alone." *New York Times* (21 February): A29.
Brusberg-Kiermeier, Stefani, and Jorg Helbig, eds. 2004. *Shakespeare in the Media: From the Globe Theatre to the World Wide Web*. Frankfurt am Main: Peter Lang.
Brzezinski, Zbigniew, 2004. *The Choice: Global Dominance or Global Leadership*. New York: Basic Books.
Buhler, Stephen M., 2002. *Shakespeare in the Cinema: Ocular Proof*. Albany: State University of New York Press.
Burnett, Mark Thornton, 2003. "Review." *Shakespeare Quarterly* 54/4 (Winter): 470.
Burt, Richard, 2002. "Introduction." *Shakespeare, the Movie II: Popularizing the Plays on Film, Tv, Video, and Dvd*. London: Routledge: 14–36.
———. 2002. "Slammin' Shakespeare." *Shakespeare Quarterly* 53/2 (Summer): 201–226.

———. 2000. "No Holes Barred: Homonormativity and the Gay and Lesbian Romance with *Romeo and Juliet*." *Shakespeare Without Class: Misappropriations of Cultural Capital*. Donald Hedrick and Bryan Reynolds, eds. New York: Palgrave, 153–186.

——— and Boose, Lynda, 1997. eds. *Shakespeare, the Movie: Popularizing the Plays on Film, TV, and Video*. London and New York: Routledge.

Charnes, Linda, 1997. "Dismember Me: Shakespeare, Paranoia, and Mass Culture." *Shakespeare Quarterly* 48: 1–16.

Clarke, Richard, 2004. *Against All Enemies: Inside America's War on Terror*. New York: Free Press.

Cohn, Ruby, 1976. *Modern Shakespearean Offshoots*. Princeton: Princeton University Press.

Corn, David W., 2003. *The Lies of George W. Bush: Measuring the Politics of Deception*. New York: Crown.

Coursen, H.R., 2002. *Shakespeare in Space: Recent Shakespeare Productions on Screen*. New York: Peter Lang.

———. 1999. "Filming *Richard III*." *Shakespeare: The Two Traditions*. Madison, N.J.: Fairleigh Dickinson University Press: 137–161.

———. 1993. *Watching Shakespeare on Television*. Madison, N.J.: Fairleigh Dickinson University Press.

Crowl, Samuel, 2003. *Shakespeare at the Cineplex: The Kenneth Branagh Era*. Athens, Ohio: Ohio University Press.

Davies, Anthony, 1988. *Filming Shakespeare's Plays*. Cambridge: Cambridge University Press.

Dean, John W. 2004. *Worse than Watergate: The Secret Presidency of George W. Bush*. Boston: Little, Brown & Company.

de Johgh, Nicholas, 2000. "This rare remarkable Prince gives the Hamlet of a lifetime." *Evening Standard* (9 June).

Denby, David, 2004. "The Current Cinema." *The New Yorker* (23 March): 84–85.

Dessen, Alan, 1986. "The Supernatural on Television." *Shakespeare on Film Newsletter* 11/1: 1 and 8.

Dobree, Bonamy, 1961. "The Last Plays." *The Living Shakespeare*. Robert Gittings, ed. New York: Fawcett.

Donaldson, Peter S, 2002. "Cinema and the Kingdom of Death: Loncraine's *Richard III*," *Shakespeare Quarterly* 53. (Summer): 241–259.

Ebert, Roger, *1999*. "William Shakespeare's 'A Midsummer Night's Dream.'" http://www.suntimes.com/ebert/ebert_reviews/1999/05/051404.html.

Fergusson, Niall, 2004. *Colossus: The Price of America's Empire*. New York: Penguin.

Forker, Charles, 2003. "Review." *Shakespeare Bulletin* 53/3 (Fall): 71 & 82.

Foster, David, 1994. "*Lion King*: Critics Say It's Full of Stereotypes." *Reading Eagle* (27 July): A12.

Frontline, 2004. "The Jesus Factor." Public Broadcasting Service, 29 April.

Frutwangler, Albert, 1991. *Assassin on Stage: Brutus, Hamlet, and the Death of Lincoln*. Urbana: University of Illinois Press.

Fuller, Graham, 1989. "Two Kings." *Film Comments* 25: 6.

Galli, Giancarlo, 2004. *Finanza Bianca: La Chies, I soldi, Il Potere*. Rome: Mondadori.

Gates, Anita, 2002 "Review." *New York Times* (1 June): A20.

Gleiberman, Owen, 2001. "*O*." *Entertainment Weekly* (29 August): 2, 8.

Goldman, Michael, 1985. *Acting and Action in Shakespearean Tragedy*. Princeton: Princeton University Press.
Greif, Mark. 2004. "Life After Theory," *The American Prospect*. 13/8 (August): 62–65.
Hapgood, Robert, 1999. "Kurosawa's Shakespeare Films." *Shakespeare and the Moving Image*. Anthony Davies and Stanley Wells, eds. Cambridge: Cambridge University Press, 234–249.
Hardison, O. B., 1969. "Three Types of Renaissance Catharsis." *Renaissance Drama*. New Series II. Evanston, Illinois: Northwestern University Press: 3-22.
Hardt, Michael, and Antonio Negri, 2004. *Multitude: War and Democracy in the Age of Empire*. New York: Penguin.
Hassel, Sven, 1996. *Gestapo*. New York: Bantam.
Hawking, Stephen, 1988. *A Brief History of Time*. New York: Bantam.
Helbig, Jorg, 2004. "Cinematic Intertextuality." *Shakespeare in the Media*. Edited by Stefani Brusberg-Kiermeier and Jorg Helbig. Frankfurt am Mein: Peter Lang: 169–180.
Henderson, Diana, 2000. "A Shrew for the Times." *Shakespeare the Movie: Popularizing the Plays on Film, TV, and Video*. Lynda Boose and Richard Burt, eds. London: Routledge: 148–168.
Heywood, Thomas, 1941. *An Apology for Actors*. ed. Richard A. Perkinson. New York: Scholars' Facsimiles & Reprints #27.
Hodgdon, Barbara, 2002. "From the Editor." *Shakespeare Quarterly* 53/2 (Summer): iii–x.
———. 1992. "Katherina Bound: or Play(K)ating the Strictures of Everyday Life." *PMLA* 107/3: 538–553.
Hodgson, Geoffrey, 2004. *More Equal than Others: America from Nixon to the New Century*. Princeton: Princeton University Press.
Howard, Tony, 2000. "Shakespeare's Cinematic Offshoots." *The Cambridge Companion to Shakespeare on Film*. Russell Jackson, ed. Cambridge: Cambridge University Press: 295-313.
Hughes, Thomas B., 2004. *Human-Built World: How to Think about Technology and Culture*. Chicago: University of Chicago Press.
Ignatieff, Michael, 2004. *The Lesser Evil: Political Ethics in the Age of Terror*. Princeton: Princeton University Press.
Ivins, Molly, and Lou Du Bose, 2003. *Bushwacked: Life in George W. Bush's America*. New York: Random House.
Jacoby, Russell, 2004."The Three P's: Publishing Perishable Prose." *New York Times Education Life* (1 August).
Jameson, Frederic, 1998. "Postmodernism and Consumer Society." *The Cultural Turn: Writings on the Postmodern: 1983–1998*. London: Verso, 1–20.
———. 1991. *Postmodernism: The Cultural Logic of Late Capitalism*. Durham, N.C.: Duke University Press.
———. 1981. *The Political Unconscious: Narrative as a Socially Symbolic Act*. Ithaca: Cornell University Press.
Johnson, Samuel, 1960. *Samuel Johnson on Shakespeare*, W. K. Wimsatt, Jr., ed. New York: Dramabooks.
Kahn, Coppélia, 1993. "They'll All Kow-Tow." *Shakespeare and the Classroom* 1/2 (Autumn): 4.

Kaminer, Wendy, 1994. Review of *The Strange Case of Dr. Kappler*. New York: Free Press. *New York Times, Book Review* (27 November): 27.
Kauffman, Michael W., 2004. *American Brutus: John Wilkes Booth and the Lincoln Conspiracies*. New York: Random House.
Keller, James R., and Leslie Stratyner, eds. *Almost Shakespeare: Reinventing His Work for Cinema and Television*. Jefferson, N.C.: McFarland.
Kenny, Glenn, 2001. "O." *Premiere* (September): 88.
Klawans, Stuart, 2004. "Blind Faith." *The Nation* (15 March): 26.
Konstein, Daniel J., 1994. *Kill All the Lawyers?: Shakespeare's Legal Appeal*. Princeton, Princeton University Press.
Krugman, Paul, 2003. *The Great Unraveling: Losing Our Way in the New Century*. New York: W. W. Norton.
Lanier, Douglas, 2002. "Shakecorp Noir." *Shakespeare Quarterly* 53/2 (Summer): 162–172.
Lardner, John, 1999. "Close Up on Will." *Newsweek* (15 February): 62.
Lasch, Christopher, 1991. *The Culture of Narcissism: American Life in an Age of Diminishing Expectations*. New York: W.W. Norton.
Lehmann, Courtney, 2002. *Shakespeare Remains: Theater to Film: Early Modern to Postmodern*. Ithaca and London: Cornell University Press.
——— and Lisa Starks, eds. 2002. *The Reel Shakespeare: Alternative Cinema and Theory*. Madison, N. J.: Fairleigh, Dickinson University Press.
Levine, Lawrence W., 1988. *Highbrow/Lowbrow: The Emergence of Cultural Hierarchy in America*. Cambridge, Mass.: Harvard University Press.
Long, Michael, 1976. *The Unnatural Scene*. London: Metheun.
Lyall, Sarah, 1998. "The Muse of Shakespeare Imagined as a Blonde." *New York Times* (13 December): B22.
Mann, James, 2004. *Rise of the Vulcans: The History of Bush's War Cabinet*. New York: Viking.
Margolis, Joe, 2004. "Box Office Campaigns." *New York Times* (17 August): 27.
Martel, Ned, 2004. "Goodbye girl grows up and loses her gags." *Financial Times* (10/11 January): W7.
Maslin, Janet, 1998. "Shakespeare Saw a Therapist?" *New York Times* (13 December): B16.
Maus, Katharine E., 1997. "Introduction to *Titus Andronicus*." *The Norton Shakespeare*. New York: W. W. Norton, 371–377.
McKernan, Maureen, 1957. *The Amazing Crime and Trial of Loeb and Leopold*. New York: Basic Books.
Menand, Louis, 2004. "Nanook and Me." *The New Yorker* (August 9 & 16): 96.
Meyerson, Harold, 2004. "Prince Hal vs. King Henry." *Washington Post* on-line (28 April).
Mitchell, Elvis, 2001. "The Moor Shoots Hoops." *New York Times* (31 August): B1 and B12.
Nelson, Tim Blake, 2001. "There's a Price You Pay for Getting Too Real: Delay." *New York Times* (26 August): 2, 8, 15.
Oruch, Jack, 1987. "Shakespeare for the Millions." *Shakespeare on Film Newsletter* 11/2 (April): 7.
Osborne, Laurie E., 1998. "Mixing Media in Shakespeare: Animating Tales and Colliding

Modes of Production." *Post Script* (Winter/Spring): 73–89.

———. 1997. "Poetry in Motion: Animating Shakespeare," *Shakespeare: The Movie*. Lynda Boose and Richard Burt, eds. London: Routledge, 103–120.

Oxman, Steven, 2002. "PBS 'Othello': Update of a Creepy Masterpiece." Reuters. Etonline.com. (28 January).

Pagels, Elaine, 2004. *Beyond Belief*. New York: Random House.

———. 1988. *Adam, Eve, and the Serpent*. New York: Vintage.

———. 1979. *The Gnostic Gospels*. New York: Vintage.

Pendleton, Thomas A., 1992. "Animated Shakespeare on HBO." *The Shakespeare Newsletter* XLII: 3/214 (Fall): 38, 40.

Pennington, Michael, 1996. *Hamlet: A User's Guide*. New York: Limelight.

Rainer, Peter, 2001. "The Moor's Last Sigh." *New York* (10 September): 166.

Rich, Frank, 2004. "3 Hours, 4 Nights, 1 Fear." *New York Times*, Section 2 (25 July): 1.

———. 2004. "Review." *New York Times* Arts (14 March): 2.

———. 2004. "Saving Private England." *New York Times* Section 2 (18 May): 1 and 8.

Richie, Donald and Joan Mellen, 1973. *The Films of Akira Kurosawa*. Berkeley: University of California Press.

Rose, Lloyd, 2000. "In London, a Truly Great Dane: John Caird's Haunting 'Hamlet.'" *Washington Post* (6 September).

Rosenthal, Daniel, 2001. "Inspector Moor." *The Observer*. Screen (25 November): 1.

———. 2000. *Shakespeare on Screen*. London: Hamlyn.

Rothwell, Kenneth S., 1999. *A History of Shakespeare on Screen: A Century of Film and Television*. Cambridge: Cambridge University Press.

———. 1998. "Orson Welles: Shakespeare for the Art Houses." *Cineaste* 14, no. 1.

——— and Annabelle Melzer, eds. 1990. *Shakespeare on Screen: An International Filmogaphy and Videography*. Boston: Neal-Schuman.

Ruggles, Eleanor, 1953. *Prince of Players*. New York: Norton.

Shattuck, Charles, 1976. *Shakespeare on the American Stage*. Washington, D.C.: Folger Library.

———. 1969. *The Hamlet of Edwin Booth*. Urbana: University of Illinois Press.

Siegel, Ed, 2002. "Modern *Othello* shows that Shakespeare still endures." *Boston Globe*. Living Arts (28 January): 1.

Singer, Peter, 2004. *The President* of *Good and Evil: The Ethics of George W. Bush*. New York: Dutton.

Smith, Gene, 1992. *American Gothic*. New York: Simon and Schuster.

Spencer, Charles, 2000. "Beale's great Dane rescues his master." *Daily Telegraph* (9 June).

Sprague, Arthur Colby, 1946. *Shakespeare and the Actors*. Cambridge, Mass.: Harvard University Press.

Steiner, George, 1961. *The Death of Tragedy*. New York: Knopf.

Stenberg, Douglas, 1996. "The Circle of Life and the Chain of Being: Shakespearean Motifs in *The Lion King*." *Shakespeare Bulletin* 14/2 (Spring): 36–37.

Suskind, Ron, 2004. *The Price of Loyalty: George W. Bush, the White House, and Paul O'Neill*. New York: Simon and Schuster.

Traister, D., 1999. "Review." *Choice* (September).

University of Chicago Law Review 22 (1955): 317ff.

Vitkus, Daniel J., 1997. "Turning Turk in *Othello*: The Conversion and Damnation of the Moor." *Shakespeare Quarterly* 48 (Summer): 145–176.

Wayne, Valerie, 1997. "*Shakespeare Wallah* and Colonial Specularity." *Shakespeare: The Film*, edited by Lynda Boose and Richard Burt. London: Routledge: 95-102.

Wheeler, Elizabeth, 1991. "Light It Up and Move It Around." *Shakespeare on Film Newsletter* 16/1 (December): 5.

Williams, Wendy, 1998. "Fonda Takes On *The Tempest*." *Satellite TV Week* (22–28 November): 2.

Willson, Jr., Robert F., 2003. "Scotland, PA." *Shakespeare Bulletin* 20/3: 41–42.

———. 2000. *Shakespeare in Hollywood: 1929–1956*. Madison, N.J.: Fairleigh Dickinson University Press.

———. 1978. "Shakespeare in *The Goodbye Girl*." *Shakespeare On Film Newsletter* II (2 April): 1, 3, and 4.

Wilson, J. Dover, 1935. *What Happens in 'Hamlet.'* Cambridge: Cambridge University Press.

Woodward, Bob, 2004. *Plan of Attack*. New York: Simon & Schuster.

Woodward, Kenneth L., 2004. "Do You Recognize this Jesus?" *New York Times* (25 February): A27.

Index

A

Aaliya, 50
ABC, 29
Abu Ghraib, 12
Achilles, 123
Ackland, Joss, 112
Adler, Luther, 120
Adorno, Theodor, 23, 25
Aeschylus, 139
Afrika Korps, 43
Agincourt, 7, 47
Agrippa, Cornelius, 21
Alamo, 127, 129
Alcott, Bronson, 52
Alexander, Louis, 68
Alexandria, 43
Ali, Mohammed, 113
Allen, Marcus, 51
Almagor, Gila, 42
Almereyda, Michael, 62, 63, 64, 77, 104
Altofronto (*The Malcontent*), 72
Amaya, Carmen, 40, 41
American Civil War, 21
American Tragedy, An, 30, 139
Anderson, Anthony, 50
Anderson, Judith, 27
Andy Hardy Gets Spring Fever, 33
Annie Hall, 18
Annie, Get Your Gun, 135
Antigone, 139
Antoinette, Marie, 32
Antonio (*The Tempest*), 130
Antony and Cleopatra, 131, 137, 141
Archibald, Tiny, 109
Arena Stage (D.C.), 93
Arendt, Hanna, 23

Ariel (*The Tempest*), 68
Aristotle, 22, 79, 102, 139
Arnt, Charles, 65
Arts & Entertainment Network, 93
Astaire, Fred, 27, 29
Atkinson, George, 32
Atlantic City, 125
Atzmon, Anab, 43
Auden, W. H., 59, 81
Audley, Eleanor, 67
Augustine, 3
Austin, William, 15
Autobiography of Malcolm X, The, 95
Avengers, The, 63

B

Babes in Arms, 134
Bacon, Francis, 78
Bad Sleep Well, The, 71, 72, 140
Ballard, Robert D., 55
Ballet Nacional de Espana, 41
Balzac, Honoré, 33
Barcelona, 41
Barrett, Lawrence, 67
Barrymore, Lionel, 34
Barton, John, 85
Bauer, Steven, 127
Bay of Pigs, 39
Bazin, André, 66, 122, 123, 124
BBC, 119
Beale, Simon Russell, 60
Beck's Beer, 30
Beetles, 29
Beleta, Francisco Rovira, 40
Ben-Hur, 33
Benjamin, Richard, 18
Benjamin, Walter, 23, 25

Bennett, Edward, 91
Bennett, Rodney, 61
Berger, Helmut, 126
Bergin, Patrick, 129
Bergman, Ingmar, 73
Berlin, 37
Bernard of Clairvaux, 3
Bernstein, Leonard, 44
Bertini, Francesca, 119
Beverly Hillbillies, The, 131
Bewitched, 20
Bickford, Charles, 67
Bicycle Thief, The, 37
Biel, Steven, 55
Biletnikoff, Fred, 51
Billa, Salvatore, 126
bin Laden, Osama, 6
Bir Hacheim, 43
Bird, Larry, 106
Birth of a Nation, 123
Bizet, Georges, 63
Black Like Me, 95
Blackburn, Ken, 78
Blanchard, Rachel, 53
Blanda, George, 51
Bledel, Alexis, 51
Blood and Sand, 33
Bloom, Harold, 24
Blos, Peter, 29
"Bluebirds Over the White Cliffs of Dover", 43
Bobbit, Lorena, 87
Bogues, Mugsy, 109
Bohdanova, Blanka, 36
Bohr, Nils, 79
Bolshoi Ballet, 38
Boose, Lynda, 23
Booth, Asia, 67, 68
Booth, Edwin, 67, 68
Booth, John Wilkes, 68, 69
Booth, Junius Brutus, 67, 68
Borgnine, Ernest, 100
Borowitz, Katherine, 13
Bradley, A. C., 95, 106, 117, 118
Bramley, Flora, 14
Branagh, Kenneth, 62, 77, 90, 111, 135, 142
Brancato, Lillo, 90
Branch, Cliff, 51

Brecht, Bertolt, 37
Bride Comes to Yellow Sky, The, 67, 123
Brocklebank, Daniel, 31
Broken English, 55
Broken Lance, 120, 123, 124
Brook, Peter, 6, 62, 119
Brooke, Arthur, 26
Brooks, David, 6
Brown, Clarence, 63
Brown, Tim, 51
Bruno, Giordano, 21
Brutus, Junius, 86
Brzezinski, Zbigniew, 10
Buchanan, Colin, 92
Bugs Bunny, 29
Burbage, Richard, 136
Burr, Raymond, 28
Burroughs, Edgar Rice, 34
Burt, Richard, 7, 23, 55, 131
Burton, Richard, 67, 100
Bush, George W., 10, 11, 74

C

Cagney, James, 28, 120, 133
Caird, John, 60
Calvary, U.S., 123
Calvi, Roberto, 126
Camus, Albert, 84
Cannon, Billy, 51
Cantinflas, 27
Capote, Truman, 91
Capulet, 32
Carlson, Richard, 35
Carlson, Richard, 36
Carney, Art, 120
Carnovsky, Morris, 118
Caron, Leslie, 27
Carpenter, Jeanne, 27
Carpenters, The, 53
Carrey, Jim, 53
Carroll, Tim, 9
Cassevetes, Paul, 19
Cazale, John, 125
CBS, 12
Chabrol, Claude, 93
Chadimova, Karla, 36
Chamberlain, Neville, 82
Chamberlain's Men, 136

Chan, Jackie, 50
Chang, Sari, 44
Chater, Geoffrey, 99
Cheers, 100
Cheetah, 34
Cheney, William, 74
Chertsey, 134
Chimes at Midnight, 62
China Girl, 44, 54, 126
Christ, 11, 47
Christie, Julie, 62
Christmas Carol, A, 73
Clarke, Warren, 92
Claudius (*Hamlet*), 58, 117
Cleopatra, 41, 122
Clift, Montgomery, 30
Cloisters, The, 3
Cloutier, Suzanne, 39
Clueless, 52
CNBC, 93
Cohn, Ruby, 1
Colasanto, Nicholas, 101
Colbert, Claudette, 140
Coleridge, S. T., 47, 88
Collingwood, Eugenia, 49
Colman, Ronald, 100, 101
Columbine, 44, 104, 108
Combs, Puffy, 107
Comedians, The, 100
Connery, Sean, 63
Conrad, Joseph, 110
Conti, John, 120
Conti, Tom, 49
Convicts Oath, The, 66
Cook, Christopher, 68
Coppola, Frances Ford, 125, 127
Coppola, Sophia, 126
Coriolanus, 11
Cornell, Katherine, 27
Cosby, Bill, 49
Court TV, 87
Cox, Julie, 127
Coyle, Richard, 109
Coyote, Peter, 76
Crane, Michael Patrick, 53
Crane, Stephen, 67, 123
Crawford, Joan, 35
Crispin's Day, 43

Crosby House, 134
Crowl, Samuel, 4, 139
C-Span, 83
Cuban Missile Crisis, 39
Cuban Revolution, 125
Cukor, George, 100
Cukor, George, 34
Cumming, John Parker, 23
Cummings, Quinn, 18
Cusack, Joan, 29
Czechloslovakia, 37

D

Dachau, 36
Daddy Long Legs, 27
Dallas Cowboys, 51
Dancing Coed, The, 35
Daniels, Jeff, 16, 17
Danson, Ted, 101
Darden, Seven, 101
Darrow, Clarence, 87
Daves, Delmer, 100
Davies, Marion, 134
Davis, Al, 51
Davis, Georgia, 63
Day in the Races, A, 27
de Bracton, Henry, 86
De Niro, Robert, 125
De Sica, Vitorio, 37
Dead Poet's Society, 15, 52
Dee, Frances, 30
Dee, Sandra, 38, 39
Delevanti, Cyril, 63
Delgado, Miguel M., 28
Demaurey, Edna, 32
Denby, David, 5
Denver, Bob, 63
Department of Health and
   Human Services, 12
Derek, John, 68
DeVito, Danny, 89
Devlin, Mary, 67, 68, 69
Diaz, Justino, 100
Diaz-Fernandez, José Ramon, 29, 55
DiCaprio, Leonardo, 49
Dillon, Matt, 29
Disney, 33, 45, 48, 54
Dives-Lazarus, 118

Dmytryk, Edward, 124
Dobree, Barnaby, 21
Domingo, Placido, 100
Donaldson, Peter, 2
Donnelly, Donal, 126
Donovan, Elisa, 52
Dooley, Paul, 76
Dorsey Brothers, 29
Dorsey, Tommy, 36
Double Indemnity, 100
Double Life, A, 22, 100, 101, 140
Doucette, John, 68
Doug, Doug E., 49
Douglas, Gordon, 35
Douglas, Paul, 13
Dowden, Edward, 8
Down with the Old Canoe, 55
Dr. Faustus, 77
Drake, Alfred, 15, 69
Dreiser, Theodore, 30, 139
Dressen, Alan, 24
Dreyfuss, Richard, 16, 17
Duke of York, 131
Dunne, Irene, 63
Dunne, Philip, 67
Dylan, Bob, 49

E

Ebert, Roger, 142
Eccleston, Christopher, 109, 111, 112
Eddy, Nelson, 35
Edmund (*King Lear*), 115, 130
Eggers, Per, 75
Egypt, 43
8 1/2, 41
Eilers, Sally, 64, 65
Einstein, Albert, 79
Eisenberg, Kate, 18
El Alamein, 43
Elizabeth I, 136
Elizabeth, West Virginia, 12
Elliot, Michael, 120
England, Lynndie, 12
Enobarbus (*Antony and Cleopatra*), 131
Epson, Buddy, 131
Erskine, Thomas, 86
Euripides, 122
Everytime We Say Goodbye, 42

Eyre, Richard, 120

F

Fahrenheit 9/11, 11, 140
Faithfull, Marianne, 61
Falstaff (*I Henry IV*), 38, 68
Farrell, Nicholas, 91
Faulkner, William, 19
Faustus, 135
Feldman, Meyer, 83
Feldman, Thomas, 83
Fellini, Federico, 41
Fielding, Emma, 135
Fiennes, Joseph, 31
Finlay, Frank, 102, 111
First Wives Club, 18
Firth, Colin, 31
Fishburne, Laurence, 75
Fisher, Frances, 49
Fitzgerald, F. Scott, 45
Fitzgerald, Zelda, 53
Fleisher, Ari, 72
Flirting Widow, The, 14
Fonda, Henry, 66
Fonda, Peter, 20
For Whom the Bell Tolls, 100
Forbes-Robertson, Sir Johnston, 86
Forbidden Planet, 19
Ford Tri-motor, 12
Ford, Francis, 66
Ford, Glenn, 100
Ford, John, 66
Forker, Charles R., 9
Fort Ashby, West Virginia, 12
Franks, Bobby, 87
Franz, Eduard, 124
Frappiér, Jill, 76
Freud, Sigmund, 8
Frost, Robert, 140
Fujiwara, Kamatari, 71
Funeral March, 37

G

Gabcik, Josef, 37
Gades, Antonio, 41
Galli, Giancarlo, 131
Gangbusters, 14
Garcia, Andy, 126

Garson, Barbara, 11
Gates, Anita, 128
Gatsby, 32
Gavin, John, 38
Gazala Line, 43
General Accounting Office, 12
Get Over It, 15, 56
Gibson, Mel, 4, 5, 11, 62
Gielgud, Sir John, 85
Gilbert, Helen, 33
Gilbert, John, 34
Gillespie, A. Arnold, 19
Gilligan's Island, 63
Gillingwater, Claude, 14
Gilmore Girls, The, 51, 54, 56
Ginsburg, Justice Ruth B., 83
Gleiberman, Owen, 104, 107, 108
Glenville, Peter, 100
Globe Theatre, 9, 134, 136
Glover, John Parker, 20
Godfather I, 125
Godfather II, 124, 125
Godfather III, 124, 125, 127
Golden Gate Bridge, 70
Goldiggers of 1937, 134
Goneril (*King Lear*), 49, 116
Goodbye Girl, The, 16, 17, 138
Goodman, Benny, 29
Goodwin, Paul, 92
Gordon, Ruth, 100
Gotterdammerung, 37
Gounod, Charles, 35
Graham, Julie, 92
Graham, Lauren, 51
Grant, Cary, 12, 69
Grant, Ulysses S., 19, 96
Grayson, Katherine, 15
Greed, 32, 33
Greenblatt, Stephen, 60
Greene, Graham, 100
Greif, Mark, 23
Grey, Virginia, 39
Grier, David Alan, 130
Griffin, John Howard, 95
Griffin, Lynne, 76
Griffith, D. W., 32, 123
Guiness, Alec, 100
Guttheil, Dr. Thomas, 83, 85

H

Hadfield Case, 86
Hale, Barbara, 28
Hale, Lord, 86
Haley, Jack, 27
Hamilton, Mahlon, 27
Hamlet Goes Business, 77
Hamlet, 8, 9, 12, 25,36, 38, 56, 57–94, 102, 103, 104, 114, 125, 128
Hangment Also Die, 37
Hanks, Tom, 42
Hansen, Elden, 105
Hapgood, Robert, 71, 72
Harden, Marcia Gay, 127
Harding, Warren, 32
Hardy, Thomas, 49
Harry and Tonto, 120
Harvard University, 83, 84
Hassel, Sven, 55
Hasso, Signe, 100
Hawes, Keeley, 109, 111
Hawking, Stephen, 79
Hawks, Howard, 12
Hawley, Richard, 92
Hayward, Susan, 121
Hazard, Jayne, 64
HBO, 101
Heaton, Patricia, 16, 18
Heigl, Katherine, 20
Heisenberg, Werner, 79
Helbig, Jorg, 142
Helmore, Tom, 69
Hemingway, Ernest, 100
Henerson, James, 20
Henry IV, 12, 22, 87, 131
Henry O, 50
Henry V, 7, 62, 68, 90
Henry VI, 141
Henslowe, Philip, 136
Heraclitus, 45
Heydrich, Reinhard, 36, 55
Hieronimo (*The Spanish Tragedy*), 72, 86
Hill, Reginald, 91
Hiller, Arthur, 76
Hines, Gregory, 89
Hitchcock, Alfred, 69, 126
Hitler, Adolph, 2, 37, 43, 82, 88, 95, 112

Hizkiyahu, Avner, 41
Hodgdon, Barbara, 6, 53
Hold that Kiss, 27
Holland, Sean, 52
Holly, Lauren, 129
Hollywood Revue of 1929, 34
Holm, Ian, 120, 131
Holmes, Phillips, 30
Homer, 57
Homicidal Ham, 100
Hood, Darla, 35
Hooker, Richard, 21
Hopkins, Anthony, 61, 99
Hopkins, Miriam, 140
Horan, Gerald, 91
Hordern, Michael, 119
Hoskins, Bob, 99
House of Strangers, 120, 124
Howard, Leslie, 30, 34, 77
Howard, Tony, 45, 55, 73
Howell, Jane, 141
Howlett, Kathy M., 22
Hubble, Edwin, 79
Huckleberry Finn, 67
Hughes, Thomas, 10
Huston, Patricia, 28

I

I Dream of Jeannie, 20
Iachimo (*Cymbeline*), 130
Iago (*Othello*), 130
Iman, 82
In and Out, 29
Internal Revenue Service, 96
Intolerable Cruelty, 140
Iraq, 12
Ireland, 128
Ivory, James, 41

J

Jackson, Bo, 51
Jackson, Russell, 55
Jacobi, Derek, 61, 62, 86
Jacoby, Russell, 24
JAG, 93
James, Harry, 29
Jameson, Frederic, 23, 25, 31
Jarvet, Yuri, 131

Jefferson, Joe, 67
Jerusalem, 42
Joe Macbeth, 13, 128
John Paul I, 126
Johnson, Lyndon, 11
Johnson, Samuel, 118
Jones, Allan, 35
Jones, Ora, 54
Joudry, Patricia, 39
Jubal, 100
Judas, 2
Judge, Ian, 135
Judges, Book of , 21
Jules et Jim, 76
Julia, Raul, 15, 19
Julius Caesar, 68, 142
Junger, Gil, 14
Jurado, Katy, 124

K

Kagawa, Kyoko, 71
Kahn, Coppélia, 4
Kahn, Michael, 7, 85
Kaminer, Wendy, 87
Kanal, 38
Kanin, Garson, 100
Kapoor, Shashi, 41
Kato, Takeshi, 71
Kaurismaki, Aki, 77
Kautner, Helmut, 39
Keaton, Diane, 18, 125
Keats, John, 8, 137
Keegan, Andrew, 105
Keel, Howard, 15
Keidor, Avi, 43
Keim, Betty Lou, 28
Kelley, DeForest, 82
Kendal, Felicity, 41
Kennedy, John, 11
Kennedy, Justice Anthony, 83, 86
Kenny, Glenn, 104
Keyishian, Harry, 55
Keyton, Bustor, 33
Kilian, Victor, 12
Killing Kindness, A, 91
King James I, 14, 128
King Lear, 6, 11, 14, 62, 105, 115–131
King of Texas, 127–130, 141

Kingsford, Walter, 36
Kinney, Terry, 54
Kiss Me, Kate!, 15, 22, 134
Kitchen, Michael, 119
Klan, Ku Klux, 123
Klawans, Stuart, 4, 5
Kliman, Bernice, 124
Kline, Patsy, 29
Knox, John, 42
Korea, 116
Kott, Jan, 77
Kozintsev, Grigori, 119
Kuhn, Thomas, 9, 78
Kurosawa, Akira, 71, 72, 74, 75

L

La Historia de los Tarantos, 41
La Scala, 100
LA Story, 63
Lake Tahoe, 125
Lake, Veronica, 36
Lane, Nathan, 135
Lang, Fritz, 37
Lange, Jessica, 18
Lanier, Douglas, 25, 62
Lardner, John, 138
Lasch, Christopher, 3
Last Action Hero, 63
Law and Order, 63
Lawrence, Steven, 110
Lazana, Sara, 40
Lee, Peggy, 28
LeGallienne, Eva, 68
Lehmann, Courtney, 7, 10
LeMay, Curtis, 74
Leopold, Nathan, 87
Letscher, Matt, 130
Lewis, Grandet, 32
Li, Jet, 50
Lidice, 37
Light in August, 19
Limited Test Ban Treaty, 39
Lindsay, Margaret, 39
Lion King II: Simba's Pride, 46
Lion King, The, 46, 48, 87
"Little Rascals, The", 35
Lloyd, David, 100
Loeb, Richard, 87

Lombard, Carole, 140
Loncraine, Richard, 2
London, 68, 69, 110, 112, 128, 133, 134, 141
Lonesome Dove, 127
Long, Michael, 112
Long, Shelley, 76, 100
Los Tarantos, 40, 41, 44
Louis, Joe, 96
Love Story, 30
Love's Labour's Lost, 62, 135
Lowell, Abbe, 83, 84
Luhrmann, Baz, 8, 31, 49, 108, 143
Lydon, James, 64
Lynch, Jessica, 12
Lysander (*A Midsummer Night's Dream*).., 17
Lyth, Ragnar, 61, 75

M

Macbeth, 13, 14, 25, 28, 57, 76, 87, 89, 113, 114, 120, 133, 137
Macbeth and the Estate, 14
Macbeth, Lady, 49
MacBird, 11
MacDonald, Jeanette, 35
Mackaill, Dorothy, 14
MacKenzie, Will, 15
Madden, John, 51
Malevole (*The Malcontent*), 86
Mama Day, 19
Mana, Alfredo, 41
Mann, James, 10
Mantegna, Joe, 126
Marcinkus, Paul, 126
Margolis, Joe, 140
Marks, Arthur, 28
Marlowe, Christopher, 77
Marshall, Alan, 63
Marshall, E. G., 123
Marsillach, Cristina, 42
Martin, Daniel, 40
Martin, Dorothy, 54
Martin, Jose Manuel, 40
Martin, Steve, 63
Marx, Groucho, 27
Maslin, Janet, 136
Mason, Marsha, 16, 18

Massey, Raymond, 67
Mathis, June, 33
Mature, Victor, 66
Maus, Katharine E., 138
Mayne, Eric, 32
Mazursky, Paul, 19, 75
McCallister, Lon, 27
McFarland, George, 35
McGroth, David 100
McKellan, Ian, 111
McKellan, Scott, 72
McLeod, Mary, 65
McNamara, Maggie, 67
McNaughten Rules, 86, 87
McVicker, Mary, 68
Meaney, Colin, 130
Measure for Measure, 141
Medea, 122
Medicaid, 12
Men of Respect, 13
Menand, Louis, 11
Menendez, brothers, 87
Mercer, Johnny, 45
Merchant of Venice, 34, 141
Metro, 33
Meyer, Nicholas, 81
Meyerson, Harold, 23
MGM, 35, 36
Midler, Bette, 76
Midsummer Night's Dream, A, 15, 30, 31, 133, 134
Midwinter's Tale, A, 90
Mifune, Toshiro, 71
Mihashi, Tatsuya, 71
Millais, Sir John, 61, 70
Miller, Glenn, 29
Miller, Jonathan, 15, 99, 141
Miramax, 104
Mistrik, Ivan, 36
Mitchell, Elvis, 106, 107
Mitchell, Thomas, 12
Mitsude, Ken, 71
Mizrahi, Moshi, 42
Modenessi, Alfredo Michel, 55
Monkey Boy, 53
Montgomery, Field Marshal Sir Bernard, 43
"Moon River", 45

Moonlighting, 15
Moore, Michael, 11
Moreau, Jeanne, 76
Mori, Masayoki, 72
Morison, Patricia, 15
Morrison, Paul, 55
Morrow, Jeff, 28
Mortimer (*Henry VI*), 131
Moshonov, Moni, 43
Moubray, Alan, 66
Mouse that Roared, The, 38
Muir, Esther, 27
Murray, Chad Michael, 51
My Darling Clementine, 66, 68, 93
My Own Private Idaho, 22

N

National Endowment for the Humanities, 4
Native Son, 95
Naylor, Gloria, 19
NBC, 19, 20, 128
Negulsco, Jean, 27
Neibuhr, H. Richard, 5
Neilsen, Asta, 61
Nelson, Tim Blake, 106, 107
Nemoy, Leonard, 82
New Place, 133
New York Shakespeare Festival, 15
New York Times, 137
New York, 44, 69, 128
New York, Museum of the City of, 69
New Zealand, 55
Newberger, Carolyn, 87
Newton, Sir Isaac, 79
Nextel, 26
Nicholson, Jack, 18
Nicolas, Gregor, 55
Nieland, Marshall, 27
Nigger of the Narcissis, 110
"Nightingale Sang on Berkeley Square, A", 43
Nishimura, Ko, 71
Nixon, Richard, 81, 112, 117
Norgaard, Dag, 75
Northern Ireland, 116
Novak, Kim, 69
Nunn, Trevor, 13, 111, 131, 133, 134, 138, 141

Index 169

O

O, 44, 103, 108, 141
O'Keefe, Dennis, 27
O'Neal, Tatum, 18
O'Sullivan, Maureen, 27, 34
Oakland Raiders, 50
Occurrence at Owl Creek Bridge, An, 79
Odysseus, 123
Oedipus, 57, 122
Ohio University, 4
Oklahoma, 69, 128
Old Bailey, 110
Old Vic, 111
Oldman, Gary, 78
Olick, Cynthia, 93
Olivier, Sir Laurence, 18, 47, 61, 62, 67, 81, 86, 97, 102, 111, 120
Olson, Theodore, 83
On Adolescence, 29
Only Angles Have Wings, 12
Ontkean, Michael, 75
Open City, 37
Ophelia (*Hamlet*), 41, 58, 93
Orestes, 139
Oruch, Jack, 15
Orwell, George, 140
Osborne, Laurie E., 101, 103
Othello, 1, 41, 44, 54, 95–114, 141
Otto, Jim, 51
Our Town, 39, 73
Outinen, Kati, 77
Outrageous Fortune, 76
Oxman, Steven, 111

P

Pacino, Al, 3, 124, 125
Padelcki, Jared, 51
Pagels, Elaine, 11
Pagliacci, 33
Palermo, 126
Paltrow, Gwyneth, 31
Panebianco, Richard, 44
Papp, Joseph, 15
Paramount, 33, 64
Parfitt, Judy, 61
Parker, Dolores, 121
Parker, Oliver, 107, 111, 112

Passion of the Christ, The, 4, 140
Patten, Luana, 39
Patton, George, 90
Paul, Praveen, 42
PBS, 109
Peacock, Trevor, 62
Pendleton, Thomas A., 114
Pennington, Michael, 61
Peret, 41
Perineau, Harold, 19
Perry Mason Show, The, 28
Petelius, Pirkka-Pekka, 77
Peters, Jean, 123
Petruchio (*The Taming of the Shrew*), 68
Phantom Lady, 63
Phifer, Mekhi, 104
Phoenix, Rain, 105
Pickford, Mary, 27
Pickleman, Brenda, 54
Pinocchio, 20
Pious, Minerva, 13
Pitt, Brad, 53
Place in the Sun, A, 30
Plath, Sylvia, 129
Plummer, Christopher, 50, 82
Pocahontas, 33, 45, 56
Poindexter, Adm., 62
Poland, 119
Polanski, Roman, 13, 113
Porter, Cole, 15, 43, 76, 134
Postman Always Rings Twice, The, 100
Pouyet, Eugene, 32
Powell, Richard, 18
Prague, 36, 37
Presley, Elvis, 29
Price, Jonathan, 85
Prieto, Antonio, 40
Prince Hal, 7
Prince of Players, 67, 69
Prokofiev, Sergi, 41, 48, 54
Prosky, Robert, 76
Prospero (*The Tempest*), 20, 63, 131
Puccini, Giacomo, 35
Puck (*A Midsummer Night's Dream*), 17
Pyper-Furgeson, J, 19

Q

Quince, Peter (*A Midsummer Night's Dream*), 133

R

Radovitch, Eugene, 35
RAF, 2
Rainer, Peter, 107
Ran, 71
Rashad, Phylicia, 49
Raskin, Bonnie, 21
Rathbone, Basil, 15
Raver, Lorna, 51
Reagan, Ronald, 11, 23
Reason, Rex, 28
Redgrave, Vanessa, 20
Regan (*King Lear*), 49, 119
Regas, Pedro, 12
Reid, Carl Benton, 123
Reisner, Charles, 34
Renaissance Man, 89
Restless Years, The, 38, 39
Revenger's Tragedy, The, 73
Rice, Condoleeza, 6
Rice, Jerry, 30
Rich, Buddy, 36
Rich, Frank, 5, 12, 23
Richard II, 9, 11, 117, 130, 141
Richard III, 2, 3, 16, 17, 18, 32, 50, 51, 128, 130
Richardson, Tony, 61
Rielly, Don, 90
Ritchie, General, 43
Robinson, Edward G., 120
Roman, Ruth, 13
Romanov and Juliet, 38
Rome, 138, 139
Romeo and Juliet, 6, 8, 12, 25–56, 63, 67, 68, 89, 108, 123, 124, 134, 135, 137, 140, 143
Romeo Et Juliette, 35
Romeo, Juliet and Darkness, 36, 37, 54
Romeo Must Die, 44, 50, 54
Romeo + Juliet, 108, 143
Romeo y Jolieta, 28
Romeus and Juliet, 26
Rommel, Ervin, 43
Rooney, Mickey, 33
Rose Theatre, 136

Rose-Marie, 35
Rosencrantz and Guildenstern Are Dead, 78, 136
Rosenthal, Daniel, 24, 55, 87, 110
Rossellini, Roberto, 37
Rota, Nino, 53
Roth, Tim, 78
Rothwell, Kenneth S., 22, 72, 73, 93, 138
Rowe, Nicholas, 85
Rowland, Roy, 28
RSC, 11, 135
Ruggles, Eleanor, 67
Russo, James, 127
Rutherford, Ann, 33
Rutherford, Ann, 36
Rylance, Mark, 9

S

San Sebastian, Order of, 125
Saphead, The, 33
Save the Last Dance, 53, 106
Savo, Elina, 77
Saxe, Geoff, 110, 111, 112
Saxon, John, 39
Scarsgaard, Stellan, 61
Schaefer, Goerge, 15
Scheider, Roy, 129
Schell, Maximilian, 63
Schmeling, Max, 96
Schumann, Robert, 64
Schwarzeneger, Arnold, 63
SciFi Channel, 63
Scofield, Paul, 119
Scotland, 128
Scotland, PA., 14
Seigfried, 37
Seiter, William A., 14
Sejbalova, Jirina, 36
Sellars, Elizabeth, 67
Sellers, Peter, 38
Seneca, 82
Sex in the City, 138
Shakespeare in Love, 7, 8, 31, 67, 133, 134, 135, 138
Shakespeare Theater (D.C.), 85
Shakespeare Wallah, 55, 140
Shakespeare, Our Contemporary, 77
Shatner, William, 81

Shaw, Artie, 36
Shaw, Fiona, 141
Shawn, Wallace, 52
Shayne, Tamara, 38
Shearer, Norma, 301, 34, 35
Sheik, The, 33
Shell, Art, 51
Shepherd, Cybill, 15
Shimiura, Takashi, 72
Shimizu, Gen, 73
Short, Martin, 16, 56
Show People, 134
Shylock, 32
Sicily, 125
Sidney, Sylvia, 30
Siegel, Ed, 112
Silverstone, Alicia, 52
Simmons, Jean, 61, 102
Simmons, Peter, 90
Simon, Neil, 16, 18
Simon, S. Sylvan, 35
Simpson, Nicole Brown, 95
Simpson, O. J., 44, 87, 95, 104, 142
Singin' in the Rain, 134
Siodmak, Robert, 63
Smart, Pamela, 87
Smiley, Jane, 113
Smollett, Jurnee, 49
Smutna, Dana, 36
Snakepit, The, 100
Solomon and Gaenor, 55
Somorrostro, 41
Sonny and Cher Show, 51
Sons of the Pioneers, The, 49
Sophocles, 57, 139
Sorel, Sonia, 65
Soul on Ice, 95
Soviet Union, 119
Sovscope, 119
Spanky, 35
Spellman, Francis Cardinal, 126
St. Patrick's Cathedral, 125
Stabler, Ken, 51
Stagedoor Canteen, 27, 55
Stalin, 10, 95
Stanley, Allessandra, 56
Star Trek, 81

Star Trek VI: The Undiscovered Country, 81
Starr, Fredo, 54
Steiger, Rod, 100
Steiner, George, 77
Stenberg, Doug, 48, 87, 88, 89
Stevens, K.T., 28
Stewart, Patrick, 61, 91, 127, 131
Stiles, Julia, 53, 104, 106
Stirling, Rachel, 109
Stoll, E. E., 88
Stone, Dr. Alan, 84, 85
Stone, Lewis, 33
Stoppard, Tom, 78, 79, 80, 81, 136
Strange Brew, 76, 140
Strange Illusion, 64, 141
Strasberg, Lee, 124
Stratford (Canada), 90
Stratford (Connecticut), 118
Streep, Meryl, 15
Stroheim, Erich von, 32
Stuart, Jeb, 19
Stubbs, Imogen, 133
Sumpter, Donald, 78
Sweet Light in a Dark Room, 36
Switzer, Carl, 35
Synott, Del, 110

T

Taming of the Shrew, The, 14, 15, 18, 134
Tamiroff, Akim, 38
Tarzan the Apeman, 34
Tate, Nahum, 115
Tatum, Art, 51
Taylor, Benedict, 43
Taylor, Elizabeth, 18, 30, 100
Taymor, Julie, 10, 134, 138, 139, 140
Tchaikovsky Overture, 34, 36
Tchaikovsky, Peter Ilich, 34, 53, 54
Teach Me How to Cry, 39
Tempest, The, 19, 21, 22, 24, 33, 45, 128, 130, 131, 137
Temple, Shirley, 18
Ten Things I Hate About You, 14
Tennant, Victoria, 63
Tennyson, 82
Texas, 127, 128, 133, 141
Thacker, David, 141

Thalberg, Irving, 34
Thalberg, Irving, 35
Thames TV, 13
Thelma and Louise, 18
"There's No Business Like Show Business", 135
These Wilder Years, 28
Thomas, Isaiah, 106
Thomas, Sean Patrick, 54
Thomas, William, 35
Thousand Acres, A, 113
Thrill of Romance, 36
Throne of Blood, 71
Titanic, 49
Titus (Taymor), 11, 139, 140
Titus Andronicus, 10, 134, 138, 143
TNT, 16
Tobruk, 43
Toomey, Regis, 65
Tootsie, 18
Torturro, John Parker, 13
Tracy, Justice, 86
Tracy, Spencer, 18, 123
Truffaut, Francois, 76
Turner, Lana, 35
Twain, Mark, 67
Twelfth Night, 133, 135, 138
Two Gentlemen of Verona, 136, 137

U

Uccello, 102
Ukraine, 10
Ulmer, Edgar G., 64
United Nations, 38
Universal International, 100
Universidad de Malaga, La, 29
Upshaw, Marvin, 51
Urlacher, Brian, 50
Ustinov, Peter, 38

V

Valentine (*Two Gentlemen of Verona*), 135
Valentine, Paul, 121
Valentino, Charles, 32
Valentino, Rudolph, 33
Vallone, Raf, 126
Van Dyke, W. S., 34
Van Dyke, Wally, 34
Van Nutter, Rik, 38
Van Zant, Gus, 22
Vancouver, 50
Vatican, 5, 126
Vendice (*The Revenger's Tragedy*), 72
Verdi, 100
Vertigo, 69, 70, 71
Vestris, Auguste, 01
Vietnam, 6, 90, 116, 119
Visa, 30
Vitkus, Daniel J., 1, 2

W

Wagner, Robert, 123
Waite, Liam, 130
Wajcla, Andraez, 37
Walgren, Pernilla, 61
Walker, Eamonn, 109, 111
Walker, Robert, 36
Wallace, Morgan, 27
Wallison, Peter, 83
Waltons, The, 130
Wanamaker, Sam, 134
Warner Electronovision, 69
Warner, David, 81
Warner, Deborah, 141
Wars of the Roses, 10
Washington, Kerry, 54
Watergate, 11, 142
Waterson, Sam, 63
Wayne, Valerie, 42
Webster, John, 136
Weil, Lisa, 51
Weiss, Jiri, 36
Weissmuller, Johnny, 34
Welles, Orson, 62, 142
Wells, Dawn, 63
West Side Story, 29, 38, 41, 44, 45, 47, 52, 55
Wexley, John, 37
"What Is this Thing Called Love?", 76
Wheeler, Elizabeth, 78
White Cliffs of Dover, The, 63
Whitefriars Theatre, 134
Whitmore, James, 39
Whitmore, James, 40
Widmark, Richard, 124
Wieck, Clara, 64

Wilcox, Fred, 19
Wilkinson, Tom, 136
William, Warren, 64, 65
Williams, Robin, 15, 52, 63
Williamson, Nicol, 61
Willie and Phil, 75, 76
Willis, Bruce, 15
Willson, Robert F., Jr., 13, 16, 66, 100, 114, 123, 124
Wilson, Dover, 86
Wing, Ward, 32
Winslet, Kate, 49, 77
Winter's Tale, The, 40
Winters, Shelley, 30, 100
Wishbone, 48
Witham, Charles W., 69
Withers, Grant, 66
Wizard of Oz, The, 19, 27
Wood, Clive, 135

Wood, Natalie, 76
Woodward, Kenneth L., 5
Woolf, Virginia, 135
Worth, Irene, 119
Wright, Ben, 69
Wright, Teresa, 39

Y

Yamamoto, Admiral Isoroku, 37
Yordan, Philip, 124
Young, Steve, 30
Yugoslavia, 116

Z

Zane, Billy, 49
Zeffirelli, Franco, 31, 62
Zimbalist, Efrem, Jr., , 121
Zohn, Harry, 23

STUDIES IN SHAKESPEARE

Edited by Robert F. Willson, Jr.

This series deals with all aspects of Shakespearean drama and poetry. Studies of dramatic structure, verse and prose style, major themes, stage or performance history, and film treatments are welcomed. The editor is particularly interested in manuscripts that examine Shakespeare's work in its American setting—in the academy, on stage, and in popular culture. Inquiries and manuscripts should be sent to the series editor:

> Robert F. Willson, Jr.
> Department of English
> University of Missouri-Kansas City
> College of Arts & Sciences
> 106 Cockefair Hall
> Kansas City, MO 64110-2499

To order other books in this series, please contact our Customer Service Department at:

> (800) 770-LANG (within the U.S.)
> (212) 647-7706 (outside the U.S.)
> (212) 647-7707 FAX

or browse online by series at:
> WWW.PETERLANGUSA.COM